CREATING YOUR BEST LIFE

CREATING YOUR BEST LIFE

The Ultimate Life List Guide

CAROLINE ADAMS MILLER, MAPP
and DR. MICHAEL B. FRISCH

STERLING

New York / London
www.sterlingpublishing.com

To my extraordinary family—my husband, Haywood, and my three marvelous children, Haywood IV, Samantha, and Bayard. Their steadfast belief in me and my ability to write this book, as well as their bottomless love, gave me what I needed to pull this off. I am richly blessed and very grateful.

—CAM

To Ed Diener, my inspiration, and to my dear ones, Jacob, Ron, and Hope.

—MBF

Text from p. 213 (Four Point List) from *Changing for Good* by James O. Prochaska, Ph.D., John C. Norcross, Ph.D., and Carlo C. DiClemente, Ph.D. © 1994 by authors James O. Prochaska, Ph.D., John C. Norcross, Ph.D., and Carlo C. DiClemente, Ph.D. Reprinted by permission of HarperCollins Publishers.

Library of Congress Cataloging-in-Publication Data is available

2 4 6 8 10 9 7 5 3 1

Published by Sterling Publishing Co., Inc.
387 Park Avenue South, New York, NY 10016
© 2009 by Caroline Adams Miller and Dr. Michael B. Frisch

Distributed in Canada by Sterling Publishing
c/o Canadian Manda Group, 165 Dufferin Street
Toronto, Ontario, Canada M6K 3H6
Distributed in the United Kingdom by GMC Distribution Services
Castle Place, 166 High Street, Lewes, East Sussex, England BN7 1XU
Distributed in Australia by Capricorn Link (Australia) Pty. Ltd.
P.O. Box 704, Windsor, NSW 2756, Australia

Manufactured in the United States of America
All rights reserved

Sterling ISBN 978-1-4027-6259-8

TEXT DESIGN BY PAULINE NEUWIRTH, NEUWIRTH & ASSOCIATES, INC.

For information about custom editions, special sales, premium and corporate purchases, please contact Sterling Special Sales Department at 800-805-5489 or specialsales@sterlingpublishing.com.

CONTENTS

FOREWORD

W HAT IS SO wonderful about psychological theory is that it enables us to predict, explain, and influence behavior. Because I am a scientist-practitioner employed in an academic setting, I hope you, the reader, will indulge me a moment while I deliberately write as one. This book is a "must read" because it brings science to life—your life. It explains in everyday language how scientific theories and the empirical research that underlie them can have a positive impact on what you think and how you behave in regard to yourself and those around you.

The first theory, goal setting, which Edwin Locke and I developed, states that (1) a specific high goal leads to higher performance than does no goal setting, or even urging people to do their best; (2) given goal commitment, higher goals lead to higher performance than easy goals; and (3) praise, money, and participation in decision making lead to an increase in your performance only if they lead you to set and commit to specific high goals. Satisfaction comes from the attainment of goals that are important to you. More than a thousand studies conducted between the 1960s and today show the validity of this theory.

Albert Bandura's social cognitive theory explains how to get goal commitment. The first step is to focus on outcome expectancy: Discover the relationship between what you do and the outcome (good/bad) you can expect. Change the outcome you expect, and you will change your behavior. Second, find ways you can increase your self-efficacy, a can-do mind-set that a high goal is attainable. This book shows you how to take these two steps.

The third theory is based on Martin Seligman's research: learned optimism. If people can be convinced to confront the evidence by answering three straightforward questions, reality leads to resiliency following the inevitable setbacks life deals all of us: (1) Is the setback temporary or will its effects plague you forever? The answer is that it's almost always temporary. (2) Does the setback pertain to everything you do or to just one thing you tried? The answer is almost always one or two things rather than everything. (3) Are you alone responsible for the setback or were there other factors involved such as time, people, resources? Get the picture? Now, get back on your feet and try again. This book explains multiple ways to do this.

As the boxer Muhammad Ali is fond of saying: "It's goals that will keep me going." Goals will keep you and me going. Read this book with the confidence that the content is based on solid scientific findings, and then get going.

GARY P. LATHAM
Secretary of State Professor of
Organizational Effectiveness
Joseph L. Rotman School of Management
University of Toronto

INTRODUCTION

WHEN I WAS small, I listened wide-eyed to my father's stories about his uncles, Platt and Ben Adams, and how they had won gold, silver, and bronze medals in the 1912 Olympics in Stockholm, Sweden, as members of the U.S. Olympic Team. Instead of emphasizing their obvious athleticism, my father always focused on how they'd created a mind-set of success that allowed them to become, and remain, the only sibling pair to ever go one-two in a summer Olympic event.

My dad's example stuck with me: Set your goals high, work as hard as you can, and then create a positive belief system if you want to create your best life.

My family's natural competitiveness found its outlet in my life through swimming, academics, and then my struggle to overcome bulimia in my early twenties. Success in these disparate areas required that I harness the exact same resources—persistence, grit, self-efficacy, and the ability to set and achieve short- and long-term goals. I began to experiment with life lists, creative visualization, and related goal-setting fields throughout my early adulthood while I wrote books, started and ran a nonprofit, had three children with my husband, and worked with clients on strategies for how to achieve a healthy mind and body.

My fascination with the pursuit of individual excellence deepened, and I created a niche as a life coach with a specialty in goal setting, devouring all the information I could find to make me better and more knowledgeable at my chosen calling.

Coaching is a thriving profession that differs from therapy and consulting in important ways: Coaches partner with healthy, high-functioning clients to help them strategize and accomplish meaningful goals. For a high-quality coach, I believe that effective goal-setting knowledge is necessary, so this is where I have focused my study and energy for years.

In 2005, I was fortunate enough to be admitted to the first class of students at the University of Pennsylvania for the new master's degree in applied positive psychology, where I was tutored by the best in the world in this subject. It was there that I found a way to marry the science of goal accomplishment with the science of happiness, and my capstone project laid the groundwork for this book.

In the fall of 2007, Sterling Publishing approached me about writing a comprehensive guide to happiness and life lists, because the connection between these two topics was undeniable, and I had become a regular in the media discussing the link. At that time, I was also teaching a teleclass with Dr. Michael B. Frisch of Baylor University called Quality of Life Therapy and Coaching.

Mike's interest in goal accomplishment and well-being dates from 1989, when he delivered a paper at an international conference at Oxford University. Until that point, psychology was focused on studying human deficits instead of innate strengths and talents. Mike's paper was an early version of what eventually became Quality of Life Therapy and Coaching, which posits that meaning and contentment come from setting and achieving goals in sixteen key areas of life, and that overall meaning and satisfaction with life improve when an individual accomplishes goals in the particular areas of life that he or she cares about, such as love, work, and spiritual pursuits.

In my coaching practice, I have discovered that successful people almost always have life lists. These lists enable them to be more joyful, proactive, and accomplished. The most current research underscores that establishing clear-cut goals—and a path to accomplish them—contribute to a meaningful and flourishing life, and *Creating Your Best Life* is the first step-by-step guide to show you how to do just that.

Creating Your Best Life is revolutionary in its content and approach. This is the first comprehensive guide that combines the science of goal setting with the science of positive psychology to help you conceive and achieve the goals that contribute to your quality of life. Using an easy-to-follow, step-by-step approach, we show you:

- Why life lists contribute to happiness and success
- Why our daily happiness has such a major impact on goal accomplishment
- How to measure and enhance your own well-being
- How to make a life list with the most appropriate and beneficial goals in sixteen areas of your life

- ■ The most important qualities necessary for success, such as grit and self-regulation, as well as how to enhance your abilities in these and other areas
- ■ How your social circle can help or hinder the accomplishment of your goals
- ■ How to become more resilient while also learning how to savor each of your wins

The many exercises and worksheets in the book are designed to help you to maximize the information, research, tips, and advice that we've poured into each chapter. Inspired and informed by leaders in the goal-setting and happiness fields, we've also given you methods of evaluating your own strengths in several areas, such as self-control and savoring.

We want you to use this book often and with passion. Carry it with you, write in it, and use our sample life lists as guides for your own dreams. Our goal is for you to create a life of engagement, meaning, and pleasure by using the tools and research you find here so that your life list is a vibrant reality and not a distant dream.

Now, go and create your best life!

CAROLINE ADAMS MILLER, MAPP
July 2008

PART

1

WHY LIFE LISTS MATTER

In this section of the book, we share the cutting-edge
research on the importance of life lists and happiness,
and how they tie together. Understanding these two
concepts will give you a solid foundation upon which
you can set and achieve the goals that will bring you
the greatest fulfillment and day-to-day joy.

▼

1

THE ROYAL ROAD
TO HAPPINESS AND SUCCESS

Twenty years from now you will be more disappointed by the things
that you didn't do than by the ones you did do. So throw off
the bowlines. Sail away from the safe harbor. Catch the
trade winds in your sails. Explore. Dream. Discover.

—MARK TWAIN

I F YOU'VE TUNED in to any popular media, glanced at advertisements on billboards, or even attended a mainstream church service in recent years, you have probably heard or seen something about the power of goal setting, and more specifically about the importance of having a "life list" or "bucket list." You've also undoubtedly heard about the science of happiness and the usefulness of living each day as if it were your last if you want to inject your goals with passion.

Sometimes these concepts are packaged as encouragement to travel to a list of must-see marvels before it's too late, and even financial-planning companies want you to have a life list to ensure that you have the funds to pay for your goals. At least one major credit card company has touted itself as the plastic of choice to pay for the realization of all these globe-trotting and acquisition goals, while a department store chain advertises itself with a to-do list, reminding you to check your daily goals off your list by spending your money there.

Life Lists Come to the Silver Screen

Hollywood brought heightened attention to the topic of life lists, producing two movies in the early 2000s that focus on the intersection of life lists with the regrets that can occur when you fail to make progress toward the accomplishment of those goals while you still have time.

In *Last Holiday*, Queen Latifah stars as an ordinary working-class woman who is galvanized into action by an inaccurate diagnosis of a medical condition that leaves her with just a few weeks to live. She takes her "Book of Possibilities"—a scrapbook filled with pictures of places she would visit and meals she would eat "someday"—and turns it into her "Book of Realities" by emptying her savings accounts and doing everything she has ever wanted to do. Queen Latifah giddily sleeps on satin sheets, wears beautiful clothes, travels first-class, eats desserts without guilt, and skis down some of Europe's finest black-diamond slopes before she wistfully sums up her new life philosophy near the end of the film.

"I wish I'd known that happiness comes from going after your goals while you are alive—not from waiting for that day to occur at some point in the future," she notes in a toast to a group of fellow diners. Luckily, she discovers that she's not on death's doorstep, which frees her up to return home to marry the man of her dreams and become the chef at her own restaurant—the goals she had only dreamed about while marking time as a department store housewares rep.

Another popular film, *The Bucket List*, featuring Jack Nicholson and Morgan Freeman, tells a similar story of how the prospect of death made friends of two strangers, who went from sharing a hospital room to traveling around the world to see the pyramids, skydive, and even heal fractured family relationships before they "kicked the bucket." The theme of both films is that it isn't enough to just have a list; you must go after the goals on your list with gusto and the companionship of others while life is there for the taking. By pushing the envelope on life, taking risks, articulating your deepest desires, gathering support, and being fearless, you will not only become happier; you'll die without regrets.

Life Lists Inspired by Near-Death Experiences

Although we can't all finance trips to Egypt or stays in five-star hotels—and those goals may not even be on our life lists—it is accurate to say that brushes with death can prompt a reevaluation of one's purpose and can result in the creation, or refinement, of one's life goals, thus leading to a happier, more meaningful existence. Ted Leonsis, a billionaire businessman who has made a name for himself through his leadership at America Online, his ownership of several Washington, D.C.–area sports teams, and his burgeoning career as a film producer, likes to talk about his life list, which came about as a result of thinking he would die when a plane he was riding in developed engine trouble.

It was 1983, and at the age of twenty-five, Leonsis had just sold his first company for a cool fifteen million dollars, vaulting him into the heady stratosphere of self-made millionaires. On a routine business trip, his plane encountered trouble, prompting the young mogul to grab an envelope and quickly scribble everything he wanted to do with his life if God would allow him a second chance. Instead of just wanting to pile up more money, Leonsis wrote things like "Take care of in-laws" and "Support someone who makes a great breakthrough in science or art." Fortunately, the plane landed safely, but Leonsis alighted from the plane a changed man who decided to use the hastily created list as his guide for a reinvigorated life.

Twenty years later, this list has become his calling card at fund-raisers, during corporate speeches, and at charity events, where he encourages everyone to create their own life lists. "If you write it down, you have a road map," he told one interviewer in 2001. "It makes it seem more bite-sized, and there's nothing more fulfilling than getting that check mark off."

Phil Keoghan, the TV host of *The Amazing Race*, tells a similar story of running into trouble while scuba diving in an underwater wreck in New Zealand at the age of nineteen. Rattled by his youthful brush with mortality, Keoghan surfaced and reconsidered his carefree and aimless existence. Now he has a mission of leaving no opportunity wasted and works professionally and personally to help others do the same. Like Leonsis, he has made his life goals public, adding that extra oomph of accountability for staying on track.

High Performers

A person should set his goals as early as he can and devote all his energy and talent to getting there. With enough effort, he may achieve it. Or he may find something that is even more rewarding. But in the end, no matter what the outcome, he will know he has been alive.

—WALT DISNEY

Edwin Locke, the codeveloper of goal-setting theory, studied the traits of what he called "prime movers"—people he termed "great wealth creators," who had "moved the world" with their passion, vision, energy, and perseverance. Over many years, Locke refined his list of "prime mover" traits down to the essential seven, two of which are "vision" and "action." Because of their abundant vision and action, the men and women Locke profiled were all renowned goal setters; the items on their lists ranged from "very difficult" to "impossible."

Locke paid special tribute to well-known business icons such as General Electric's former CEO Jack Welch, who encouraged "stretch" goals, and Mary Kay Ash, the founder and president of Mary Kay Cosmetics, who started every day with a list of prioritized goals that were tied in with longer-term goals. She typically started each day by tackling the hardest goal first, and encouraged every-one in her company to do the same. Her methods were so successful that major corporations copied her goal-setting strategies, just one of the reasons why Ash was named one of the most successful businesspeople of the entire twentieth century by Harvard Business School.

Permission to Live More Fully

Watching a loved one die before he or she even has a life list can open the door for an individual to become more proactive. Chris Duffy lost his life when terrorists attacked the World Trade Center, where he perished along with sixty-seven of his investment bank colleagues at Keefe, Bruyette and Woods. Duffy's father, John, also a member of the firm, was late getting to work that day, along with colleagues Andrew Cullen and Will DeRiso. All three men told a reporter six years later that they'd been transformed by the tragedy in terms of how they now view risk taking and the necessity of a carpe diem outlook.

Cullen noted, "I think I have accelerated things in life that I have wanted. Whether it is going out to the Grand Tetons and hiking through Cascade Canyon, or going to Albuquerque to watch the mass ascension of the balloons, or climbing Mount Washington, instead of saying, 'I will get to those things in the future,' I say, 'These are things I want to do, and I will do them now.'"

Duffy elaborated on the impact of losing his son and how it had caused him to have a profound respect for approaching each day as if it were his last. "It has made me more decisive in terms of doing things. You have a different appreciation of time and how much time you have. . . . If there is stuff I want to do or a decision I have to make, I just make it now. Why wait? You may not be around tomorrow."

Many were also inspired to live with courage by the phone call made by Tom Burnett to his wife, Deena, as he sat on United Flight 93, which was the only hijacked flight on 9/11 that did not crash into a building. He told his wife that his flight had been hijacked, that a man had already been knifed to death, and that he thought the plane was on a "suicide mission." Deena responded that planes had already crashed into the World Trade Center and the Pentagon, to which Tom said, "They're talking about crashing this plane into the ground. We have to do something. I'm putting a plan together." In his next and final phone call to his wife, he said, "We're going to take back the airplane. . . . Don't worry, we're going to do something." Then he hung up.

The Pursuit of Happiness

We are all of us resigned to death; it's life we aren't resigned to.

—GRAHAM GREENE

It was a remarkable sight. On September 18, 2007, a handsome, dark-haired man stepped to the microphone to give his "last lecture" at Carnegie Mellon University. The tradition of a "last lecture" is usually reserved for tenured professors who are at the end of their teaching days, when they impart their final words of wisdom in a farewell address to their students. Some American schools, such as Stanford University, have leaped on this idea and featured a Last Lecture series, in which they ask esteemed colleagues to give a hypothetical last lecture on a topic that is meaningful to them. The philosophy behind these talks is "If I had just one more chance to tell the world what matters most to me, what would I say?"

For Randy Pausch, the married father of three young children, his last lecture was not hypothetical. He had been diagnosed with late-stage pancreatic cancer, which was no longer responding to treatment, so this was, indeed, one of his last opportunities to make any kind of speech, and its impact was so profound that within weeks of its posting on YouTube, more than six million people visited his home page to watch his speech.

What did Pausch talk about in this emotional and riveting last lecture? He called it "Really Achieving Your Childhood Dreams," and in it he paid homage to the power of not only having a life list, but pursuing it with vigor and allowing its energy to drive you forward as you live your life with gusto and gratitude. /

The audience watched a slide show packed with photographs from his life, as Pausch illustrated how he'd pursued and accomplished most, if not all, of his childhood dreams, from experiencing zero gravity to winning huge stuffed animals at amusement parks. He made the audience laugh heartily, but also drove home the point that going after your dreams and never losing your childhood sense of wonder is crucial to your well-being. He encouraged his listeners to know and assist others with their goals. "As you get older," he noted, "you may find that enabling the dreams of others is even more fun." Pausch finally succumbed the following summer to the cancer, but not without impacting countless lives with his brave speech, which also was the inspiration for a book that came out in the months before his death.

Fearless Forties and Nifty Fifties

Life list goals have also become more fashionable among adults who have accumulated the money and time to pursue their childhood dreams. A survey released by the Adventure Travel Trade Association in March 2007 noted that the typical adventure traveler is "female and fortyish," with South America being her most popular destination. Many travel organizations cater to this group, assembling "girlfriend getaways" that whisk travelers to dude ranches, yoga retreats, and other exciting destinations that stimulate the imagination.

The British government has even identified a new subset of British adults called the "Nifty Fifties," who are going after their goals with renewed gusto. Their most common aspirations are to travel to Nepal, drive a convertible, write a novel, experience true love, skydive, and go white-water rafting, according to Tesco Life Insurance, which conducted the survey. Tesco's report explained, "They've decided to take the five-star version of the student gap year [a year between high school and college during which many European students traditionally work and travel to gain maturity and life experience], encompassing all of the adventure with none of the discomforts. Neither burgeoning waistlines nor graying hair is going to hold them back."

Life lists are also proliferating in these age-groups because we are living longer and healthier lives, which has changed the midlife crisis into the midlife opportunity. Experts who have studied this trend call it "creative aging," and they say that any depression or sadness noted in this group is often transformed into initiatives that lay the groundwork for substantive, long-term growth. "People are aware that they have more years in front of them, and they feel really creative about it, and so for them, it's more what the Chinese call a crisis of opportunity," says Judith Sherven, a clinical psychologist in New York. "They want to do something different."

Why the Best Athletes Have Life Lists

Elite athletes have a lot at stake. They often have the eyes of the world upon them, and many have financial incentives in the form of sponsorships, salaries, and bonuses that are tied to their performance. With a compressed time span in which to enjoy their physical prowess, they have to be more goal focused, diligent, and resilient than the rest of us if they are going to succeed. Many also work with sports psychologists to ensure that they benefit from the latest developments in visualization, peak performance, and nutrition.

It's no surprise, then, to learn that one of the world's all-time finest swimmers, American Michael Phelps, keeps his list of life goals on his nightstand so that it's the first thing he sees when he wakes up in the morning to begin the first of several grueling daily practices. Kate Ziegler, another internationally ranked American swimmer, keeps her goals posted on her bedroom walls, frequently checking them to gauge her progress and create a new set of challenging missions. Both swimmers work with coaches who weigh in on these short-term and long-term goals, providing them with feedback, tools, and the motivation to keep going when the list feels daunting, or when short-term obstacles arise.

In fact, sports coaches are often renowned for their own personal goal setting, and not just how they work with their athletes. Eric Mangini, the youngest coach in the National Football League in 2006, had a goal of running his own team for years before the opportunity actually arose. His partner in running the New York Jets, Mike Tannenbaum, was no different in terms of long-term goals and a ferocious belief in himself. As a college student, he'd researched and written a paper on how he planned to run a football team one day, which he was doing just ten short years later.

The iconic Lou Holtz, coach of the legendary Notre Dame University football team, made his own life list in his twenties when his wife persuaded him to do so to counteract his depression about losing his job at the time. Holtz took her challenge to heart and wrote down 107 goals, including seeing his children graduate from college, becoming the coach of a national championship football team, and dining at the White House. Of these 107 goals, at least 93 have been accomplished, according to Holtz, who says, "An unwavering commitment to your goals will turn today's tragedies into tomorrow's triumphs."

Not a New Phenomenon

Life lists aren't restricted to the current generation, however. Leonardo da Vinci, who has often been called the most exceptional genius and inventor of all time, was a renowned goal setter who was never without his famous notebooks, in which he jotted down ideas for inventions, questions he wanted to learn the answers to, and elaborate mind maps of solutions to problems. As he got older and became more aware of his mortality, da Vinci often spoke of the importance of having clear personal goals that were followed through to completion.

"Think well to the end" and "Consider first the end" were pieces of advice that he gave to his students about crafting their own goals, which he also felt ought to be represented visually. That being said, da Vinci was bereft on his deathbed about the goals he failed to accomplish, apologizing to "God and man for leaving so much undone."

It's No "Secret"

It appears obvious that accomplishing goals leads to greater joy. After all, who wouldn't want to win Olympic gold, dine at the White House, marry the love of one's life, or see one's children graduate from college?

The real reason why a life list can bring you more joy, however, is a bit more complex, even though it's not a "secret." This is where our book is revolutionary and different from every other book that has ever been published on the topic of goal pursuit and how it is connected with life satisfaction. Our theory doesn't involve any magical thinking, chanted affirmations, or the visualization of fancy red sports cars and lavish homes. We also do not pass along unproven anecdotes that don't offer empirical evidence to support our step-by-step guide to creating, and then accomplishing, the goals that matter most to you.

Proven, Time-Tested, and Simple

Findings from thirty years of research on life satisfaction show that happiness requires having clear-cut goals in life that give us a sense of purpose and direction. When we make progress toward satisfying our most cherished needs, goals, and wishes in the sixteen areas of life that contribute to contentment, we create well-being. Our research also shows that when we make progress toward attaining goals in one area of life, we raise our overall life satisfaction in other areas because of the potent "spillover" effect.

Our life list theory includes tenets from Quality of Life Therapy and Coaching, a science-based system that comes from working with hundreds of clients for more than thirty-five years, and that has been held up to the most rigorous standards of testing by well-established organizations such as the National Institutes of Health. Our approach also includes some of the most recent findings in the emerging science of positive psychology, a rapidly growing movement comprised of scholars, academics, and clinicians who are finding that we can become happier through such practices as gratitude, using our strengths effectively, and accomplishing goals that are tied to our values. We also bring decades of our own experience of working with clients all over the world to the table, and we share many of their stories here with you.

If you follow our step-by-step method, you will learn what areas of life matter most to you, what types of goals will bring you the greatest satisfaction, how to pursue them to completion, and how to flexibly disengage from goal pursuit that no longer suits your day-to-day reality. You will also learn happiness-boosting strategies that will increase your persistence and zest, as well how to cope with the inevitable disappointments and setbacks that can threaten to undermine all goal pursuit. In short, we give you a complete step-by-step guide to understanding how to set and achieve goals, and we show you how and why this pursuit has the impact of making you happier, too.

A Fun Enterprise

Too often, we resist setting goals because of failed attempts at New Year's resolutions, or because we equate goals with tasks, which can feel more like a burden than anything else. With Americans spending less and less time on leisure pursuits and more time juggling job demands, parenthood, aging parents, and other challenging situations, having one more thing to do can be overwhelming.

The purpose of this book is to show you how creating a life list can be effective as well as fun. Identifying goals that involve creative pursuits, and that put you into a state of "flow," can be fun, and it's also fun to have travel goals that give you something to plan for and anticipate. Sharing your goals with other proactive people, and finding ways to brainstorm about them so that you wake up with a contagious feeling that life is filled with opportunities, is also a lot of fun!

Goals should never be designed to punish us, and they should never be goals that we adopt because someone else feels they would be good for us. Rather, our work with clients has shown that clearly chosen goals that are anchored in our own values and the areas of life that matter to us give us an exciting feeling that others will recognize as zest and a can-do attitude, and by the end of this book, we believe you will feel this way, too.

A Hopeful Outlook

What keeps me going is goals.
—MUHAMMAD ALI

A good life list is one that makes you feel hopeful about yourself, your future, and the manifold opportunities that will arise as a result of your endeavors. Rick Snyder, the founder of hope theory, said that when a person has goals, he or she begins to think more creatively about how to achieve them, and that this "pathways thinking" results in a more hopeful outlook on life. People who are hopeful are happier, and they work much more persistently and flexibly toward goal completion. Not only will our life list theory show you how to be more hopeful, but you'll discover for yourself why it pays off handsomely in goal accomplishment.

Positively Contagious

Groundbreaking work at Harvard Medical School by Dr. Nicholas Christakis has shown that one's likelihood of becoming obese is more closely correlated with who your friends are than with what you eat. He has also discovered that smokers don't quit smoking alone; they quit in clusters. We also see this "social contagion" factor in our work with clients, who find that becoming more focused about setting and attaining goals in the domains of life that are important to them has the result of making those around them more proactive, too. They also find themselves drawn to spending more time with people who share their upbeat outlook.

Consider the case of Bob Perini, the founder of DrinkMoreWater, a company in Maryland. Bob decided that he wanted to break into the list of the five hundred fastest-growing companies charted in *Inc.* magazine, so he posted that goal—along with a number of other personal and professional goals—on a list outside his office. Everyone who came to speak to him had to pause and look at Bob's goals before they met with him.

The results astounded Bob, even though he already believed in the power of life lists. Not only did his company vault into *Inc.* magazine's lists, rising steadily for several years in a row, but goal lists became commonplace at DrinkMoreWater.

"I put a dry erase board in a common area in the company headquarters," Bob recounted later. "People wrote down their goals on this huge board, and I got a huge kick out of knowing that people could see me standing in front of the board, looking at their goals."

It's no wonder that the company has become so successful that Bob has gone into semiretirement and now lives on a multiacre spread in the bucolic suburbs of Washington, D.C., and that he has time to pursue other goals on his life list, such as traveling extensively with his wife and children and mountain biking with friends throughout the American Southwest.

Every List Is Unique

We are often asked whether life lists should be studded with exotic trips that drain our bank accounts, particularly after *The Bucket List* depicted daring and expensive escapades that most of us can only dream about. The emphatic answer is no. Your life list is unique, and if you follow our step-by-step approach, it will not replicate anyone else's list, nor should it. Just as we are all distinct individuals with different chromosomes, backgrounds, and family situations, we all have our own passions, longings, strengths to tap, and goals that reflect where we want to go and what we wish to leave behind as our legacy.

Even after years of working with clients, we are always fascinated by the extraordinary variety of meaningful goals we see on their life lists, from "Tell my father I love him before he dies," to "Retrace Odysseus' voyage around the Greek Islands," "Anonymously donate all of the presents for an underprivileged family's Christmas," "Rollerblade through Holland," "Wear a bikini at the age of sixty," and "Make other people laugh every day." Let your imagination, your heart, and your soul be your guides as you go through this process, but don't be afraid to peek at someone else's list from time to time, because you never know what it might trigger inside of you!

Where Your Life List Is Now

At the moment, your personal goals are probably swirling through your head in a mad rush of pictures and words, and your pulse might be slightly quicker because you're beginning to dream about your immediate and long-term future. Decide right now if you'd like to dedicate a special journal to the process of creating your life list, or if you'd like to scribble notes in the margins of this book as you read and fill in the exercises at the end of the book. Of course, you can do both. There is no right or wrong way to go through this process, but we do encourage you to give this book a workout, regardless of your approach. This guide has been designed to provide you with all the tools and checklists you need to understand and refine the process of goal accomplishment, but we expect that you may want to add a notebook or binder to this process, and we encourage you to use whatever tools make creating your own life list fun and easy. Before we get to the actual making of the lists, however, we will provide a bit more background on just how important they are in the creation of one's happiness, and why understanding and applying the findings from the new science of positive psychology can make or break your efforts to accomplish your goals. By the time we get to Chapter 5, where you will read about a variety of new ways to create your own life list, you will have a solid grounding in the research about how and why this all fits together.

Life List Exercises and Worksheets

❏ Complete the "Portrait of Your Life" exercise on page 249. This is a one-paragraph writing exercise designed to help you think about how you would like to be memorialized in a newspaper obituary that would focus on your key strengths and gifts to the world.

❏ Take a few minutes now to jot down five goals that have emerged since you picked up the book:

1. _____

2. _____

3. _____

4. _____

5. _____

❏ Rent and watch *The Bucket List* or *Last Holiday.*

❑ Begin to fill in "One Hundred Things to Do before I Die," a popular "bucket list" approach (see page 225) that will help you brainstorm ideas for your own life list. After finishing this book, you will probably have completed the entire list, as well as accomplished a few of your goals, but you can get started now, and return to your list to add and tweak it as you experience more insights.

❑ Make a list of people you know who are goal setters. Do they have life lists?

❑ Watch Randy Pausch's "Last Lecture" online, where he describes the importance of going after your dreams, and helping others accomplish theirs, as well (www.cmu.edu/uls/journeys/randy-pausch/index.html).

❑ Visit a social networking site that is devoted to listing, tracking, and achieving your life goals so that you can get a sense of what others are doing. A comprehensive site is www.your100things.com, where you can even hear short interviews with people who have accomplished some of the goals that might be on your list, too. See page 266 for names of other sites like this.

❑ Read or listen to biographies of people who are famous goal setters, such as Lou Holtz, Tiger Woods, and Mary Kay Ash.

2

WHAT'S ALL THE FUSS ABOUT HAPPINESS, ANYWAY?

It is not God's will merely that we should be happy,
but that we should make ourselves happy.
—IMMANUEL KANT

Perhaps you have read or heard something about the new science of positive psychology and the importance of understanding and cultivating happiness if you want to have a meaningful, healthy life. Appropriate goal pursuit is also one of the chief hallmarks of a happy person, so it is important for anyone who is making or pursuing life list goals to understand some of the research on well-being and why learning how to become even a little bit happier can have such a massive impact on your success. This connection will also interest you if you have made happiness the number one goal on your life list.

Happiness Is Not Just a Warm Puppy Anymore

The theme of happiness is everywhere, from the cover of *Time* magazine to the ad campaigns that increasingly link your well-being to something as frivolous as the consumption of a grilled cheese sandwich. *U.S. News and World Report* begins each year with an issue devoted to fifty ways to improve your life in the coming year, and the magazine's top suggestion for 2006 was to "get happier." And just as it did on the subject of life lists, Hollywood has weighed in on the happiness topic, giving us its rosy interpretation of what life satisfaction consists of in the 2006 Will Smith tearjerker, *The Pursuit of Happyness.*

Happiness is now seen as a commodity that we can seek and attain if we work hard enough. While this is good news for those who are looking to enhance their well-being, it's also important to understand that achieving happiness can be a hard-fought battle, particularly if you were born with a temperament that tends toward pessimism or introversion. Our life list approach blends the best of current well-being and goal-accomplishment science to give you the tools you need to enhance your own daily experience of contentment so that your goal pursuit has the best chance to succeed.

Happiness at Harvard

Some of the most avid seekers, and discriminating consumers, of happiness are young adults. At Harvard University, arguably one of the most elite learning institutions in the world, students expressed their enthusiasm for this topic by voting with their feet during the 2005–2006 academic year. A record-setting number of students enrolled in Professor Tal Ben-Shahar's undergraduate class on positive psychology that year, with more than eight hundred undergraduates packing the cavernous Memorial Hall, where they quietly took notes on the philosophy of happiness, historical attempts to change well-being, and the research to date on the topic. The noteworthy success of the class was described in hundreds of newspapers and television shows, and even in late-night comedy programs, as the most popular offering in the history of the institution, and one that students often told reporters was the most life-changing and practical educational experience they'd ever had.

Harvard wasn't alone. The University of Pennsylvania opened its doors for a new master's degree in applied positive psychology in September 2005, and increasingly turns away hundreds of applicants from around the world who continue to vie for the opportunity to study at the feet of the "father of positive psychology," Dr. Martin E. P. Seligman, for one year. The first PhD program in positive psychology was not far behind, beginning at Claremont College in California in 2007 under Hungarian researcher Mihaly Csikszentmihalyi, who coined the term "flow" as a way of describing our emotional state when we engage in challenging pursuits that cause us to lose track of time. Business schools and corporations also upped their attention to happiness, devoting money, class time, and conferences to helping graduate students explore "appreciative inquiry"—the process of asking questions to elicit information about how and when individuals and organizations function at their highest and most positive levels—as well as strengths-based approaches to hiring, management, and performance reviews.

Is More Happiness Better?

We are not all born for happiness.

—SAMUEL JOHNSON

As often happens, when the pendulum swings too far in one direction, there is a correction at the other end of the arc. This has been seen in the happiness movement, which initially attracted scores of motivational speakers, life coaches, new-age gurus, and wide-eyed positive psychology devotees who believed that if some happiness was good, more was undoubtedly better. Unfortunately, that's just not true.

Researchers have found that extreme happiness is not the optimal state for day-to-day functioning, particularly if we ignore or try to quash normal feelings of sadness or guilt that prompt us to do valuable soul-searching or simply move through normal life transitions, such as the death of a loved one or the loss of a dream. When we are sad and wear a look of distress, it also signals to those around us that we can use help in getting through these times, which bolsters the social support so necessary to ongoing well-being.

In surveys of 118,519 people from ninety-six countries, scientists studied how closely well-being matched up with reports on income, education, political participation, volunteer activities, and positive relationships. University of Illinois psychologist Ed Diener, one of the most respected researchers in the field of happiness, analyzed the results of this study with his colleagues and distilled the essence of the findings in an article in *Perspectives on Psychological Science.*

"Once a moderate level of happiness is achieved, further increases can sometimes be detrimental" in some areas of life, Diener and colleagues noted. People who rated as "8's" and not "9's" or "10's" were more likely to use slight discontent as motivation to improve their education, their community, and even their jobs. This could be why "8's" and "9's" were found to be not only healthier, but also wealthier than people who strove for a constant "10."

That's not to say that sadness should be the norm, or that striving for greater fulfillment and life satisfaction doesn't have a place in your life. The dangers of discontent and unhappiness are profound and well-known. For example, following is a small sample of the possible negative outcomes of living with depression or low life satisfaction.

- Money spent on visits to the doctor's office
- Chronic pain syndrome
- Job accidents and low worker productivity
- Heart problems
- Fewer and worse social relationships

Unaddressed depression is also thought to contribute to the recent 20 percent spike in suicide among Americans between the ages of forty-five and fifty-four. Experts studying this trend have noted that a frayed social support network, resulting from the breakup of families and a disintegration of extended family support, could be behind this surge. Unhappy people are also thought to be abusers of prescription medications, which are easily available online, because a number of suicides result from overdoses of these drugs.

Happiness as Character Strength

We see happiness in a new and exciting way: as a character strength that, if persistently cultivated, will give you greater zest, persistence, and energy for accomplishing your goals. Our program doesn't take a get-happier-at-all-costs and check-goals-off-your-life-list-now approach that glosses over what research tells us about optimal well-being, however. We believe that positive and negative affect are both necessary in one's life, and that both are important barometers that play a role in optimal well-being. Following our life list approach will result in a richer and deeper level of happiness—an élan vital that will give you not only enthusiasm for life, but also a deep sense of excitement that will allow you to have more success with your goals than you ever thought possible.

How Did It All Start?

Although philosophers, sages, and biblical prophets have been theorizing and writing about happiness since the beginning of time, the idea of studying happiness and its components experienced its tipping point at the end of the twentieth century. At that time, Marty Seligman, a highly respected researcher in the fields of depression and learned helplessness, sounded a clarion call in his role as president of the American Psychological Association for a dramatic shift in how his profession approached human functioning.

"Sadly, while plumbing the depths of what is worst in life, psychology lost its connection to the positive side of life—the knowledge about what makes human life most worth living, most fulfilling, most enjoyable and most productive," he noted, asking that psychology now turn its attention to studying the conditions that contribute to human flourishing as opposed to the study of how to fix what is broken or diagnosable.

Seligman was, in many ways, the ideal person to pull this movement together, because he is a self-described "grump" who points out that his normally pessimistic outlook on life responds to the exercises that he and others have fine-tuned in recent years to enhance well-being. In fact, Seligman was the young researcher at the University of Pennsylvania who discovered "learned helplessness" when he noticed that a certain percentage of dogs refused to give up even after being repeatedly shocked and given no means to escape their cages. What made some dogs lie down and give up while others remained resilient fascinated him. Creating the positive psychology movement allowed him to bring the study of this resilience, and how to cultivate and teach it to others, to the forefront.

As Seligman and other noted researchers aptly pointed out in the late 1990s, thousands of research papers existed on the topics of dysfunction, sadness, illness, and breakdown. Studies about joy, gratitude, character strengths, and positive emotions were almost nonexistent. At Seligman's urging, more and more people around the world turned their attention to identifying what conditions allowed people and institutions to be at their best. Cultivating these positive emotions and understanding how they fit into the puzzle of well-being attracted some of the best minds of our time, giving the movement credibility.

BETWEEN 1887 AND 2000, the number of research papers and studies on negative emotions such as anger and depression outnumbered the study of positive emotions such as gratitude and happiness by fourteen to one!

A Happiness Set Point

Since Seligman birthed the science of positive psychology, the world of psychology has literally turned upside down, with the popular media breathlessly reporting on its every development. In fact, a January 2005 *Time* magazine cover story was largely devoted to this topic, exploring the various components of well-being, including how it is created, why it matters, and what we can do to impact our mind-sets and behaviors in ways that allow us to flourish.

For example, it's now known from studying identical and fraternal twins that we inherit a genetically determined happiness set point (a hardwired predisposition to feel and express emotions within a certain range), but that we also have more discretion and power than previously thought to override that inheritance. In fact, although the percentages vary slightly from study to study, it's safe to posit that 50 percent to 80 percent of our daily contentment is completely under our control.

There is even a widely accepted equation for happiness that was devised by researchers Sonja Lyubomirsky, Kennon Sheldon, and David Schkade to illustrate how powerful our daily behaviors and circumstances are in contributing to our happiness:

$$S(et\ point) + C(ircumstances) + V(oluntary\ behaviors) = H(appiness)$$

Our program is a voluntary activity that can boost your happiness because a proactive pursuit of deliberate goals is just one of the ways we can create beneficial circumstances that contribute to a happier and more productive life.

The Hedonic Treadmill

Many people labor under the assumption that becoming lastingly happier involves accumulating things, such as bigger houses or fancier cars. But the newest research shows that we experience mostly temporary changes to our well-being when we get a raise or acquire granite counters for our state-of-the-art kitchens, even if those particular goals have been in our crosshairs for a while. A simple analogy helps to explain this puzzling discrepancy. Remember when you (or your child), begged and pleaded for a certain toy (trip, romantic relationship), and once it was received, the amount of joy derived from this possession or experience didn't provide the same oomph as time went by, and another thing became the object of desire?

This common occurrence has been dubbed the "hedonic treadmill," a moniker that suggests we are destined to always crave more in order to maintain a current level of happiness. Thus, we adapt to good things and then begin to crave more, which is why the treadmill analogy exists. Advertisers understand this phenomenon, which is why they are always ready to sell us a new item to replace the one we are already bored with—and because a new purchase temporarily works to make us happier, we always fall for it.

Although the hedonic treadmill predicts that we tend to adapt to the good things that happen in our lives, and gradually lose pleasure in what initially made us happy, researchers have found that there are some things that we never get used to experiencing as either good or bad. For example, on the plus side, it's been found that great sex is a fail-safe way to always experience more joy, while loud noises never cease to make us unhappy.

An International Perspective

As researchers have increasingly turned to the study of individual happiness, they have begun to determine which countries have the happiest citizens. A recent Gallup World Survey demonstrates that circumstances clearly play a role in self-reported well-being, because the happiest citizens are from wealthy, stable countries (Scandinavians are at the top), while the unhappiest citizens inhabit countries with poor infrastructure, human rights issues, and poor health care (Ethiopia and Niger round out the bottom).

But Ruut Veenhoven, a professor of sociology at Erasmus University Rotterdam, and director of the World Database of Happiness, is quick to note that while national wealth matters in global well-being surveys, that figure isn't necessarily correlated with the personal well-being of individual citizens of each country, for whom it's more important to "invest in good social relationships."

The tiny Buddhist country of Bhutan in the Himalayas has elevated the pursuit of happiness to a level of importance not seen anywhere else in the world. Bhutan's former king Jigme Singye Wangchuk decided to eliminate the gross national product as the barometer of ultimate flourishing in his realm in the 1980s, noting that "Gross National Happiness is more important than Gross National Product." Instead, he focused on the "four pillars" of Gross National Happiness: socioeconomic growth, cultural values, environmental conservation, and good governance. Bhutan even has a happiness commissioner, whose job is to monitor shifts in the national mood as the country moves toward modernization, and to survey residents regularly to determine how to preserve national traditions such as respect for nature, something the residents say makes them happier.

Getting happier in Great Britain has also caught the attention of its political leaders, who have met with Seligman and other leaders in the positive psychology movement to find out how to make happiness more of a governmental priority. Their concerns are well founded, since the United Kingdom came in at the bottom of a UNICEF survey of life satisfaction among children in twenty-one developed countries; and the number of children reporting emotional difficulties or committing suicide has more than doubled in the United Kingdom over the past twenty-five years. In the meantime, the venerable British Broadcasting Corporation (BBC) got in on the act by bringing a thirteen-part series called *Making Slough Happy* to the airwaves. This down-on-its-luck British mill town tried positive psychology on for size and reported in weekly, with the end result that certain happiness prescriptions such as socializing more often and even remembering to say "thank you" did, indeed, make Slough happier.

There is also a new international happiness measure based on blood-pressure readings. A random sample of fifteen thousand people from across European countries found that hypertension troubles matched reports of low well-being, leading the researchers to conclude, "We found that a measure of a nation's rate of hypertension is a good predictor of its overall happiness. That surprised us. . . . Perhaps blood-pressure readings will one day replace or augment GDP as a measure of the success of a country. Maybe economists and doctors are going to have to work together in the design of future economic policies."

Are We at Our Lowest in Our Forties?

A comprehensive study of eighty countries released in early 2008 found that happiness follows a U-shaped curve, with men and women gradually sinking from happiness highs in their twenties to depressing lows in their forties, and then rising again. The researchers noted that one of the reasons why women appear to hit their nadir at age forty-four and men a few years later was because they lose faith in their abilities to achieve their life goals, and may have trouble finding ways to energize themselves through this tough period.

Although most men and women begin to feel happier as they get older, research shows that women are usually more unhappy than men later in life because they feel less able to accomplish their life goals. We believe that our life list approach can help both men and women with their goals and provide them with fresh, research-tested approaches to accomplishment that are successful and fun. For women, especially, this book could be exactly the medicine they need to survive their tough midlife challenges and to have the knowledge to turn their dreams into happiness-producing accomplishments.

The Happiest among Us

Periodically, the National Opinion Research Center surveys Americans about how happy they are. Six in ten of those surveyed report that they are "pretty happy," and three in ten say that they are "very happy." These positive self-reports are thought by researchers to be fairly reliable over time, especially because studies have found that they match reports given by friends and family members.

Since we have created so many measures to rank and quantify our well-being, there are multiple studies confirming that the happiest people among us:

- Enjoy what they do for a living, and regularly experience "flow" during the workday (they feel that they are challenged and that their skills match those challenges)
- Enjoy close, intimate relationships with family and friends
- Are happily married
- Have a strong spiritual faith
- See life through an optimistic lens
- Are healthy
- Compare themselves favorably to people who have less, instead of focusing on those who have more
- Are not constantly concerned about whether they can put food on the table and a roof over their heads

Flourishing Families

We are even now learning that happy families have their own idiosyncrasies that distinguish them from less happy families. Not surprisingly, happy families don't feature rigid thinking or harsh punishments, and they are not defined by affluence, either. Rather,

- There is an emphasis on hard work as opposed to "being the best."
- Everyone has privacy within the home, if desired, and can retreat to his or her own space, as needed, without intrusion.
- There is a central gathering place within the home where others, such as neighborhood children, also feel warmly accepted and welcome.
- Differences are tolerated, and family systems feature oddball aunts and goofy cousins who are treated with tolerance, demonstrating that everyone has a place in the world.
- Rituals exist for the celebration of birthdays and getting one's driver's license, lending themselves to raucous celebrations and storytelling.
- There are just a few household rules that everyone knows (such as "Be honest" or "Do your homework") as opposed to multiple rules for many occasions.
- Punishments are consistent and fair, with no surprises about why, when, or how they are inflicted.
- There is often an abundance of plants, pets, and photographs in common living areas (it's theorized that happy families extend themselves to care for objects outside of themselves more often, which explains the presence of pets and plants).

The "Big Four"

Because we're able to pinpoint the people and families who are happiest as well as the conditions that contribute to or detract from their well-being, we're also able to specify which personality characteristics are common to those happy people. There are several different ways to describe the qualities of happy people, but we focus on what is commonly described as the "big four":

1. **Optimism.** Happy people are optimistic because they tend to believe that they will experience happy outcomes and resolve problems more quickly than do pessimists. They are quick to pat themselves on the back for a job well done, and when they experience setbacks, they do not personalize them or see the issues as persistent and pervasive problems that are likely to recur.
2. **Self-confidence.** Happy people are self-confident and like themselves. Their self-confidence stems from high self-regard, and they tend to see themselves as kinder, more generous, ethical, intelligent, healthy—and freer from prejudice—than others.
3. **Extroversion.** Happy people are extroverted and thrive on the energy that is created by interacting with others, joining groups, and helping others feel at ease.

4. Self-efficacy. Happy people have self-efficacy, which simply means they not only set goals but have a strong belief in themselves that they either have what it takes to get something done or can learn how to get it done. Self-efficacy also implies the belief that your life is in your hands, and that you have the ability to control your own behavior and shape your own destiny.

One of the reasons we like this list of traits is because they are not hardwired from birth; they can be cultivated. For example, optimism training is quite well-known and very effective, and natural introverts can fake extroversion. In fact, one study of college students found that those who made deliberate efforts to socialize with others despite a desire to be alone experienced all of the benefits that natural extroverts get from being in the social swirl. This outcome is thought to stem from the benefits of being distracted from our own problems when we interact with others, as well as the powerful impact of creating bonds and experiences with people.

Our approach focuses quite strongly on building self-efficacy. When we learn how to enhance this quality through the process of having "wins" on the road to goal accomplishment, we are creating a solid foundation on which we will experience lasting and valid happiness, while establishing unshakeable self-esteem.

Self-Efficacy Theory

Albert Bandura is a much-beloved figure in the world of psychology, particularly when it comes to understanding how people motivate themselves. From his perch at Stanford University, Bandura developed his theory and methodology of self-efficacy, which has revolutionized such diverse fields as management, sports, counseling, coaching, and the self-help world. In fact, self-efficacy theory is so well accepted as an integral component of human motivation and achievement that we cannot write about goals without explaining Bandura's contribution to our approach.

As Bandura described in his seminal volume, *The Social Foundations of Thought and Action,* we can "failure proof" our lives by building the self-efficacy that is needed to accomplish all of our life goals. People with high self-efficacy see difficult tasks as interesting challenges to be mastered instead of as impossible, scary threats to be avoided. They bounce back from failure with resilience and a healthy perspective, and they don't denigrate themselves as bad or flawed people. Instead, they resolve to improve their efforts with better skills, role models, and knowledge, and they don't shrink from trying again and again until they get it right.

You might be wondering if you have "the right stuff" to be self-efficacious and turn your dreams into reality. You may even wonder if goal accomplishment is for the favored few who are born upbeat and resilient, and who live and work with people who validate them and help them achieve their goals.

The answer is yes, you have what it takes, and no, self-efficacy is not just for the favored few, or for those who won the genetic lottery. Self-efficacy is one of those qualities that are earned, not given, but it also comes only through determination, focus, and hard work. We are not promising anything that is unreachable, but we do want to caution you that it is only through the careful application of our methods, and the persistent use of certain skills, that you will become both happier and more successful. The prize is there for anyone who wants to work for it, and there is no shortcut.

How to Build Self-Efficacy

Self-efficacy is just like a muscle that you can build in four ways that are simple to understand but not easy to accomplish. Whenever you run into a roadblock with one of the goals on your life list, take a look at the four steps of self-efficacy to see if you are missing a step. Self-efficacy can be enhanced in the following ways:

- **Having role models.** Although high achievers have been found to be voracious readers of biographies of successful people, it's also important to have role models in your day-to-day life who demonstrate what you need to do to accomplish your goals. Countless athletes attest to the power of training in the presence of other athletes who have accomplished the same goals, which helps demystify and put a familiar face on a goal you may have only dreamt about. Sponsors perform this function in twelve-step groups such as Alcoholics Anonymous, and the role of mentors in Big Brother / Big Sister programs is built around this same premise.

- **Having a cheerleader.** If you have someone in your life who believes in you, and who has also earned your trust because his or her feedback is on-target and helpful, you can increase your belief in your own skills and take risks that you might not otherwise take. This is why mentors, coaches, and wise elders can have such a dramatic impact on our emotional development, and why having the right kinds of cheerleaders can be so powerful. The wrong kinds of cheerleaders are those who simply tell us what we want to hear, or who never encourage us to stray outside our comfort zones.

- **Managing stress appropriately.** People who don't have high self-efficacy often allow bad moods and physical pains to keep them from doing their best. When we learn to manage stress and its physical symptoms appropriately, we persevere and bring a more optimistic mind-set to goal pursuit.
- **Having mastery experiences.** This is the most powerful way any of us can build self-efficacy—by having "wins" that allow us to redefine who we are. Watching someone succeed, being encouraged by others to succeed, and managing our moods so that we can give our tasks our best efforts are all important pieces of the puzzle, but it's only by breaking goals into small pieces and mastering the action steps along the way that we can truly believe in ourselves.

The Bottom Line

So far, we've communicated two basic ideas:

1. Life lists are common to high achievers, and the creation and pursuit of a life list promotes happiness.
2. Happiness is a hardwired trait, but your daily behavior and actions are just as important in the expression of this quality as your genetic heritage.

In the next chapter, we detail the exquisite interplay of these two forces and what the research tells us about the success-happiness topic. We will also show you proven ways to change your own well-being, and help you create your own recipe for daily joy.

Where Your Life List Is Now

You have probably written down a few goals and are crossing them off or refining them as you think about the joy you might or might not experience from accomplishing them. For example, did you finish Chapter 1 thinking that a new Corvette might be on your life list, but now you're thinking that it might just keep you stuck on the hedonic treadmill? Take a few minutes to think about how your goals might have changed in light of what you've learned about happiness.

Life List Exercises and Worksheets

❑ Try the BAT Form on page 252. This research-supported exercise builds self-esteem, self-efficacy, and self-confidence. It also encourages celebration of past joys and achievements, and helps us to spot our unique strengths and talents, which we can use in our quest toward goal accomplishment.

❑ List five goals that you believe will bring you lasting happiness, and why.

1. _____

2. _____

3. _____

4. _____

5. _____

❑ Read or listen to a biography of someone who is considered a happy person and a high achiever, such as Oprah Winfrey, Harry Truman, or Ben Franklin. Do you think that an upbeat personality helped them to achieve more than someone else might have?

3

HOW HAPPY ARE YOU?

Happiness is . . . wanting what you want, getting what you get,
and hoping that the two will coincide.
—HOWARD MUMFORD JONES

I N THIS CHAPTER we help move you farther along the path of life list fulfillment by sharing the conclusive evidence that happiness precedes goal success
and demonstrating how many of your own ambitions can be fulfilled by learning
how to create and maintain optimal happiness levels. We also show you a new way
to take a snapshot of your current emotional temperature and overall life satisfaction, as well as provide a means of charting your progress with goal accomplishment as you move closer to fulfilling your life list ambitions. When you match
these results with our exercises, you will be able to start setting goals in the areas
of life that mean the most to you and that can have the biggest impact on your life
satisfaction. We also share some proven ways to enhance personal happiness. While
daily well-being can vary from person to person depending on genetic predisposition—and there is a limit to just how happy any of us can or should aspire to
be—there are some "silver bullets" emerging from the study of positive psychology that have been proven to evoke a positive mood by altering our body chem-
istry.

Happiness = Success

We now know that happiness is a key ingredient in living a healthy and contented
life, and that cultivating your own well-being has many implications for life list

success. But the tie-in between happiness and success is even more profound than was once thought. In fact, researchers have only recently compiled hundreds of disparate studies to conclusively answer the question, "Does success produce happiness, or does happiness produce success?"

Sonja Lyubomirsky, Ed Diener, and Laura King—all top researchers and scholars in the field of positive psychology—have methodically examined reams of data and concluded that the happiest people among us actually draw success to themselves in areas ranging from work to friendships, and that the benefits of becoming even a little bit happier on a daily basis can favorably impact the achievement of our goals in every area of life. The types of goals that researchers have studied undoubtedly include some of the ones that are on your own list, such as having a satisfying job, enjoying stable friendships, and experiencing good health, so it's helpful to know what scientists have learned and how we can apply their findings to our own lives.

Here is a sample of how happiness can affect some of the most important areas of your life:

- **Work.** Happy people are more likely to get job interviews and land jobs, be productive, avoid "job burnout," have positive relationships at work, receive high supervisor and client ratings, and earn high salaries.
- **School.** Happy people are more likely to stay in school and succeed from elementary school right through high school and college.
- **Helping others and community service.** Happy people are more deeply involved in charitable and volunteer work, and derive more satisfaction from doing it.
- **Social relationships.** Happy people have more friends and enjoy the quality of these relationships more than unhappy people. In fact, friendship has been found to be one of the strongest correlates with happiness, while having few friends predicts depression. Social isolation hurts us more than either smoking or cholesterol in shortening our life!
- **Romantic relationships.** Happy people tend to be happily married or happy in romantic relationships, and tend to describe their partners as their "great loves." Marital satisfaction has a big impact on overall life happiness, as well.
- **Health and longevity.** Happy people are healthier, have stronger immune systems, and even live longer, and this connection has been found across multiple types of illnesses such as asthma, cancer, and sickle-cell anemia. Happy individuals are also less likely to engage in substance abuse or other detrimental behaviors.
- **Leisure activities.** Happy people are much more likely to pursue recre-

ational activities, and to be interested in learning new skills and taking new classes. Not surprisingly, happy people also report much more zest and vitality, which helps them to partake of these activities.

■ **Creativity.** Happy people score very high on tests of creativity, and are more likely to be curious and open-minded than others.

The connection between happiness and success is so profound, and the list of desirable outcomes so long, that we encourage you to start your life list program by gauging how happy you are, and then learn the different ways you can voluntarily improve your well-being in order to function at your highest and most productive levels.

Resetting Your Emotional Thermostat

Some of you already know that you could stand to be a little bit happier, either because you've become aware that life has lost its zip, or maybe someone close to you has mentioned that you don't seem to be as upbeat or happy as you once were. One of our clients mentioned that she realized that she needed to work on her well-being when she was asked what brought her joy, and she couldn't think of anything!

We know that it helps immeasurably to start your life list program in a positive frame of mind, so we have devised a test of overall life satisfaction that is based on a popular measure used to assess happiness.

You can use "The Ladder of Fulfillment and Contentment" assessment, below, to gauge how happy you are right now, but you can also use it to chart your progress from time to time and see if there are other areas of your life where you would like to achieve certain goals.

The Ladder of Fulfillment and Contentment

Think of this happiness assessment as a ladder, and use it to rate how successful you have been in achieving your life goals. The top of the ladder represents complete success, while the bottom rung indicates complete lack of success. Take a few minutes to review the list, and then circle the ladder step or number that best describes where you are right now:

[10] Completely successful—so far, I have gotten the important things I want in life.

[9] Very successful

[8]

[7] Mostly successful

[6]

[5] Moderately successful

[4]

[3] Somewhat successful

[2]

[1] Slightly successful

[0] Completely unsuccessful—so far, I have not gotten any of the important things I want in life

The following table tells you how to interpret your score on the Ladder of Fulfillment and Contentment:

[10] Completely successful— so far, I have gotten the important things I want in life [9] Very successful [8] [7] Mostly successful	You are generally happy and satisfied with life. You are skilled and able to fulfill many or all of your most cherished needs, goals, and wishes. You achieve most of your goals and have found or created rewarding circumstances in which to live. Any score in this range indicates general success in your efforts to carry out a life list program. Movement up or down one point in this range indicates a significant change in life satisfaction and happiness.
[6] [5] Moderately successful [4] [3] Somewhat successful	You are fairly happy and satisfied with life but could use some improvement. You have some skills and are able to fulfill a few of your most cherished needs, goals, and wishes. Still, you do not achieve many of your goals and you may live in unrewarding circumstances that need to be changed or improved. Movement from position 6 to position 7 on the ladder indicates significant progress in life satisfaction and happiness, although any score in this range indicates only a little success in your efforts to carry out a life list self-improvement and achievement program. Even the most successful and happy people score this way when they are blocked or frustrated when they attempt major goals. This score is a wake-up call that something is wrong and that you need to take some action to achieve your goals and have your needs in life met. Pursuing a program like ours can be a good place to start. Movement up or down one point in this range indicates a significant change in life satisfaction and happiness.

	(continued)
[2] [1] Slightly successful	Movement up or down one point in this range indicates a significant change in life satisfaction and happiness. These scores signal that, in general, your most cherished needs, goals, and wishes are not being met or fulfilled. You are unsuccessful and unhappy, and you may be unskilled in meeting your needs. You may also be stuck in unrewarding and difficult circumstances that make it hard for you to fulfill your most cherished needs, goals, and wishes. This score is a wake-up call that something is wrong and that you need to take some action to achieve your goals and to get your needs in life met. Pursuing a program like ours can be an excellent place to start. Scores this low may be a sign of serious unhappiness that could lead to health problems and a lack of success and enjoyment in major areas of life such as love, work, or school.
[0] Completely unsuccessful— so far, I have not gotten any of the important things I want in life	This score signals that all of your most cherished needs, goals, and wishes are not being met or fulfilled. You are unsuccessful and unhappy, and you could be unskilled in having your needs met. You might also be stuck in very unrewarding and difficult circumstances that make it hard, or even impossible, for you to fulfill any valued goals. Scores this low may be a sign of serious unhappiness that could lead to health problems and a lack of success and enjoyment in major areas of life such as love, work, or school.

Your score is not meant to alarm you. In fact, the lower it is, the greater the possibility of finding this program affirming, hopeful, and life enhancing. It is just a starting point, and it can change quickly if you attack goals in areas that are especially important to you. If you start near the top of the scale, we also have good news—our program will enhance your goal pursuit, as well, and show you new and valuable ways that will deepen your own satisfaction in areas of life that you may not have previously considered.

Personal Pep-Ups

Now that you have taken your emotional temperature and know where you are as far as life satisfaction goes, we'd like you to jot down what you already know about activities, thoughts, or situations that consistently make you feel calm, contented, and joyful.

Marilyn responded to this request this way:

While I love spending time with my close friends, I consider myself an introvert because I draw a lot of energy from spending time alone. Ideally, this alone time is spent doing the things that make me feel most refreshed, centered, and happy: exercising, seeking natural beauty, listening to music I love, and expanding my mind in some way, like reading or learning new things.

Gerry had a slightly different take:

My favorite thing is to get in my truck and drive alone. When I have time on the open road in a car I love, I have my best thoughts, and I'm usually able to calm myself down about anything that is upsetting me. I also enjoy watching the Comedy Channel—especially the *Blue Collar Comedy Tour*—which I watch with one of my sons when we have time. I also feel better whenever I ride my bike on the weekends. My wife says I'm happier when I get home from a long ride, and I think she's right because she has known me the longest, and I know she cares about me and wouldn't say something that wasn't true.

Carolyn's list had more overtly religious and spiritual items:

When I'm sad, I duck into a Catholic church near my house that is always open, and I go into a side room that has a quiet place where I can pray and light a candle. When I sit there and pray or meditate, I feel more peaceful. I'm also at my best if I include at least one giving activity during the week that has nothing to do with me, but that helps someone else. I've volunteered to serve coffee after our Sunday service, and I've also participated in building homes with a local organization that assists the needy. That's probably my favorite thing because I feel like a million bucks when I give to people who have less than I do, and I've used my time and energy to help someone instead of just giving them my money.

Happiness boosters have been found to be most effective when you find the right fit between your own personality and lifestyle, and a behavior or activity that can improve your well-being. Take a moment to consider what you already know about yourself and what has typically boosted your mood before. For example, an introvert may find more enjoyment from solitary activities, while an extrovert may naturally thrive on group activities. By the end of this chapter, you will have a list of "jolts of joy" that will help you write your own prescription to change your mood voluntarily and at will—barring the normal sadness, anxieties, and anger that even the happiest among us go through when we are frustrated in our pursuit of the things that are most important to us.

Happiness Promotes "Inner Abundance"

When you know how to restore your equilibrium and soothe your frazzled nerves, and you follow through on these techniques, you are practicing good self-care. We believe that self-care builds something called "inner abundance," which is a condition that means you are rested, calm, and able to face the challenges in your life. Having good self-care has been found to assist in the creation of and adherence to higher professional ethical standards, but it's also important for your personal life list success, too.

Sample Booster Shots

To get you started, here are a few things we've seen on other people's lists of happiness boosters that you may not have considered before, but that might remind you of a time when you experienced a similar positive surge of emotion:

- Making breakfast and serving it on a tray to someone you love
- Giving a one-dollar bill wrapped around a PowerBar to every homeless person you encounter, along with directions to a shelter that has free meals
- Rocking in a rocking chair
- Reading a feel-good book
- Calling a repair technician, handyman, or other worker after you've received exceptional service, just to say "thank you"
- Walking at the same speed as an elderly person crossing the street, just to convey that he or she is not holding you up
- Trying something new and different, just for the heck of it, like attending a musical concert of a genre you are unfamiliar with, or watching a how-to show about a hobby that interests you

With these suggestions in mind, write down a few happiness boosters that come to mind (fill in five now, and visit page 241 for a more comprehensive worksheet, "Jolts of Joy." This list will become an invaluable source of ideas to bring a smile to your face when you need it most, and can spell the difference between having a bad day or turning it around with a well-timed and carefully chosen boost.

1. _____

2. _____

3. _____

4. _____

5. _____

p.38

Outside Opinions

Many of our clients also find it very helpful to include friends and family in their quest to discover what makes them feel good and act upbeat. Gerry told us that his wife notices how happy he is after long bike rides. In the same way, people around us often have observations about when they think we are at our happiest. You might want to solicit their opinions; you never know what people around you might have noticed that isn't quite as apparent to you. For example, one client of ours was told by some of her classmates that she always smiles when she's in a certain class with a certain professor, which she had never noticed before. Upon reflection, she realized that the professor's zany sense of humor *did* have the reliable impact of putting her in a better mood, which reminded her that offbeat humor is a definite booster for her.

Research-Tested Happiness Boosters

Why do you spend your money for that which is not bread,
and your labor for that which does not satisfy?

—ISAIAH

What brings a smile to your face could be very different from what brings a smile to someone else's face. There are certainly many opinions about what works. The Enlightenment philosopher Jean-Jacques Rousseau thought that happiness consisted of "a good bank account, a good cook, and a good digestion." Dr. Samuel Johnson asserted, "[T]here is nothing which has yet been contrived by man, by which so much happiness is produced, as by a good tavern or inn." According to author John Gunther, "all happiness depends on a leisurely breakfast." In a similar vein, Mark Twain's recipe for "the ideal life" was "good friends, good books, and a sleepy conscience."

When you strip away public opinion, and turn to what the science of positive psychology says, you can discover what researchers are both finding and confirming about a handful of proven happiness boosters that have been shown to change mood significantly. Some of these methods, which we call "above-the-neck boosters," work by changing our thinking and perception, while others—"below-the-neck boosters"—change our behavior.

▶ Proven Booster #1: Journaling

Words are, of course, the most powerful drug used by mankind.
—RUDYARD KIPLING

Dr. Laura King and Dr. James Pennebaker have done some of the earliest and most profound research on the power of journaling. They've found a number of interesting outcomes, whether someone is writing about past trauma or about their hopes and dreams for the future. Self-disclosure through writing appears to regulate our moods by giving us a safe emotional outlet, a way to put life into perspective, and a fresh way to ignite hopefulness about the future.

Even nursing home residents benefit from journal writing, which is sometimes used as "reminiscence therapy." Writing about one's life helps to "make meaning" for those who may not live much longer, providing them with comfort and psychological benefits.

One of the most intriguing findings about journaling came when King asked research participants to write down their hopes and dreams for the future in a "Best Possible Self" exercise. The instructions were to write for twenty minutes a day, four days in a row, about their life in the future if everything had gone as well as possible and all of their goals were realized. Not only did the participants feel "significantly happier" after this assignment, but the positive impact—including improved health—lasted for weeks afterward.

The types of words you use while journaling might even have a surprising long-term impact on your health. For instance, Sarah Pressman and her colleagues at the University of Pittsburgh combed the autobiographies of almost one hundred psychologists looking for words that reflected a sense of humor. They found that those who used the words "smile," "laugh," or "chuckle" frequently in their writings lived six and a half years longer than those who used the words less often or not at all.

Carly decided to make daily journaling as easy for herself as possible, because even as a child she had discovered that writing in her diary had been an enjoyable pastime, but she had gotten out of the practice as she got older and busier. Every morning at work, she decided to spend a few minutes journaling about her life, her children's lives, her experiences at work, and her hopes for the future. She decided to type her journal entries into a password-protected file on her computer, which for privacy reasons she never printed. Overall, Carly was really happy to find a modern and efficient way to incorporate the power of journaling into her busy life, and she also noticed—as did people around her—how much more contented she was on the days when she sat down and gave herself time to simply think and type.

Takeaway: There are many different ways to journal, including writing in notebooks, typing into private files, making bulleted lists of thoughts, and creating scrapbooks with words and pictures.

▶ Proven Booster #2: Expressing Gratitude

> Gratitude is the memory of the heart.
> —J. B. MASSIEU

Michael McCullough and Robert Emmons are two of the leading scholars on the topic of gratitude, and they have researched and written extensively about its power to boost happiness. They have found that people who express gratitude in any number of ways—such as thanking someone else verbally, writing down a list of blessings on a regular basis, or mailing a letter to someone who has made a difference in your life—have the power to increase life satisfaction and hope. Gratitude is also linked with lowering depression and anxiety, and may be the most powerful and long-lasting way to make someone happier.

Marty Seligman has explored the power of gratitude in his work and has found that writing down a list of things you are grateful for, as well as why those things happened to you, has the power to shape your moods in lasting ways. He also assigns an exercise called "the Gratitude Visit" to many of his students to explore whether writing—and personally delivering—a letter to someone who has changed your life, but whom you've never thanked appropriately, can make you happier. He's found that every exercise that promotes gratitude works well—some better than others, depending on the person.

Susie decided to write down the things she was grateful for every night before she went to bed. She found that her list was somewhat perfunctory at first, and included standard items like food and shelter. It wasn't long before her list expanded to items she had never properly taken the time to be grateful for, like the fact that her husband made enough money that she didn't need to work while her children were small, and how much she loved sleeping on special flannel sheets every night. Susie discovered that her gratitude list became longer and longer, and that she consciously noticed things she was grateful for throughout each day. For example, when she got the perfect parking spot when she was running late, or she learned a new skill easily, she'd make a mental note to put it on her gratitude list that night, which made her feel thankful throughout the day. Susie definitely feels happier as a result of doing this exercise, and she thinks that it will be a lifetime habit that she hopes to pass along to her children.

Takeaway: Expressing gratitude takes many forms, and there are countless ways to do so. Saying "thank you" to people who help you is a great place to start, or you can express your gratitude through an anonymous donation to a worthy cause in someone's honor. Many people find that prayers of thanks are daily gratitude exercises that make them feel better, too.

Proven Booster #3: Physical Exercise

Lack of activity destroys the good condition of every human being, while movement and methodical physical exercise save it and preserve it.
—PLATO

Physical exercise isn't just good for your body; it's good for your soul, too. Oxford University psychologist Michael Argyle was one of several prominent researchers to pinpoint the many ways that exercise makes people happier. For example, people who regularly break a sweat are more self-confident, happy, energetic, and "prosocial" (behaving in empathic, kind, and altruistic ways) with others than people who plead "too tired" and "too busy" to exercise. Exercise also reduces tension, anxiety, and depression. Regular exercisers even report mild "withdrawal" symptoms when they cannot exercise, while people who start exercising for the first time say that they get the biggest happiness boosts of all!

It's not uncommon for doctors to now prescribe exercise to clients who are suffering from depression, and there are now therapists who use their time with clients to walk and talk their way through their sessions because of their clients' noticeable boost in mood and energy after doing so.

Researchers have now proven that the so-called runner's high is an actual phenomenon and not just an anecdotal observation. Dr. Henning Boecker at the University of Bonn gave distance runners psychological mood tests before and after training sessions, and also did PET scans of their brains to note any chemical changes that had occurred during their runs. He found that the prefrontal and limbic areas of the runners' brains—the areas associated with mood—were studded with endorphins after the runs, and the more euphoria the runner noted, the more endorphins Boecker found in the brain.

> Len couldn't make it around the track at the local high school when he first decided to give running a try. His goal sheets for coaching sessions for months included walking and running to gain mileage, and although Len felt discouraged at times, he persisted until running became a regular part of his life. Within one year, he had joined a running group and had completed his first 10K race. Within three years, he had lost thirty-five pounds and successfully completed the Marine Corps Marathon in Washington, D.C. Len knows that running changed his mood for the better, and that it also gave him more persistence and energy in his work as a photographer. He believes that accomplishing the goals on his life list became easier the more he ran, and now he also lifts weights and swims to augment his regular fitness program.

Takeaway: Exercise is one of the best ways you can improve multiple areas of your life, including your happiness. Regular exercise not only releases endorphins into the bloodstream; it also helps people socialize with other exercisers, lose weight, and enjoy the outdoors.

▶ PROVEN BOOSTER #4: VOLUNTEER WORK AND ALTRUISTIC BEHAVIOR

Volunteers do not necessarily have the time; they just have the heart.
—ELIZABETH ANDREW

The more you give, the more you get—or so they say. But in this case, it's true. Researchers who studied adult men in Michigan found that those who volunteered their time, money, and energy felt happier than—and also outlived—their less altruistic peers. Random acts of kindness performed over a week also have been shown to boost well-being, as do working as a volunteer firefighter and helping to rebuild homes for people who have lost everything, such as the victims of Hurricane Katrina. Laura King even said at a conference that the link between well-being and altruism was so clear that people should "quit reading self-help books and start helping others."

Why does this type of behavior have such an impact on people's well-being? Researchers believe that it might be a hardwired characteristic that promotes the survival of our species and enables reciprocal generosity when we need a hand. But it also feels great on a chemical level. Studies of macaque monkeys have found that the more monkeys a female macaque grooms, the more stress hormones she expels!

Melissa decided to join an organization in her city that matches twentysome-things with volunteer opportunities. Every week, she went to a Web site and looked for a volunteer activity that matched the openings in her work sched-ule, and over several months she found herself doing a variety of volunteer activities, such as reading to individuals who were blind, weeding an overgrown community lot, and driving disabled senior citizens to doctor appointments. When she first started to volunteer, she had hoped to meet new people and expand her social horizons, which she did. What Melissa found most enjoyable about her volunteer work, though, was how she felt at the end of every week when she realized that she had made a difference in other people's lives, which made her happier and boosted her gratitude for her own blessings, as well.

Takeaway: Giving to others is one of the biggest gifts we can give to ourselves. Homebound men and women can write newsletters for nonprofit organizations, and even children can organize fund-raising efforts for those less fortunate by setting up bake sales at school or spearheading a campaign to donate backpacks filled with school supplies for students who have lost everything, which was one of the many efforts launched after Hurricane Katrina. Search for a community Web site that lists volunteer opportunities, or scan the local newspapers for ideas if you don't know where to start. Many churches are also involved in volunteer efforts that are not necessarily limited to members of their parish.

▶ Proven Booster #5: Savoring Happy Memories

God gave us memories that we might have roses in December.

—J. M. BARRIE

Researcher Fred Bryant of the University of Chicago has done some of the finest investigations into how the process of recalling happy memories can impact hap-piness. In one of his studies, he asked participants to vividly recall happy times in their lives and to think about them for ten minutes, twice a day, for one week. In the same study, participants in another group were asked to hold memorabilia while they thought about a happy time associated with it for the same period of time, while a third group didn't do any "savoring"—defined as attending to, appreciating, and enhancing positive experiences in one's life—during that exper-imental week.

Bryant found that recalling happy times had a reliable impact on making peo-ple feel happier, especially compared to a control group who didn't do any savor-ing. This type of research could help explain the exponential growth of scrapbooking, which is now considered one of the top leisure hobbies in the world! Scrapbookers preserve family memories and other life highlights by creating photo albums, often with decorative touches, a process that undoubtedly promotes savoring, and which might also explain why studies of happy families show that photos are often found in abundance all over the home.

> Stephanie loved the idea of using more photographs around her house to help her savor memories, so she covered her refrigerator with snapshots from family vacations and memorable occasions. Then she heard about a new product that would allow her to create a magnetized wall with paint, so she painted one wall in her son's room while he was away at college, and then covered it with hundreds of magnetized frames containing pictures of him throughout his life with his siblings, parents, and friends. When he came home from college and saw the wall, he was momentarily speechless, and then said it was the best gift anyone had ever given him. Now he takes all of his friends immediately to his room to show them his "scrapbook wall," where they laugh and reminisce about their shared adventures, and the changes in each other's appearances. Stephanie's son also makes a point of e-mailing pictures from college with the request, "Can you put it on the wall, Mom?" Stephanie says that not only has the magnetized wall promoted her own savoring, but she and her other children find themselves in the room, rearranging and dis-cussing the pictures with laughter and delight on a regular basis, and that the other children have asked for magnetized walls for pictures, too!

Takeaway: Whenever you can stop and take a moment to recall the memo-ries that have brought you joy, you are essentially giving thanks and promoting happiness at the same time. Find unique ways to recall and share your blessings, a regular activity that might include initiating conversations with other people about their favorite memories or blessed times.

▶ PROVEN BOOSTER #6: FORGIVING

To be wronged is nothing unless you continue to remember it.
—CONFUCIUS

A remarkable movement has emerged among people who have been victimized directly or indirectly by someone who is still incarcerated. This project brings prisoners together with their victims, or relatives of their victims, with the sole purpose of allowing prisoners to express their remorse for their crimes while being forgiven by those they have harmed. Those who have participated say that moving through this difficult process and forgiving people who have done them unspeakable harm is the only way they have found that they can free themselves of anger and hurt, and move into a happier and more peaceful existence.

When we decide to let go of old hurts or fresh insults, we foster compassion for others and enhance social bonding, which build inner reserves of well-being. Forgiveness isn't always easy, and might need to be given in stages, but John Maltby, a psychologist at the University of Leicester, found that thoughts and behaviors associated with forgiveness produce happiness.

Having a "forgiving" personality also helps with health issues. One study found that people who discussed an old injustice with a researcher, but who were described as typically forgiving, experienced an elevated heart rate while discussing the injustice, but their heart rate returned to normal relatively soon after the discussion. People who were not as skilled at forgiving had heart rates that became elevated, and remained elevated after the conversation, leading researchers to speculate that the inability to forgive—and excessive rumination about hurts and insults—could lead to and fuel illness, depression, and, eventually, cardiac issues.

Larry was skeptical when he read about a group of disabled veterans that was going to Vietnam for the purpose of forgiving the people they had once fought against. He finally decided to join the group, however, after realizing that it might help him deal with some of his own issues with anger and cynicism. Once he got to Vietnam, Larry met with aging Vietnamese soldiers who greeted him as a respected military brother, and who forgave him for his role in the war. They also shed tears and asked Larry for his forgiveness of their part in killing his comrades. Larry was not only profoundly moved by this experience; he discovered that the person who most needed forgiving was himself. "I realized that going to Vietnam allowed me to forgive myself for being young and naive, and for doing things that I never would have done otherwise, but that were expected of me as part of my job. Forgiving others opened up my heart and allowed me to finally forgive myself, and that is something I hadn't expected."

Takeaway: Forgiving others and forgiving yourself are good for your health and well-being. Forgiveness cannot always be rushed, but once you are ready to experience its benefits, experts suggest that you create a forgiveness ritual—such as writing a letter to the person who has harmed you, and then either sending it or burning it to signify closure.

► PROVEN BOOSTER #7: APPLYING YOUR STRENGTHS

Use what talents you possess; the woods would be very silent if no birds sang except those that sang best.

—HENRY VAN DYKE

Perhaps the most touted happiness technique that has emerged from positive psychology is the encouragement to use our strengths more often, and to avoid spending too much time fixing our weaknesses. Researchers are finding that people are happier when they know and embrace the personal qualities that come most easily to them—their talents—and use them in new and clever ways to accomplish their goals. One study found that employees who had been passed over for partner in a large accounting firm, and who were subsequently coached on how to discover and use their strengths as they handled a variety of interpersonal and professional challenges at work, learned how to be more genuine and comfortable in their daily interactions, and all made partner the following year.

Esther felt despondent about how overwhelmed she was by her job and responsibilities to her autistic son, until she took a strengths test and found that leadership was her number one strength. Esther realized that she was a natural leader in many settings, but that she wasn't using this innate talent to handle her son's diagnosis and the confusing suggestions that poured in from others. Esther worked very hard to see herself as the leader of her son's treatment team, and whenever she went into a medical appointment, she humorously described herself as the "quarterback of the Justin team," who was gathering information to write the winning plays. Transforming her self-image as a defeated, sad mom into an empowered leader allowed Esther to regain the vitality and hope that she had been missing, and it gave her the ability to accomplish other goals, as well.

Takeaway: We all have strengths that are unique to us, but we don't always notice or appreciate them. When we come from a position of strength, though, we appear comfortable in our own skin, and have more natural tools at our disposal to be successful.

► Proven Booster #8: Meditation

Prayer is when you talk to God; meditation is when you listen to God.
—DIANA ROBINSON

Once the exclusive domain of Far Eastern mystics, meditation has gained a solid foothold in the world of positive psychology through the pioneering work of University of Wisconsin researcher Richard Davidson and others, who have discovered that meditation can rewire our brains so that we experience significant changes in happiness, health, relationship quality, empathy, and resilience. Barbara Fredrickson, the 2000 Templeton Prize winner and professor of psychology at the University of North Carolina at Chapel Hill, has also done exciting research on the results of practicing "loving-kindness" meditation for as little as twenty minutes each day. Her findings show that workers at a computer company who meditated over an eight-week period experienced all of the benefits listed above, with the results becoming especially noticeable after the sixth week of regular practice. In particular, Fredrickson found that for every minute put into meditation after the sixth week, meditators reported experiencing triple the benefits they had experienced in the early weeks, including more rewarding interactions with others, more energy, less stress, and greater empathy for themselves and others.

> Lindsey started to meditate at the encouragement of a therapist, who felt that her problems with compulsive eating would improve if she could learn to sit quietly, and not respond impulsively to every urge or thought that crossed her brain. Although it was initially difficult to sit for just two minutes, Lindsey found that she was calmer, happier, and more focused as her meditation practice deepened. Eventually she built up the courage to go on an all-day meditation and yoga retreat. Through regular practice, Lindsey has found that she doesn't instinctively turn to food when she is under stress, and is able to take a few deep centering breaths instead, which has helped her in other areas of life, too, because her focus has improved and her anxiety is greatly reduced.

Takeaway: Meditation can take many forms, including walking silently through a labyrinth, repeating a soothing phrase to yourself, or even singing. Practicing meditation is a wise step for anyone who wants to have a positive exercise that can be practiced anywhere, at any time, and without any special gear.

Where Your Life List Is Now

At this point, your list of goals is probably embryonic, but hopefully you are actively creating lists of happiness boosters, writing your thoughts about what you most want to leave behind as your legacy in terms of accomplished goals and memories that others will have of your life. In the next chapter, we will help you understand how to construct some of your goals so that they reflect your innermost values, harness your strengths and energy, and bring you the joy you desire.

Life List Exercises and Worksheets

❏ Try the "Three Blessings" exercise on page 254, and see if this daily ritual helps you to feel happier or more grateful over a two-week period.

❏ Begin to fill in the "Jolts of Joy" worksheet so that you can identify the people, places, situations, and activities that bring you happiness. Add to this list as you continue to spot joy boosters in your life, and refer to it whenever you feel the need to take a break and recharge your batteries with a much-needed mood lifter.

❏ Read the "Meditation and Mindful Breathing for Beginners" guide on page 243, and consider adding a regular meditation or yoga class to your life.

❏ Take the "VIA Signature Strengths" Test at www.authentichappiness.com. This free test was designed by Marty Seligman and Chris Peterson, who authored the comprehensive *Character Strengths and Virtues*, a book that outlines twenty-four character strengths such as gratitude, humility, diligence, bravery, and creativity. Review "The BAT Form" (on page 252) and add any new strengths to your list, and begin to consider how you can use your greatest strengths to assist you in accomplishing your goals.

CREATING YOUR BEST POSSIBLE LIFE LIST

This section is devoted to the mechanics of creating
a life list that is filled with the goals that are most
authentic and meaningful for you, as well as some of the
cutting-edge techniques that can help you bring them
to fruition. We also show you how you can augment
your willpower stores, become grittier, and select the
best possible relationships that will maximize your
likelihood of success and happiness.

▼

4

LIFE-CHANGING GOALS

An average person with average talents and ambition and average
education can outstrip the most brilliant genius in our society,
if that person has clear, focused goals.

—MARY KAY ASH

ONE OF THE most common misconceptions about goal setting is that there are only a few things we need to know in order to achieve our goals. Often, the acronym SMART is used to help people to remember to set goals that are specific, measurable, attainable, realistic and time-sensitive. While this is a nice start, the acronym doesn't do justice to some of the tremendous complexities that motivational specialists and researchers have discovered are important to an individual's success.

In fact, having a "realistic" goal may not stretch your own imagination and abilities as far as possible, while a goal that is very audacious might be appropriate for your particular emotional makeup and situation, but not someone else's. So before you begin your list in earnest, we'd like to introduce you to some new facets of goal setting that you may not have read or heard about before.

Why New Year's Resolutions Often Fail

People who don't set any goals are the ones whom life will pass right by. In fact,
most people say they wish they could live their lives over again because a high
percentage of people realize too late that they have frittered their lives away.

—GARY LATHAM, PHD, COFOUNDER OF GOAL-SETTING THEORY

One of the reasons why some people shy away from goal setting is because they have made New Year's resolutions in the past that didn't give them the results they desired. Egged on by television commercials featuring buff models, men and women often join gyms or weight-loss programs, but fall off the wagon by the third or fourth week of the year, and then decide that goal setting is for the birds.

This phenomenon of failing at New Year's resolutions is so familiar to researchers that a certain day—the third Monday in January—has been dubbed "the most depressing day of the year." This is when it's thought that people give up on their goals because they've encountered one setback, they are depressed about credit card statements that reveal holiday overspending, and the weather isn't cooperating to lift their mood. Instead of examining whether or not they have set the right types of goals, in the right way, they completely throw in the towel and conclude that New Year's resolutions don't work.

What studies of New Year's resolutions have found, though, is that when they are set correctly and for the right reasons, they can make a tremendous difference in a person's life, and even set that individual up for success in the future. One study tracked the success of resolvers and nonresolvers, and found that people who set New Year's resolutions had a 46 percent success rate with their goals after six months, while those who set no goals had only a 4 percent success rate!

Clearly, the process of setting goals has a powerful impact, but we'd like to show you some of the finer points of goal setting that will dramatically increase your own odds of success, including all of the most recent research that has been found to even *triple* your odds of getting what you want.

Challenging and Specific

Edwin Locke and Gary Latham are the two brilliant men who have worked together for decades to cobble together goal-setting theory, an approach that is so powerful that it has been dubbed the number one tested management technique for achieving change in the workplace. Locke, a professor emeritus at the University of Maryland, and Latham, a professor at the Rotman School of Business at the University of Toronto, coauthored a textbook called *A Theory of Goal Setting and Task Performance* and have overseen numerous studies that underscore one of the most important points about goals, and one that is frequently not honored.

If you are seeking an outcome in a performance goal—such as achieving a certain grade, salary, race finish, or anything that can be measured—your goal must be "challenging and specific," according to Latham, and individuals' omission of this one feature is the number one reason why most goals fail: "People don't always like to work hard at their goals, and they want to wish for positive outcomes and keep the goals deliberately vague. Making performance goals challenging and specific is the only way around this trap," Latham said, adding, "Easy goals also mean you never have to get down on yourself if you fail."

After observing workers in hundreds of situations, Latham and Locke found that two goal conditions consistently lowered productivity and results: "low goals" and "no goals." Low goals, they discovered, were goals that were not particularly challenging, and that didn't require a person to exert himself or herself much. These mediocre goals were shown time and time again to produce subpar results.

Subsequent work at the University of British Columbia by Dr. Jessica Tracy and her colleagues determined that these types of mediocre goals also fail to promote "authentic self-esteem," which they concluded came only from pursuing hard tasks that took a person outside his or her comfort zone.

For this reason, we challenge the word "realistic" as a guideline for all life list goals. Some of our best goals may appear to be unrealistic at first, but when broken down, they are attainable if our best efforts are rewarded with the most promising possible outcomes.

Here's a story about a goal that appeared to be unrealistic, but that simply turned out to be "challenging and specific":

> When Michael Phelps, one of the greatest swimmers in history, was just a tadpole, his coach, Bob Bowman, called his parents into his office for a goal-setting session. Bowman outlined an audacious training plan for the next few years that eventually resulted in the attainment of an Olympic medal in Phelps's teen years. Phelps was only eleven at the time of the goal-setting conversation, however, so his astonished parents just looked at the coach and openly questioned his sanity. Bowman, who had a history of recognizing excellence, said that his goals might seem unrealistic at the moment, but that they were definitely something he felt would guide the talented young boy, and not intimidate him. To his credit, the young Phelps adopted these goals as his own, and actually accomplished all of them before Bowman's predicted timeline, proving that some goals that appear to be unrealistic are simply challenging goals that demand that we give them everything we've got.

"No goals" have an even worse result than "low goals," according to Locke and Latham. People who fail to set any goals—including people who scorn New Year's resolutions—end up in worse shape because without a goal to strive for, they have nothing to use as a yardstick for progress. In the same category as "low goals" and "no goals" are "do-your-best" goals, which are often the kinds of goals uttered by well-meaning parents who encourage children to "do their best" instead of encouraging them to strive for something specific. "Do-your-best" goals, we can report to the chagrin of many of us who have set them because we didn't know better, are detrimental to high performance in most cases, except for a condition we'll outline below.

"Challenging and specific" goals are goals that exceed your grasp, and that you can clearly define verbally and in writing. For example, a challenging and specific recreational goal might be to learn how to knit and to make two scarves as holiday gifts. A low goal—one that doesn't necessarily stretch us very far outside our comfort zone and that has a high probability of achievement—might be to look up a knitting pattern on the Internet, but that type of goal would be better suited as a step in service of the first goal, instead of as a full-fledged goal itself. No goal at all would be to simply avoid taking any responsibility for learning a new skill, which could easily leave you with regrets about not making any effort whatsoever to tackle a new and different hobby.

There Are Exceptions to Every Rule

Locke and Latham have one caveat to the "do-your-best" condition that must be noted before we go on. When we are placed in a situation where we don't necessarily have the tools or resources to succeed—and the situation is pegged as a learning challenge and not a performance challenge—"do your best" is the only way to approach the goal. For example, imagine asking your preteen to do your income tax return for you when he or she has only a rudimentary knowledge of how to fill out these types of forms. In a situation like this, which involves a "learning goal," it's appropriate to approach the task in a "do-your-best" frame of mind that allows for the possibility of success, but doesn't dictate an unrealistic performance goal that is almost certainly destined to go unrealized from the outset.

That Which Cannot Be Measured Cannot Be Achieved

Locke and Latham also found in many studies that measurable goals produced more and better efforts. "That which cannot be measured cannot be achieved," they summarized beautifully in their seminal textbook. What this means is that not only must goals be challenging and specific, but they must have some type of yardstick that adds accountability to the process, also called "subgoals." For example, winning the U.S. presidency has the measurable process of accumulating delegates to help candidates determine whether or not they should stay in the race. Having enough money to stay in a political race is another measurable part of the goal, because if you don't have some millions of dollars in the bank, that measurable statistic can undo the most polished and charismatic politician on earth.

As you think about your own goals, ask yourself if they have measurable pieces to them or not. For example, if you want to donate time to your community's efforts to rebuild decrepit homes or raise money for a school textbook drive, there must be a measurable component to the goal, for example, "Set aside two hours a week to discuss options for fund-raising if we're going to raise five thousand dollars by June." Having these types of subgoals can prevent you from being overwhelmed by the big picture, and also allows you to celebrate the baby steps of accomplishment along the way.

An unmeasurable, vague goal would be something like "Be happier." But how will you accomplish this and by what date? Which methods will you use? Becoming happier is definitely challenging and somewhat specific for some people, but without a way to measure progress, it's not a goal that's likely to be fulfilled.

Feedback

Closely tied to the need for measurable goals is the fact that regular feedback dramatically enhances success. What this means is that we must use the measurable pieces of our goals to give us feedback that will help us correct our strategy if it's not working. For example Tiger Woods performs "deliberate practice" in his quest to become the greatest golfer of all time. Like many other golfers who are trying to improve their games, Woods is often seen on the practice greens, hitting a bucket of balls.

But if you look closely, Woods exemplifies the best in goal-setting theory, which is what distinguishes him from his peers. Woods uses his bucket of balls to set challenging and specific goals; he uses a concrete measurement (hit the ball ten feet from the pin); and then he uses the feedback he gets while performing the practice drill (the ball is not getting quite as close as he wants it to be) to adjust his stance and swing.

In this way, Woods is able to use feedback to accomplish his specific goals, which makes the outcome of his strategy dramatically different from that of other golf players, who hit a bucket of balls without a specific goal or a means of measuring that goal, and who receive no feedback.

Approach versus Avoidance

The best goals have an exciting, zestful component to them. They make your eyes widen and your pulse quicken, and you can't wait to devote time to making them happen. These are called "approach" goals, and they do exactly what they say: They help you "approach" a positive outcome such as "Break 100 on our local golf course by September 1st." If playing golf is your most passionate form of recreation—and it allows you socialize and spend time with people you like—this goal will help you approach an outcome that will bring you joy.

An "avoidance" goal also implies exactly what it says. If the same golfer set the goal "To not be the worst player in my regular foursome by September 1st," that would be a goal designed to avoid a negative outcome. Not only do we think about these goals differently (one with anticipation and one with dread), but it's been found that approach goals actually use up less energy, because avoiding something takes more mental and physical energy than approaching it. As you design your goals, pay attention to the wording and sentiments behind them, and steer away from anything that smacks of avoidance.

Intrinsic versus Extrinsic

One of the slam-dunk findings in goal-setting literature is that goals that you set for yourself, and that come from your own genuine desires, values, and interests, are the goals that you will enjoy, pursue with vigor, and savor once they are accomplished. These are called "intrinsic" or "self-concordant" goals. When we are children, it's sometimes hard to distinguish what we want to do from what our parents want us to do, but in adulthood, we must be clear about what we want to accomplish and why.

"Extrinsic" goals are the opposite of intrinsic goals. These are goals that other people have set for you, or that you pursue because you think you should pursue them. This is often seen among unhappy workers in professions that they chose because they are following a family tradition (i.e., to be a doctor or teacher) or because someone else suggested them. Extrinsic goals often revolve around the accumulation of possessions, money, or fame that you believe will cause you to be admired by others.

AMERICANS HAVE INCREASINGLY theorized that money is the definition of "the good life," according to Roper pollsters. In 1975, 38 percent of Americans said that "a lot of money" would comprise the good life, while 63 percent said the same in 1996. This paralleled the responses of incoming collegians between the 1970s and 1990s, who went from valuing developing a "meaningful philosophy of life" to overwhelmingly (75 percent) favoring "making a lot of money" as their top-rated value.

Extrinsic goals have a funny way of coming back to bite you if you're not careful. For example, Tal Ben-Shahar, the Harvard author and lecturer we mentioned in the first chapter who teaches positive psychology to standing-room-only classes of students, stumbled into the field by figuring out that many of the things he had once thought would bring him joy—like being an Israeli squash champion or getting a PhD—did not. Instead, he realized that he had adopted those goals for himself out of obligation and not passion, and that was why he felt a pervasive sense of emptiness in his early thirties. When he discovered that his true passion was teaching, he redirected his energies and found the satisfaction that had previously eluded him.

Latham has likened intrinsic goals to "overarching vision goals," which are akin to creating a mission statement for your life. He noted that many people and organizations accomplish a great deal by tying goals to a big vision, such as Martin Luther King's "I Have a Dream" speech. As you set goals for yourself, remember to ask yourself: "What is my vision and how does it connect with my goals?"

Foster Independence and Competence

Richard Ryan and Ed Deci have studied human motivation and achievement since the 1970s, including what types of goals bring about the greatest fulfillment and most positive outcomes. Their self-determination theory posits that intrinsic goals have the following conditions:

- they promote autonomous and independent behavior,
- they help create competence and the ability to take care of oneself, and
- they assist people in connecting and relating well to each other

When these conditions are met, Deci and Ryan found that not only were these valuable goals, but they fostered flourishing and promoted the development of self-esteem at the same time.

Value Driven

It bears emphasizing that goals that are attached to our values are the ones that we're more likely to adopt and pursue as our own. For example, a goal attached to a value might look something like this:

Julie has always valued family time and togetherness, and she knows from her childhood that the time she spent with her parents meant more to her than any of the gifts or money they ever gave her. As a mother, she has felt increasingly conflicted by the demands of her work, which require that she travel twice a month and work long hours when she's in town. Although she can't afford to quit her job, she knows that having a strong value that isn't reflected in her current life goals is making her increasingly depressed. Julie worked to set some specific, challenging, and measurable goals around increasing the time she spent with her two children, and periodically reviewed how well she was doing at leaving work early twice a week and petitioning her manager to telecommute twice a month, an arrangement that would allow her to see her children before and after school. Julie also decided to plan an annual getaway with each child that had the goal of just being together, as opposed to visiting a particular place. Not only did Julie instantly feel happier that she had created a plan with specific goals, but she was excited that these "approach" goals reflected more of her own internal beliefs.

Nonconflicting and Leveraged

When we're young, it's not uncommon to think that anything is possible (being an astronaut and a Hall of Fame baseball player at the same time, for example) and that we can accomplish everything we put our minds to if we work hard enough. We don't want to disabuse anyone of this idea, particularly because lofty aspirations often *do* come true for people who have ambition and grit.

As we get older, though, we need to take a look at making a life list that isn't in conflict with dreams that don't support or "leverage" one another. Studies show that if we have two goals that don't logically go together, we will not make progress on either one of them. For example, one of our client's goals was to be married by the age of thirty, but she found herself avoiding commitment because of the goal her mother had set for her, which was to be mentioned in the social pages of a major newspaper for being at as many events around town as possible. Not only was the socialite goal extrinsic for our client (who didn't realize how it didn't match her values until she used our life list approach), but it prevented her from making progress on her intrinsic goal of being committed to someone and pursuing that relationship to the exclusion of others.

Goals must not only be harmonious with our own desires and dreams; they must also be leveraged. What this means is that the accomplishment of one goal on your life list will be enhanced by the accomplishment of another. For example, if your wish is to become a yoga teacher and open your own studio, this goal will benefit from other goals such as "Go on an annual yoga retreat with my best friend," "Visit India," and "Practice two new yoga poses every week." Studies show that these types of leveraged goals create well-being and momentum, and improve your chances of overall goal attainment.

Write It Down; It Will Happen

There doesn't seem to be any doubt among goal-setting experts that written goals produce better results than goals that aren't written down. Writing goals in a place where you can easily see them has the effect of reminding you of your commitment to yourself, and it also allows other people (remember Bob Perini, the founder of DrinkMoreWater, from Chapter 1) to add their support and ideas to the accomplishment of your goals. Prominent sports psychologists encourage athletes to keep their goals written down on a business card that is always within their reach, so that there is never a time during the day when they can't be visually cued, for example, to see the splits they want to accomplish in an upcoming triathlon.

Journaling researcher Laura King hypothesized that when we write down our goals, we automatically begin to scan our environment and psyche for people and situations that will facilitate attainment of those goals. The simple process of writing down a goal also seems to stimulate a more hopeful mind-set, which in turn has been found to evoke a more creative type of "pathways" thinking that generates multiple solutions. Written goals also allow us to immediately identify what is called "goal conflict" and to adjust our pursuits appropriately. For example, a college student who has the goal of being a straight-A, 4.0 student may not want to achieve his second goal, being more active in his fraternity, at the same time.

Gary Latham has also said that "behavioral contracts, which are often used in the business world to set and achieve specific, work-related goals," have an amazing power to produce superior efforts and goal success. An ideal behavioral contract specifies the following: "This is what I'm going to do, this is how I'm going to do it, and this is how I'm going to reward myself if I succeed." Studies of these types of behavioral contracts have also been done with recalcitrant students and dieters. Latham noted, "[T]he group with the contract beats the heck out of the group that doesn't have the contract every time!"

We encourage you to take advantage of the power of journaling to use this book to record and be reminded of your goals. But there are many other ways you can do this, such as making your goals into a screensaver on your personal computer, plugging them into the floating liquid display of a Fantazein clock, which flashes your goals throughout the day, posting them on life list sites, and e-mailing them to friends or to yourself.

There's also the old-fashioned method of writing in your diary, which is what Oprah Winfrey has cited as a place where her goals come to life for her. In fact, when she announced her decision to launch a television station, she added that the goal had been birthed fifteen years earlier in her journal!

_____ ⁂ _____

TOM HIGGENSON, LEAD singer for the Plain White T's, met the very beautiful Delilah DiCrescenzo in 2002 and was so smitten that he told her that he was going to write a song about her. Higgenson and DiCrescenzo stayed in touch but never dated, although he continued to tell her, before writing even one note, "I'm going to write the song, and it's going to be the best song I've written. It's going to be the song that gets us famous and wins us a Grammy!" In 2007, "Hey There Delilah" was nominated Song of the Year, and Higgenson finally got his date with his crush at the Grammy awards ceremony. He didn't win the honor, but he certainly won the heart of the public, which loved his story of accountability to the woman he hoped to impress.

Precommitment and Accountability

When you write down your goals, you precommit to a course of action, creating accountability to yourself. And when you share those goals with others, you add more accountability to the process. Writing down goals that only you know about, however, does have some benefits. For example, a study of college students found that those who wrote and signed a contract to themselves to do all of the readings and assignments for a particular class did more work than students who didn't take that step.

We believe that accountability to more than just yourself for your life list goals is in your best interests, however. When other people know about your goals, or are involved in their accomplishment, you are far more likely to follow through with your efforts. For example, people who made their New Year's resolutions public were ten times more likely to succeed than people who did not make a public proclamation. This could be for many reasons, the most obvious being that we don't want to disappoint others or "lose face" by not living up to our commitments.

Accountability to the general public, or to people we know, if it's cleverly done, can be more galvanizing to our taking action than being paid to accomplish the same goal. An economist who analyzed whether it would be useful to earn money for losing a certain amount of weight said that posting a picture of yourself in a Speedo in a public environment, like your office, was the strategy most likely to work!

A State of Flow

Mihaly Csikszentmihalyi, a Hungarian-born researcher, discovered that hiking put him into a state of "flow," a state in which you lose track of time, and your emotions are somewhat neutral. Typically, "flow" is defined as a time when you are completely engaged in the task at hand, without any feelings of worry, anxiety, or self-consciousness. Athletes refer to this condition as "being in the zone," when they are using their physical efforts to overcome a challenge or complete a race. Being in a state of flow on a regular basis is good for us, and good for our emotional well-being. Csikszentmihalyi found that the happiest people are those who regularly achieve flow at work and in their leisure activities, noting that every instance of flow creates a person who is more unique and individuated than he or she was beforehand.

Typically, intrinsic goals promote flow and extrinsic goals do not. We believe that being in the flow while pursuing your valued goals will not only help you achieve your goals; it will also help you to become happier in the process, so we would like you to use the "My Flow Chart" worksheet on page 245 to help you identify the times and places you have experienced this feeling.

One cautionary note about flow: Csikszentmihalyi reminds people that flow is not the same as losing track of time while watching television, playing video games, or being in a mindless state while overeating, overspending, gambling, or otherwise being unaware of your behavior. These conditions are known as "junk flow" and are not necessarily directed toward the attainment of valued and meaningful goals. They are, instead, pleasant and mind-numbing activities that don't involve any challenge or skill. In fact, it's been found that our brain waves resemble the brain waves seen among depressed people when we watch too much television.

Where Your Life List Is Now

You have already written down some preliminary goals that you believe will make you happier and your life more fulfilling and meaningful. You also have your "Jolts of Joy" worksheet, which gives you a personalized list of activities, thoughts, and situations that you can draw upon whenever you need a boost and the extra energy that comes from lowering your stress level and putting a smile on your face.

Now that you have learned about the types of goals that have the highest likelihood of attainment, and some of the multifaceted ways in which you can achieve them, take a look at the goals on your list and revise them in light of what you've learned in this chapter. Remember that the best goals are:

- Specific and challenging
- Approach (exciting and magnetic) and not avoidance
- Value driven

- Create feelings of independence, connectedness, and competence
- Intrinsic and not extrinsic
- Measurable and have the opportunity to produce feedback
- Nonconflicting and leveraged
- Written
- Precommitment and accountability
- Capable of stimulating "flow" states

Life List Exercises and Worksheets

❑ The "Goal Success Plan" worksheet (see page 238) will help you begin to design your specific goals and will encourage you to consider the different components of goals that have the highest likelihood of attainment. Whenever you are adding a goal to your life list, it's a good idea to use this form as a template to help you identify the various pieces that you need to consider.

❑ "My Flow Chart" (see page 245) will help you take note of times when you experience flow, both personally and professionally, which will help you better understand which goals are more intrinsic and value laden than goals that don't promote this same positive emotion and outcome.

5

CREATING THE LIST
THAT WORKS FOR YOU

Ask yourself what makes you come alive, and go do that, because what the
world needs is people who have come alive.

—HOWARD THURMAN

I T'S NOW TIME to start a task that is extremely fun and potentially life changing.
It's the moment when you sit down and make a list of your life goals, a list that
will infuse your life with hope, inspiration, passion, commitment, meaning, and
purpose. In the first few chapters of this book, we discussed the importance of life
lists, their connection with happiness, and what researchers have discovered are
the components of the most reachable and exhilarating goals. You might want to
make a copy of the "Goal Success Plan" worksheet on page 238 and keep it by your
side to help guide you as you begin your list. As time goes by, you'll make additions
to your life list as you uncover more and more buried longings that you want to
pursue when the time is right. So sharpen your pencil and let's get going.

There Is No Right Way

I did it my way.

—FRANK SINATRA

Just as religious commentators say that there are many paths to God, so there
are many ways to create a life list. All of them work, and the only key variable is
whether or not the method speaks to *you* and allows *you* to successfully follow
the necessary steps to completion. Many of our clients are visual learners, and
their lists are designed to appeal to that aesthetic sense. Some of our clients are

linear and practical thinkers who prefer businesslike spreadsheets. Others like virtual social-networking tools and enjoy the ease and practicality of the popular goal-setting Internet sites. Plenty of people like scrapbooks, diaries, or journals that they can write in and embellish. The most important thing is to pick and use the process that speaks to you.

Is There a Right Time?

Yes and no is the answer to this question. You want to embark on a life list process when you feel happy, upbeat, hopeful, energetic, and engaged in life. At the same time, you will probably derive many of those same benefits from actually creating your list, so don't be too cautious about starting out of fear that the stars have to be aligned or that you have to be perfectly healthy for you to successfully create your life list.

Some people, however, find that different times of the year are easier than others for them to begin a process of self-discovery, so pay attention to your inner clock if that's the case, and honor it while you gather the information you need to change and grow. For some, the start of the New Year signals the end of holiday parties and overindulgence, and that's why so many dieting and exercise half-price specials abound in early January. January is also traditionally a time of buying self-help books, so your local bookstores might be encouraging you to consider transformation at the start of the year.

Psychologically, some people prefer to wait for a "spring cleaning" of their lives, because the return of flowers and birds cues them to think about their lives in terms of renewal and rebirth. At the same time, many people find that the traditional start of the school year in September is when they like to de-junk their lives and consider a fresh start and new learning. We've discovered that there is never one "perfect" time for anything—but there is a perfect time *for you* to begin making the changes that matter to you.

We advise you, however, to block out some free time for the exercises and list writing we ask you to do when you begin the process of creating your life list. Ideally, you should do this when you can ignore the phone or any other interruptions that will frustrate your ability to focus. Some people like to go to a coffee shop, a park, or even a silent retreat to make headway on their list making, so do whatever you need to do to give yourself the maximum amount of time with the fewest interruptions.

The First Step

Many of our clients like to start by reminiscing about, or writing down, things they've already accomplished and are proud of. Going through this type of exercise as you embark on a goal-setting process is important for several reasons. First, remembering what you've done will flood you with positive feelings and images and create a hopeful state of mind. It will also strengthen your feelings of self-efficacy, which have been found to be predictors of goal accomplishment and happiness. Sharing these memories with other people also strengthens social connections.

Take a moment to write down five goals you've already accomplished and that you enjoy thinking about or telling others about. You might also want to refresh your memory about these experiences by looking through photo albums or other memorabilia to stimulate your thoughts:

1. _____

2. _____

3. _____

4. _____

5. _____

Now you can live in the present and move into the future with a greater feeling of power and pride. In fact, you should always be sure to have past successes captured in a way that allows you to remind yourself regularly of instances in which you've already proven that your commitment and energy get you what you want. Pictures on your refrigerator, computer, iPod, or other portable device might help you recapture these memories, as can songs that were popular during the time period when you had those big wins.

IN THE ONLY study of its kind, led by Bruce Headey in 2008, more than 3,500 people from around the world were followed for fifteen years to see what satisfied them and made their lives meaningful and happy. According to this study, the happiest people

- **are guided by clear-cut life goals;**
- **are risk takers who never make excuses and never give up; and**
- **have goals in the areas of friendship, love, and helping others.**

You Need a Vision

Perhaps you already know where you want to be in one year, in five years, and even at the end of your life, and you're just itching to get those goals on paper or somewhere else that appeals to you. If not, it's time to start, and we have a variety of fun and appealing ways to do this. For example, as mentioned earlier, the "Best Possible Self" journaling exercise used by researchers such as Sonja Lyubomirsky and Laura King to clarify one's most-hoped-for life has been shown to enhance well-being and reduce goal conflict, as well as create hope among people who did it. King even found that simply writing down short-term goals and projects had the ability to boost subjects' mood and health, too.

We have a quick version of "Best Possible Self" called "The Magic Wand." This simple exercise encourages you to imagine that you have a magic wand that can create the life and situations you most long for, with no limitations on its power. Imagine that each of your personality deficits, financial dilemmas, and all the seemingly "unfixable" problems in your life are solved and anything is possible. If you take a moment to think about your life in this way, you might get an immediate snapshot of what you most desire. Use these lines to record what your life might look like:

_____

_____

_____

One More Day with . . .

Another way to go about uncovering secret, or less obvious, goals is to ask yourself whom you would spend another day with if you had the chance. A recent best-selling book posed this hypothetical question and struck a chord among readers, encouraging them to think about the opportunities they might be missing in their own lives to spend time with a valued person, like a grandparent or friend. Posing questions in terms of potential regrets is an interesting way to uncover your values and shape current goals.

For some of our clients who have had brushes with death, this type of all-too-real exercise—"If you had limited time to live, what would you do and with whom would you spend time?"—has been one of the most life-changing experiences they've had, and it has turned many of them into inveterate goal seekers in the present who refuse to ever take another day for granted.

You may find that a goal or set of goals emerges from this thought-provoking exercise:

1. If I could spend one day with someone who has passed away, who would it be and what would I ask or tell him or her?

_____

_____

2. If I could live without regrets and spend the day with anyone of my choosing, who would that person be and what would I ask or tell him or her?

_____

_____

Thirty Days to Live

Many Christian-based congregations have adopted a movement called "30 Days to Live," which encourages worshippers to live their best life now, and to spend the next thirty days of their lives striving to be as kind, loving, giving, and spiritual as possible. This movement has benefited many who found that imagining an imminent death prompted them to become better people, and to strive to leave a more positive legacy than their current life. If this idea is appealing, visit the Web site www.30daystolive.tv and ponder the questions presented there, or write your ideas here:

IF I HAD 30 DAYS TO LIVE, I WOULD:

1. _____

2. _____

3. _____

What Are Your Values?

As we mentioned in Chapter 4, identifying your goals as uniquely yours and connecting them with your values are two key indicators of whether or not you will pursue your goals with vigor and excitement. If you are a bit unclear about your values, or don't know how to describe them, we have a fun way to help. Quickly think of who your favorite characters are from books, movies, plays, or any other type of literature or popular media. Then write down each of their most obvious qualities. This will give you a clue about what you admire most in others, and what you also probably hold dear and consider a code that you try to live by, too.

For example, one of our male clients grew up at a time when typically "masculine" traits, such as those personified by John Wayne, were admired, and as a result he internalized a value system based on being tough, resilient, and honest. Another male client who did the exercise described above immediately mentioned the movie *Rudy*, which is about the scrappy football player who never abandoned his dream of making it onto the legendary Notre Dame football team, and whose perseverance earned him the respect and friendship of the coaches and the rest of the team. Some of our clients name biblical figures as favorite role models, and will point to Job's grit or Jesus' kindness in the face of anger as the values they most admire. Generally speaking, a worthwhile value will elicit your best behavior and make you a better person.

Take a moment to write down the names of five characters, as well as the qualities they embody:

CHARACTER	QUALITY
1.	
2.	
3.	
4.	
5.	

Sneak a Peek

We don't want you to be intimidated or overly influenced by other people's goals, but occasionally it can be helpful to look at—and get great ideas from—other people's lists. Countless clients have uttered, "Oh! I forgot about that one!" when they've taken a look at an Internet goal site devoted to this topic. (See page 266 for Web addresses and other helpful resources.) One college student saw a classmate's list of life goals and was struck by one of the altruistic ones: "Endow a library and name it after my father, who taught me how to read." The student immediately connected with the value and love behind the goal, and thought of one that embodied his own love for his grandmother, which he put near the top of his list.

Why Not?

As you embark upon the process of writing down your goals in the format that best suits you, we also would like you to ask yourself the question "Why not?" as you create your future. This type of limitless thinking has set a number of people free as they have designed their goals. Instead of approaching the process with a "Why me?" attitude, they have transformed this question into "Why *not* me?" and have thereby altered their perceptions of themselves and changed their goals accordingly. In upcoming chapters, we'll feature some of the people who dared to think this way, and who not only did amazing things, but also inspired many people around them to do more than they thought possible, too.

Here's an example of someone who thought, "Why not?" and did something significant for herself, which then led her to set other kinds of joyful goals:

> Alison Sigethy came to the realization in her forties that she'd stopped going after her life goals out of fear. "It's safe and easy to think 'I can be a great artist,' but once you commit, you lose that cushion. You can fail." She changed her life by unexpectedly announcing to her kayaking friends that she was going to compete in multiple events in the Greenland National Championships the following year. Almost immediately, she turned her life upside down and began to train for the frigid waters of Greenland by biking in a walk-in freezer and running up and down the steps of buildings with a kayak on her head. Pushing through fear and exhaustion, she learned to roll her boat in icy waters, harpoon, and compete on a grueling ropes course. Her midlife makeover continued as she used her excitement about the Greenland National Championships to set goals that had lingered in the back of her mind for years. Instead of just singing in the car at stoplights, she decided to sign up for singing lessons and planned to sing in public at an artist's café before the year was over.
>
> "Life is so much fuller if you dive in," she explained to a reporter with a smile on her face, thrilled that she had the guts to go after her midlife makeover with verve and commitment.

The Happiness House

There are a number of ways we encourage clients to make their life lists, but we'll start with a simple cut-and-paste exercise called "Happiness House," which will help you clarify your values and set your goals at the same time. The foundation of this exercise is Quality of Life Therapy and Coaching, a research-supported process of assessing your well-being and moving toward the fulfillment of goals that will help you improve your quality of life. By doing this exercise, you'll ensure that the areas of life that mean the most to you are represented in your life list.

Our theory is that 50 percent to 80 percent of your happiness is under your control. More specifically, we believe that this percentage is made up of your satisfaction with sixteen specific areas of life (seventeen if "Spiritual" is separated from "Goals and Values") that have been found to be the key building blocks of happiness the world over. You can use these sixteen specific areas of life to build your Happiness House.

For the purposes of this exercise, imagine that each of the sixteen areas of life making up your overall happiness is a room. You can build your Happiness House by putting these rooms in an arrangement that reflects your values. Here's how:

1. Make a copy of the following pages of rooms.
2. Use scissors to cut out each room in your Happiness House.
3. Build your Happiness House (the areas of life that mean the most to you) with the rooms you have just cut out. Put the rooms that are *most important* to you on the first floor of your Happiness House. The areas of your life that are *important, but not extremely important* go on the second floor. The third floor is reserved for areas that are *somewhat, or fairly, important to you*. Throw away any room that does not matter to you or is not relevant to you. (Do not worry if your house doesn't look like an actual house; there is no right or wrong way to make this dwelling!)
4. Take special note of the definitions of each of the sixteen areas as you place them in your Happiness House. Our definitions for the different areas of life are broader than you may have previously considered. For example, "Money" actually consists of three things that people find important to their standard of living or financial well-being: current assets, possessions, and the expectation that you will be able to provide enough for future needs, such as college funds.
5. Write your goals for each area of life on the back of each room in your Happiness House. You might also want to type them into a computer document and massage them until they feel right. Then print and glue them to the back of the room. You might even want to take a picture of your Happiness House and post it where you will be reminded of your goals regularly.

Sarah's Happiness House

Here is a representation of a Happiness House made by one of our clients, Sarah. When she did this exercise, Sarah, a middle-aged, semiretired attorney who had just come out of a painful divorce, was looking to add more relevant goal pursuits to her life so that her retirement years would have more meaning. Sarah's initial Ladder of Fulfillment and Contentment (see page 30) score put her in the "slightly successful" range, but as she pursued and accomplished many of her goals—starting with the ones that pertained to her "ground-floor" values—her score climbed into the "mostly successful" range.

HEALTH

Being physically fit, not sick, and without pain or disability.

SELF-ESTEEM

Liking and respecting yourself in light of your strengths and weaknesses, successes and failures, and ability to handle problems.

GOALS AND VALUES
(OR PHILOSOPHY OF LIFE)

Your beliefs about what matters most in life and how you should live, both now and in the future. This includes your goals in life, what you think is right or wrong, and the purpose or meaning of life as you see it.

SPIRITUAL LIFE

Spiritual or religious beliefs or practices that you pursue on your own or as part of a like-minded spiritual community. If very strong, Spiritual Life becomes an important part of a person's Goals and Values.

MONEY (OR STANDARD OF LIVING)

The money you earn, the things you own (like a car or furniture), and believing that you will have the money and things that you need in the future.

WORK

Your career or how you spend most of your time. You may work at a job, at home taking care of your family, or at school as a student. Work includes your duties on the job, the money you earn (if any), and the people you work with.

PLAY (OR RECREATION)

What you do in your free time to relax, have fun, or improve yourself. This could include watching movies, visiting friends, or pursuing a hobby such as sports or gardening.

LEARNING

Gaining new skills or information about things that interest you. Learning can come from reading books or taking classes on subjects such as history, car repair, or using a computer.

CREATIVITY

Using your imagination to come up with new and clever ways to solve everyday problems or to pursue a hobby such as painting, photography, or needlework. This can include decorating your home, playing the guitar, or finding a new way to solve a problem at work.

HELPING (OR SERVICE)

Helping others in need or helping to make your community a better place to live. Helping can be done on your own or with a group such as your church, a neighborhood association, or a political party. Helping can include doing volunteer work at a school or giving money to a good cause. Helping means helping people who are not your friends or relatives.

LOVE (OR LOVE RELATIONSHIPS)

A very close romantic relationship with another person. Love usually includes sexual feelings and feeling loved, cared for, and understood.

FRIENDS (OR FRIENDSHIPS)

People (not relatives) you know well and care about who have interests and opinions like yours. Friends have fun together, talk about personal problems, and help one another out.

CHILDREN

How you get along with your child (or children). Think of how you get along as you care for, visit, or play with your child (or children).

RELATIVES

How you get along with your parents, grandparents, brothers, sisters, aunts, uncles, and in-laws. Think about how you get along when you are doing things together like visiting, talking on the telephone, or helping one another.

HOME

Where you live; your house or apartment and the yard around it. Think about how nice it looks, how big it is, and your rent or house payment.

NEIGHBORHOOD

The area around your home. Think about how nice it looks, the amount of crime in the area, and how well you like your neighbors.

COMMUNITY

The whole city, town, or rural area where you live (not just your neighborhood). Community includes how nice the area looks, the amount of crime, and how well you like the people. It also includes places to go for fun such as parks, concerts, sporting events, and restaurants. You may also consider the cost of things you need to buy, the availability of jobs, the government, the schools, taxes, and pollution.

The "floors" of Sarah's Happiness House were built on the following values:

GROUND FLOOR

Helping—Work with Habitat for Humanity; give money to worthy causes
Children—Get back to teaching Sunday school
Spiritual life—Meditate at the Zen Center; pray daily; listen to God more
Learning—Research feasibility of after-dark meal program
Relatives—Appreciate sister more; stay connected with Dad despite Alzheimer's
Creativity—Paint and redecorate house; return to rug hooking as a hobby
Health—Sleep eight or nine hours a night; lose weight; drink less alcohol
Friends—Be in weekly contact with close friends; listen more and judge
less when friends ask for advice

SECOND FLOOR

Love—Find a new soul mate
Money—Pay off credit cards; enter all financial transactions in computer
money-management program
Play—Garden more; laugh every day
Self-esteem—Experience less self-doubt; do things that make me feel
competent

THIRD FLOOR

Work and retirement—Remain part-time with legal work
Home—Set up timed coffeemaker every night; run dishwasher/laundry daily
Neighborhood—Learn all neighbors' names; get involved with neighbor-
hood association
Community—See more plays; participate in nature walks

Tips on Building Your Happiness House

One of the advantages of using this exercise for your goals and values is that you
can save and post the results in a place where you're likely to see them every day.
Sarah actually typed her goals into a document that was in the start-up menu of
her computer. This way she was often reminded of her goals, and it helped her
to feel more directed and successful.

Using this approach also reminds you of where you can start your goal pursuit if you are feeling overwhelmed. Typically, attacking a goal in a "ground-floor" room will bring you greater life satisfaction than the accomplishment of a goal on the "third floor." You can also juggle goal pursuit in several valued areas at once, enjoying the potent spillover effect that emerges from increasing happiness in one area of your life.

Bucket-List Approach

One of the traditional goal-setting methods that works for a lot of people, including the stars of the movie *The Bucket List*, is to sit down with a legal pad or diary and write down what you want to do before you die, or even before you hit a certain milestone, like getting married, turning forty, or retiring. Thousands of successful goal seekers have done this in the simplest possible way by going to a coffee shop, the beach, or even their own living room couch to carefully jot down their thoughts about where they want to go with their lives. These lists have become dog-eared references that serve as guiding stars, even though they are not fancy or divided into areas of life. This simple method has worked for business and sports titans who revolutionized their lives by scrawling their dreams on index cards, envelopes, and scraps of paper that they carried around until they fell apart.

If you want to follow the bucket-list approach, you can use any type of writing instrument or notebook to write down your goals. In Chapter 1 we suggested starting to fill out a form called "One Hundred Things to Do before I Die" (see page 225). If this form prompts you to get going, that's perfectly fine. Don't worry if you don't get to one hundred goals; in fact, don't worry if you don't get to even ten goals initially! The point is to simply get the ball rolling, to try to push past some of the early, easy goals, and to dig a little bit deeper into your heart.

Mind Maps

Many people swear by mind mapping as a way to organize or break down big projects and create smaller steps and goals with accountability to take them to completion. One writing coach uses mind maps to help her clients write books from start to finish, including detailed chapter outlines. Lawyers often use mind maps to create outlines and to track and organize massive amounts of information, and countless students say that traditional note taking pales in comparison to mind mapping during lectures.

Mind maps are like a wheel with spokes coming out from the center, which typically depicts the finished goal. Related goals or subgoals branch out from the spokes. The advantage of using this system is that you can actually see your goals in a visual way, and you can individualize the steps in a variety of ways, using color and varying the length of spokes and the distance between goals. Many people like to work with text that is not laid out in a traditional way, and they find this design method even allows them to think more expansively. Turn to the sample life list map on page 246 if you'd like to try this approach.

Vision Boards

If images speak to you in ways that the written word does not, you may be interested in making a vision board of your life list goals that includes any number of visual media such as photographs, magazine images, advertisements, scraps of fabric, CD covers, recipes, ticket stubs, and even jewelry. Typically, a vision board is a massive collage created on poster board; you can place one almost anywhere that regularly gets your attention—including the refrigerator door or bedroom mirror.

One of our clients, a professional photographer, decided to use her skills to make huge collages of blended images and slogans to help her stay focused on her goals for the next few years of her life. She blew up the collages to poster size, framed them inexpensively, and hung them on the wall leading up the stairs to her home office. The images included a woman crossing a finish line, which represented her goal to complete a marathon for the first time, and a picture of a peaceful lake, a representation of her goal to slow down and enjoy the small, everyday pleasures.

Another client created an unusual vision board composed of lots of Post-it notes. She divided the board into five columns and wrote a variety of goals on the Post-its, which she then placed in a column for each of the years she was targeting. She then put the vision board in her bedroom and looked at it for weeks, rearranging the notes whenever she felt compelled to do so. Finally, she invited some close friends to look at this unique life list board, and asked for their thoughts. To her surprise, one of her friends picked up one of the notes and moved it up in the timeline, saying, "You'll do this goal this year because I'm going to do it with you, and we'll push each other forward." Our client was amazed and gratified to find that her friends not only were moved to create their own boards after this, but also asked to join forces with her on certain goals so that they could help one another.

• • •

Scrapbooks

Scrapbooks are great tools for multiple activities. One of the most clever uses of scrapbooks that we've seen involves decorating each page with images of a particular goal, leaving a blank space in the middle of the page to record when the goal is actually accomplished—through either a written record or a picture of the completed goal. Scrapbooks can be tiny or large, depending on your preference, and you can create them with other people or by yourself. Some of our clients find that making goal scrapbooks allows them to use a variety of creative materials and colors, similar to the process involved in making a mind map.

Internet Goal Sites and Blogs

Advances in technology are bringing us closer to one another. As we mentioned earlier, there are several high-quality goal-setting sites on the Internet that offer virtual communities for people who wish to connect with others around the world with similar passions and goals (see page 266 for some examples). It's not uncommon to see people cheering one another on at these sites, sharing tips on different ways to accomplish goals, and commiserating when things aren't going well. Personal blogs devoted to the pursuit of goals are also proliferating, particularly in the weight-loss arena, and many that cropped up after viewing Randy Pausch's stirring "Last Lecture."

Unusual Life List Approaches

There is no limit to the ways that you can note and track your goals. Here are some of the more creative approaches that have struck us, over the years, as the most successful and that might spark you to do something a little out of the ordinary:

- **Mosaics.** One person bought unfinished tabletops and mirrors and created mosaic representations of her goals on these items. This brainstorm about how to make her life list feel "authentic" emerged from seeing gorgeous Byzantine mosaics on the floors and walls of churches she toured while vacationing in Europe.

- **Time capsules.** One of our clients had a party whose purpose was for everyone to discuss and write down their goals for the coming year, and then exchange them with another partygoer after dinner. All the guests committed to coming back in a year to open the sealed envelopes and celebrate the progress everyone had made, and then make a list for the next year!

■ **Quilting.** After seeing a quilt display at a local airport, one client decided to craft a quilt representing her life goals, including those she had already accomplished. Her finished product was stunning. Each quilt square had a picture she'd taken of the accomplished goal that had then been transferred onto cloth and sewn into the quilt. For upcoming goals, she was equally clever, using T-shirts and other items to depict her dreams. After she had made this quilt for herself, other people began to ask her to make quilts representing their goals, or their children's goals, which resulted in a niche business that earned her a nice income.

■ **Weaving and stitching.** Several people we know have had their goals woven into scarves, stitched in needlepoint canvases, and embroidered onto tote bags.

■ **License plates, security passwords, and e-mail addresses.** Vanity plates and e-mail addresses are prime places to make yourself consciously aware of at least one of your goals. A woman who was trying to save money to buy a beach house had the vanity plate "IMCHEAP" made for her car in order to remind herself to stop impulse purchases. A writer changed all of her Internet site passwords to read "BestsellerInOneYear" so that she'd always have to type that goal in order to do tasks online.

■ **Videos.** Although none of our clients have ever done this, we like the idea of people videotaping themselves stating their goals and then putting the videos on a video-sharing site such as YouTube, where they have the added bonuses of public accountability and seeing their own facial expressions.

■ **Book clubs.** We have helped people in languishing book clubs transform their monthly gatherings from wine-soaked, gossipy get-togethers into goal-setting groups, where members can share their short-term and long-term goals with one another and spend each month celebrating, brainstorming, and being proactive.

And While You're At It . . .

One of our clients worked busily on her life goals for a solid day, and when she was done, she excitedly drove to her parents' home and read them aloud over a family dinner. Within the next twenty-four hours, her father had written "Sixty Things to Do before I Turn Sixty" and started to plan an ambitious set of trips and goals.

Yet another client was surprised when her nine-year-old son presented her with a neatly printed list of his goals, which included attending a Hall of Fame induction ceremony at the National Baseball Hall of Fame. It turned out that the boy had listened to his mother talking about her own goals so much that he decided to set his own. What surprised our client the most, though, was that it had never even occurred to her to ask her three children if they had life goals. So they all sat down one day and wrote down their goals, which they put on the refrigerator. Now every summer vacation trip involves trying to help one of the children accomplish a life goal.

Our takeaway from these experiences has been that creating a life list has the power to inspire those around you, whether you know it or not. So don't be shy about sharing your goals with your family, because you might find that they will be delighted to let you know what they want to do with their lives, too.

Where Your Life List Is Now

You are now actively creating your life list, which, as we've just seen, can be accomplished in any way that suits you, whether it's visual, spoken, written on paper, or typed into a document on your computer. Whatever your preference, we encourage you to explore the method that gives you the greatest amount of flexibility, creativity, and accountability to be successful. You may even find that a combination of approaches is the best way for you to move forward. The main thing is to get started and enjoy the process. If you need a little extra encouragement, try a couple of the exercises listed below or visit some of the goal-focused Internet sites listed on page 266.

Life List Exercises and Worksheets

❑ Visit several goal-focused Internet sites. If you didn't do this as part of Chapter 1's assignments, you might want to do it now because you never know what new goals might leap out at you even if you've looked before (see page 266).

❑ Map of life list goals. Look at "My Life List Map" to consider this novel visual approach for yourself (see page 246).

6

WILLPOWER:
WHY YOU MUST SAY NO SOMETIMES

He who guards his lips, guards his life.
But he who speaks rashly will come to ruin.
—PROVERBS 13:3

THERE IS NOTHING that matters more in goal accomplishment than the ability to resist the urge to give in to little voices that tell us that it's okay to quit when the going gets tough. Researchers have studied willpower in various forms for decades, and their conclusions are consistent: The key to success with any goal is to withstand temptation and persist through discomfort. The inability to do this has far-reaching consequences, some of which are discussed in the next section.

Out of Sight, Out of Mind

In one of the most famous psychological experiments of all time, conducted on the campus of Stanford University in California, dozens of preschoolers were given a treat and told that if they could sit quietly by themselves until the tester returned in about fifteen minutes, they would be rewarded with two treats instead of one. If they couldn't wait, however, all they had to do was summon the tester with a bell, at which point the experiment would end and they could leave with the one treat they had already been given.

As the minutes ticked away, a team of observers huddled behind a one-way mirror and watched the children cope with the temptation in various ways. Some couldn't resist it and ate the treat immediately. Some waited a while, and then furtively gobbled the treat. A few rang the bell and were done with the experiment.

But plenty of others—at least 60 percent of the children—devised strategies that revolved around avoiding eye contact with the forbidden substance, ultimately allowing them to override the desire to satisfy an immediate urge for sugar. For example, a few of these prescient four-year-olds put their heads down on their folded arms. Some sang songs and distracted themselves by moving around. Still others turned their backs on the treat, refusing to even look at it. "Out of sight, out of mind" was clearly the winning approach for most of them.

From Cookies to SAT Scores

Fast-forward more than ten years. Researchers mailed questionnaires to the parents of the children in the test in which they were asked about their children's grades, SAT scores, behavior, popularity, alcohol use, and friendships. Over and over, the researchers learned that the four-year-olds who had successfully withstood temptation so that they could double their sweet rewards were judged more than a decade later to be socially competent, hardworking, verbally proficient, and mature teenagers. They were also described as more likely to deal successfully with stress, plan activities ahead of time, respond to reason, and concentrate when necessary.

For the first time, researchers had proof that teaching young children how to control their behavior might not just make parents' lives easier and less stressful. Now it was clear that saying no to one's urges at the age of four predicted the trajectory of those children's lives, including the way they viewed themselves, how others interacted with them and graded them, and even whether or not they could overcome obstacles and experience success in multiple life domains during some of the most impressionable years of their lives.

Suddenly, it was startlingly apparent that one small trait—the ability to wait fifteen minutes for a reward at the age of four—had the power to predict long-term results around life success, which is why self-control occupies such a prominent place in this book, as well as in our program. Understanding how much self-control you have now, and how to get more of it when you need it most, is one of the key building blocks in creating your best life and accomplishing your life list goals now and in the future.

Life List Goals Require Willpower

The seminal work at Stanford University on delayed gratification by Walter Mischel described above has been replicated over the past fifty years by many others who

study self-regulation (also referred to as self-control or willpower), and g‗
to the heart of whether or not we will be able to achieve life list goals and
high quality of life. If we cannot withstand temptation when it arises, contr‗
urges when we are tired, start something new and challenging, and invoke the
power of discipline when we're in the final stretches of attaining something important, we will always be destined to live the "pleasant" life, which doesn't demand
much from us, but certainly won't allow us to maximize our potential and achieve
our goals, either.

Self-control isn't essential for just goal accomplishment, though. It is viewed
by many as the bedrock of personal and social stability, and the major difference
separating animals from humans. After all, what would life be like if we all
dumped gravy on our mother-in-law's head at every Thanksgiving meal when
she criticized our cooking skills? What if we all relieved ourselves publicly because
we didn't want to wait until we found a restroom? And how well would our office
function if we told our coworkers and superiors what we thought about them
every single time we were angry or irritated about something they'd done?

Dr. Roy Baumeister, a social psychologist at Florida State University who has
spent much of his adult life studying the importance of self-control and how we
both cultivate it and lose it, believes that "self-regulation failure is central to
nearly all of the personal and social problems that currently plague citizens of
the modern, developed world." These problems include, but are not limited to,
drug addiction, violence, obesity, gambling, credit card abuse, lack of exercise,
and most self-destructive behaviors.

One of the major reasons why researchers are so eager to understand self-
regulation is because it appears to be dissipating in the face of technological advances
and their promises of instant gratification. For example, many high school students
don't bother to listen to cell phone messages because text messages can be read
more quickly. Letter writing is now bemoaned as a lost art form because e-mail
gives us quicker responses with less effort. And the long-term discipline required to
lose weight and stay out of the sun is negated by the ability to sidestep all of that hard
work through gastric bypass surgery and lunchtime acid peels.

Chris Peterson and Marty Seligman, coauthors of the definitive textbook *The
Twenty-Four Character Strengths and Virtues*, regard self-regulation as one of the most
important qualities a person can devote time toward enhancing, for many obvious reasons. They also fear that America's increasing departure from the
Protestant work ethic, coupled with the excesses of the self-esteem movement,
could be creating a generation of children who don't understand hard work and
long-term payoffs, and who may be "weak, narcissistic, and self-indulgent" as a
result. This could also be why the trait of self-regulation is usually at the bottom
of most Americans' list of strengths, and why so many New Year's resolutions
and other goals bite the dust so quickly!

Take a quick, enlightening look at your own list of life goals through the lens of self-regulation. How many of them will require that you work extra hard, hold your tongue more often, get up a little earlier, stay a little later at work, and exhibit more pronounced discipline with money? Chances are that most, if not all, of your meaningful goals will require that you exercise some measure of self-control.

The Self-Control Scale

As Mischel and other researchers have noted, some of us are naturally more cautious and prudent than others, and less prone to impulsive behavior. How else can you explain why some four-year-olds knew, without being told, how to distract themselves in order to get two treats, while others couldn't resist the temptation and got only one treat? Children with attention deficit issues, such as ADHD and ADD, are also at a natural disadvantage, which is why it's so important to know the many ways that we can help ourselves through effective behavior changes—or medication, if it's called for. It's important, too, to improve our chances of attaining our goals that we understand what science is telling us about how we can protect and replenish our self-control supplies when required to do so.

The Self-Control Scale, designed by Roy Baumeister, June Tangney, and Angie Luzio Boone, has been found to be a powerful and accurate measure of how much self-control we possess, and how well we are able to regulate our thoughts, emotions, impulses, and performance—the four actions that tend to deplete self-control—under normal circumstances.

Following is a sample of the statements used in this test, which are scored from 1 to 5 on a Likert item (a widely used psychological tool that ranks a respondent's evaluation from negative to positive).

1. I am able to work effectively toward long-term goals.
2. Pleasure and fun sometimes keep me from getting work done.
3. I often interrupt people.
4. I am always on time.
5. Sometimes I can't stop myself from doing something, even if I know it is wrong.

Regardless of where you stand right now in your ability to exercise self-control, our life list plan will help you act in ways that will make a powerful difference in many spheres of your life and will also make you feel happier in the process.

The Fallout from Poor Self-Control

As we mentioned earlier, poor self-control is not conducive to living an optimal life. But there are some especially difficult consequences of low self-regulation, which underscore the importance of paying attention to this area of your own life.

Following is a small sample of what researchers have discovered happens when we can't or won't control our impulsive urges.

- A Pennsylvania State University study of preschoolers in a Head Start program found that a child's inability to control impulsive responses or pay attention led to later difficulties in educational settings, and particularly in math.
- Teens and adults with poor self-control are more prone to problem drinking, eating disorders, criminal behavior, out-of-wedlock births, and substance-abuse problems.
- A lack of self-regulation among adults often results in poor work performance and fewer promotions.
- Low self-control is linked to poor interpersonal relationships, lack of popularity, and aggressive behavior throughout life.
- Anxiety disorders, depression, phobias, obsessive-compulsive behavior, and other psychological disorders are more prevalent among people with low self-control.

The Multiple Benefits of Exercising Self-Control

Mischel's preschoolers were the first to demonstrate, more than ten years after being tested on self-control, that willpower could predict higher grades, better SAT scores, more popularity, and the ability to reason well. But the benefits didn't stop there. Other positive payoffs included

- More resilience and ease coping with setbacks
- Better performance in school and at work
- Enhanced popularity and peer trust
- More empathy for others
- Less likelihood of feeling shame and more likelihood of experiencing appropriate guilt when necessary and taking steps to right wrongs instead of blaming others for shortcomings
- Fewer eating disorders, substance-abuse problems, and other addictive behaviors

- Greater ability to save more money and spend less impulsively
- More success in accomplishing goals that involve willpower, such as weight loss, smoking cessation, and fitness improvements

Now What?

Don't despair if you have already identified yourself as someone who could use an infusion of willpower. After working with thousands of people for decades, we know that everyone is capable of change if they want to work for it, and we've seen miraculous transformations when people understand that they can take control of their lives and successfully accomplish their goals.

Our self-control gets depleted every day in ways we may not even be aware of. It may explain that strange breakdown between lunch—when you passed up the dessert cart without a second glance—and right after dinner—when you ate a pint of ice cream in bed. Or even why you got through six hours of a tough job interview, only to find that you destroyed your chances of getting your dream job when you made a thoughtless racial joke over dinner. These types of situations are more common than you can imagine, but you can avoid them if you practice the science behind enhancing willpower.

Where Did It Go?

To understand self-control, you must first grasp that it is exactly like a muscle that gets stronger or weaker every day, depending on how much or how little you use it. Roy Baumeister and his colleagues have now determined through a variety of clever experiments that we start each morning with a certain amount of self-control that gradually gets used up when we perform deliberate acts of control, such as suppression of thoughts, behaviors, and emotions that are not automatic for us. Once this supply is depleted, we have less energy to do other things that require self-control, such as exercise, drink responsibly, avoid sexual temptations, or manage money effectively.

Here is a case history of a client, James, who exemplifies beautifully how you can have self-control in many areas during the day, but make crucial mistakes—with long-term consequences—at night when your self-control "muscle" is exhausted:

James was gunning for the vice presidency of his consulting firm, and to do this he needed to be extra-disciplined about his behavior at work with female subordinates because of a well-known weakness for pretty women. He buckled down and worked for weeks on a demanding project that involved making difficult decisions and suppressing his true emotions when he had to lay off some of his colleagues and people who reported to him. His usual fitness routine evaporated in the face of the long days at work, and before he went home at night he began to drink a bit to "take the edge off" the demands of the day. At the conclusion of this successful cost-cutting initiative, James felt emotionally exhausted and was unable to withstand the come-ons from his shapely assistant, Susanna, whom he wound up bedding in a motel near the office one night. Their behavior became office-cooler gossip, and James's hard work was destroyed by his lack of self-control in his personal life. Not only did he lose the promotion, but he lost the respect of his colleagues and his family, as well.

What Eats Up Your Self-Control and What Doesn't

Before we go on, let's recap what uses up our storehouse of self-control and what doesn't, because it's not immediately obvious unless you understand the nuances of this important point. James's story has a few clues: He had to make tough decisions that impacted other people's lives on a daily basis; he had to suppress his urges to be a friend when he fired his colleagues or cut their salaries; and he already was known as a guy who had low self-control around good-looking women. On top of that, he had let his normal fitness routine (running two miles around the neighborhood every morning) lapse, and he was drinking more than usual at night. A "perfect storm" of factors led him to abandon his normal self-control and make a mistake that had long-term consequences—something he might have been able to avoid if he'd understood what was happening to him throughout this process on a more subtle level.

The following are situations that cause you to deplete your store of self-control:

- **You suppress normal urges** like saying and doing things that are socially inappropriate, such as telling off your boss or laughing in the middle of a serious meeting.
- **You use a lot of mental energy to make decisions that involve self-control** and willful planning, like setting up the family budget.
- **You try not to think about something** in order to focus on something else—for example, trying not to think about your child's rejection from a desired college while writing an important article for your company's newsletter, or trying not to think about the sweets in the kitchen while you are trying to lose weight.
- **You have two conflicting conscious goals,** such as cooking a healthy dinner while avoiding the chocolate cake on the kitchen counter.

- **You constantly attempt to hide something about yourself** that would hurt your social standing, such as an extramarital affair or a criminal past.

In contrast, the following situations *do not* cause you to use up your valuable self-control, and should have no impact on whether or not you have willpower left at the end of the day for important tasks:

- **You do something difficult or mentally challenging.** When you do something hard, like solve math problems, you are not necessarily using willpower, and people who rate something with high "task difficulty" do not necessarily have lower self-control when tested immediately afterward.
- **You are mentally fatigued.** People who are simply fatigued don't show signs of self-control failure, and may even do well on tests of self-control when they are tired because the tests are a new challenge that engage different faculties than the ones used in self-control.
- **You have low self-esteem.** In one study, participants were divided into two groups that received positive and negative feedback about their performance on a self-control task. Regardless of their feedback, both groups showed poorer responses to a second test of willpower, which proved that there was no correlation between self-efficacy and self-control.

White Bears and Carrots

Now there is proof that self-control vanishes before our eyes, leaving us vulnerable to being ineffective and even passive if our self-control has been drained by another experience. A study at the University of Kentucky divided participants into two groups. One group ate carrots while looking at a plate of tempting sweets, while the other group ate the sweets while looking at the carrots. Then both groups were asked to work on difficult—almost impossible—anagrams. The group that had used up most of its energy avoiding the sweets showed very little persistence in solving the anagrams, while the group that had not had to exhibit self-control worked much longer and harder to solve the anagrams. In another study, research participants who focused on saying the color of the letters of a word instead of saying what word the letters actually spelled were more likely to use sexually inappropriate language or act on sexual urges than people who had not had to focus on overriding their conscious word choices. Finally, in a third study, a group of participants who were asked to refrain from thinking about white bears lost more physical strength in a hand-grip test than another group that was not asked to consciously suppress their thoughts.

Refilling the Willpower Tank

Because this is such a new and cutting-edge area of research, there are only two proven interventions thus far that have been found to immediately restore our self-control levels, giving us the energy to persevere on a subsequent self-control challenge:

- **Making yourself smile.** Participants in the white-bear study, for example, were divided into two groups that watched either a funny video or a film of a dolphin encounter. The participants who were induced to be happy by watching the funny video showed no loss of willpower in a subsequent task, while the participants who watched the dolphin video—which was nonarousing and neutral—were not able to replenish their strength as quickly.
- **Eating a small amount of sugar.** Participants in another study who used willpower on one test were found to recover completely for a second task by drinking a glass of lemonade that contained real sugar, not a sugar substitute.

Willpower Boosters

It's exciting to discover that scientists are finding ways that we can improve our willpower in many areas. These findings give fresh credence to the efficacy of behavioral exercises seen in many parochial schools, such as neat handwriting, good posture, and adherence to wearing a prescribed uniform. Public schools that have prescribed rules of behavior, such as no gum chewing, are also helping students to improve self-regulation skills, whether they are aware of it or not.

Following are some willpower boosters that have been proven to work.

- **Hide temptations.** People who had chocolate candies on their desks showed less self-control in eating them than people whose desks were placed six feet away from the same treats. Avoiding the sight of something tempting, just like Mischel's preschoolers did, allows you to be more successful at resisting temptation.
- **Follow a regular exercise program.** Participants in an Australian investigation led by Megan Oaten and Ken Cheng who embarked on

a two-month physical exercise program of weight lifting, resistance training, and aerobics experienced reduced caffeine, cigarette, and alcohol consumption. They also lowered their junk-food intake and ate more healthy food. As if that weren't beneficial enough, these participants had improved emotional control, better spending habits, and fewer hours of television watching!

- **Start a money-management program.** Oaten and Cheng did another study of self-regulation, this time asking participants to engage in a four-month program of financial monitoring. Again, they found that taking control of this one area improved self-regulation in a variety of other areas, such as healthy eating, maintenance of household chores, better study habits, less cigarette and alcohol use, and lowered coffee consumption.

- **Avoid alcohol.** Numerous studies, including those conducted by Roy Baumeister, have shown that alcohol undercuts all attempts at self-regulation, regardless of the goal, and that people who drink alcohol are more apt to fail at self-control than those who don't when it comes to spending money, handling anger, eating—and almost any behavior that requires self-control.

The takeaway for people who want to accomplish their life list goals and have more willpower is to say no to themselves on a regular basis if they want to enjoy all of the fruits of self-regulation. This is actually not a particularly new idea—Benjamin Franklin espoused the same sentiment in his famous "Character Improvement Project" at the age of seventy-six—an effort that was so successful that it was the inspiration for the noted Franklin Covey organizational system, which helps people learn how to set goals and accomplish them. To get started on tracking and improving your own behaviors, take a look at the "'Ben' There, Done That" worksheet on page 236. In the meantime, following are a few more things that have been found to help people learn to withstand temptation and improve their focus.

► MEDITATE

Scientists are increasingly finding that meditation is one of the "silver bullets" that have nothing but positive outcomes. It turns out that meditation also has the positive impact of curbing impulsive actions and helping people become kinder, more empathic, and more willing to behave in positive ways, particularly if they practice a form of meditation called "loving-kindness." Richard Davidson at the University of Wisconsin has been at the forefront of this research and has studied Tibetan Buddhists (including the Dalai Lama) in order to discover which part of their brains are stimulated when they enter a meditative state to understand a bit more about how different actions flow from different neural stimuli.

Davidson's research has found that long-term meditators who are connected to functional magnetic resonance imaging sensors show increased action in the insula—an area near the front of the brain that is connected with emotions. The stronger the meditator's experience of compassion, the more activity was observed in this area. Increased activity was also detected in the temporal parietal juncture, especially in the right hemisphere, which is a location noted for processing empathy. Davidson noted that improved self-regulation is another side effect of meditation, adding, "I think this can be one of the tools we use to teach emotional regulation to kids who are at an age where they're vulnerable to going seriously off track."

Improvements in self-regulation around overeating and impulsive behaviors with food have also been noted among women with eating disorders who were taught mindfulness meditation. Psychologists at Australia's Griffith University, Michelle Hanisch and Angela Morgan, noted that the mindfulness practice allowed the women to "learn that thoughts and emotions don't have any power over us as they are just passing phenomena and aren't permanent." They also found that the eating disorder sufferers reported less dissatisfaction with their bodies, increased self-esteem, and improved personal relationships.

► GET RID OF THE CLUTTER

> Never again clutter your days or nights with so many menial and unimportant things that you have no time to accept a real challenge when it comes along. This applies to play as well as work. A day merely survived is no cause for celebration. You are not here to fritter away your precious hours when you have the ability to accomplish so much by making a slight change in your routine. No more busy work. No more hiding from success. Leave time, leave space, to grow. Now. Now! Not tomorrow!
>
> —OG MANDINO

Technology has infiltrated our lives so dramatically that it's hard not to be beeped or text-messaged at least once an hour, while high school and college students are interrupted with even more frequency by cell phones or the distinctive sound of an instant message arriving on their computers. One Canadian study estimated that the onslaught of technological time wasters and interruptions is costing the United States fifty billion dollars annually and fueling the rise in the number of people who describe themselves as chronic procrastinators who can't start or finish projects on time.

Dr. Edward M. Hallowell, an expert on attention issues, has even coined a new phrase to describe people whose brains have been hijacked by technology—attention deficit trait. Hallowell says that formerly high performers at work are now becoming disabled by an endless amount of information that is so dizzying, it is almost impossible for them to focus on what really matters.

People with poor self-control are also habitual procrastinators, so removing the instant gratification of e-mail, online poker, and Web shopping will strengthen willpower while eliminating some of the most common causes of procrastination. Experts are unanimous in their advice on how to deal with procrastination and willpower challenges as they pertain to technology and its seductive lure:

- **Check your e-mail only twice a day.** Very few e-mails need to be attended to within five minutes of delivery.
- **Remove instant messaging programs from your computer, or use them only at designated times during the day.** One of our clients found that his work output skyrocketed when he eliminated a program that opened all of his instant messaging programs at once, which kept him tied up in reactive text conversations for hours, with no evidence of real productivity.
- **Remove all games from your computer and cell phone.**

▶ MONITOR YOUR BEHAVIOR

Behavior that is not monitored cannot be changed, and research has found that lapses in self-regulation are often preceded by a failure to monitor behavior. Roy Baumeister has laughingly said that one of the most powerful ways a person can drink less at a bar is to have the bartender leave every emptied glass on the bar in front of the drinker. That way, the person cannot lose track of how much he or she is actually drinking!

Self-monitoring through journals and charts has been found to be especially successful when a person is trying to lose weight, exercise, and accomplish any long-term goal. In fact, keeping a food diary has been found to actually double dieters' weight loss.

Where Your Life List Is Now

Your list is still new, but you need to take a look at the goals that will require extra reserves of willpower and self-control and come up with a plan to boost yours, if necessary. Any daily action you perform that involves suppressing your impulses so that you will succeed in the areas that are important to you (exercising in the morning despite being tired, putting away your credit cards when you are tempted to overspend) will make you better at self-regulation.

Life List Exercises and Worksheets

❏ Fill out the "'Ben' There, Done That" self-control worksheet. In honor of Ben Franklin's Character Improvement Project (see page 86), we have created a self-regulation worksheet to help you get started on monitoring your own self-improvement project, which could include following the posted speed limit for two weeks, refraining from whining, walking two miles every morning, or praying for others.

7

RISKS THAT PAY OFF

Risk! Risk anything!
Care no more for the opinions of others.
Do the hardest thing on earth for you.
Act for yourself.
Face the truth.
—KATHERINE MANSFIELD

Taking risks is an essential part of life list success. Engaging in appropriate but scary behavior outside of your normal comfort zone is one of the guaranteed ways you can increase your chances of positive change and lower the likelihood that you'll be doing the same old things that have gotten you the same old results that you don't want anymore. There's a phrase often heard in twelve-step meetings such as Alcoholics Anonymous about how easy it is to delude ourselves into thinking that taking the safe road will take us into more rewarding territory in life. It goes something like this: "What's the definition of insanity? Doing the same thing over and over and expecting different results."

It would, indeed, be insane to think that you will be able to accomplish aggressive goals of any kind without being uncomfortable. The problem is that it's scary to do this. Goal-setting theorist Edwin Locke noted that fear—"[f]ear of change, fear of telling the truth, fear of being wrong, fear of being different, fear of thinking for oneself, fear of failure, fear of the subconscious and of knowing one's own motives, fear of disappointment, fear of disapproval, fear of being hurt, fear of being vulnerable, fear of the new, and fear of standing up for one's values"—is the main thing that keeps people from goal accomplishment and success.

. . .

Why Risks Matter

Fear causes people to draw back from situations. It brings on mediocrity,
it dulls creativity, it sets one up to be a loser in life.
—FRAN TARKENTON

Mary, a young, college-educated woman, wanted to take the massive risk of starting her own company by the age of thirty, just like her older brother and father had done before her. She'd seen the risks they'd taken to build their companies and then sell them quite profitably, but she wasn't sure if she had the "balls," as she laughingly put it during a coaching session, to do it.

Mary was asked to take a few minutes while meeting with her coach to write down some of the biggest risks she'd ever taken in her life, and to then write next to them what payoffs she'd gotten from taking those risks. She worked quietly and then said that doing the exercise had resulted in a key breakthrough.

This is what Mary said:

> The first risk that came to mind was the application I sent to the college I really wanted to attend when I was a high school senior. I knew they'd get thousands of applications and that my chances of getting in as an out-of-state applicant would be small. So I decided to take a huge risk, and I had a snow globe made with a picture in it. The picture was of me holding up a sign with the ten top reasons why they should take me at that school, and what I'd bring to the student body with my presence. I didn't know if the snow globe would be perceived as corny, pretentious, or just plain stupid, but I knew I had to take some kind of risk if I was going to stand out. So I did it and crossed my fingers, and I got in! In my acceptance letter, they told me it was the most creative and memorable application they'd ever gotten. Taking that risk resulted in one of the biggest rewards of my life. The friends I made, the courses I took for my major, and the activities I participated in while I was there have helped make me who I am. So I get it—big risk equals big reward!

Another coaching client, Allison, was trembling with fear about taking the risk that she wanted to take more than anything else: applying to medical school. The only problem was that she was approaching thirty and was a well-paid financial consultant in a big city. She was also surrounded by friends who weren't any happier with their own career choices than she was, and none of them were taking any action to change. Allison fed her depression and inertia about not applying to medical school—even though she had satisfied most of the premed requirements in college—by hanging around with other complainers who never forced her to examine different choices or take more proactive steps toward change.

In a pivotal coaching call, Allison was asked what she'd feel like if she looked back on her life as an old woman and had never taken the risk of seeing if she could become a doctor.

Allison was thoughtful. "I'd be miserable," she said softly. She added that she had followed a boyfriend to the big city in the hopes of marrying him, but that in doing so, she had reneged on her dream of applying to medical school ("He told me he wouldn't sit around and play housewife while I was at med school") and that she'd taken an unfulfilling financial job to be more attractive to him as a potential wife.

Despite her best efforts, the boyfriend eventually dumped her, so the risk of remaking herself to suit him clearly hadn't paid off. Now Allison was nursing bitter regrets and wasn't happy about the prospects for her future. At the urging of an old friend, Allison decided to get a coach and make a life list, and she resolved to take new and more appropriate risks that reflected her own authentic goals and not someone else's.

She started by finding out the requirements to get into med school and where she could enroll to take the prerequisites she hadn't taken in college. Then she found out where those medical "prep" schools were and what it would take to get into them. After weeks of nail biting, she took the huge step of asking her supervisor for a recommendation for the school applications—a sure signal that she wanted to leave her job, one that could result in not receiving her much-needed annual bonus.

To Allison's tremendous surprise, her supervisor was excited about her medical school dreams and even asked Allison how she'd had the courage to go for it. Allison discovered that her bold move had a profound impact on her friends, her supervisor, and how she saw herself. She began to view herself as a woman who was courageous and focused, and she decided to use her burgeoning self-confidence to knock off two more goals on her life list: She trained for, entered, and completed a triathlon, and she did it in a city that she had always wanted to visit.

Allison got into the medical prep school in the city she'd always wanted to live in, and despite cutting her income down to near nothing and moving to a place where she didn't know anyone, as she set off to become the oldest doctor in her medical school class she felt surges of profound happiness that had eluded her for years.

When Risks Don't Pay Off

There are risks and costs to a program of action, but they are far less
than the long-range risks and costs of comfortable inaction.

—JOHN F. KENNEDY

Mary's and Allison's true stories demonstrate some of the typical results we see when people take scary risks to make their life lists happen. Usually, the risks result in immediate gains in confidence, forward progress toward goal accomplishment, and an increase in life satisfaction in other areas.

But that's not always the case. Allison's story is a perfect example of the risks we take and then come to regret because they don't give us what we want at that particular moment. When she gave up her dream of applying to medical school to follow her boyfriend to a city that she didn't really like, and to take a job in a field that didn't really interest her, Allison compromised on some of her important values to try to please someone else. This was a definite risk, and it didn't pay off. Allison's happily-ever-after fantasy crumbled and she subsequently became mired in misery.

▶ THE RISK/REGRET TIPPING POINT

> The follies which a man regrets most in his life are those
> which he didn't commit when he had the opportunity.
> —HELEN ROWLAND

Research explains why we try to avoid taking risks that might cause us short-term pain. Economists have found that people will do almost anything to avoid making a choice that will result in financial loss, even if it's unlikely that they'll ever recoup that money. This is also why many people balk at selling stocks at a loss; they'd rather not book the loss and face the finality of actually being poorer. Our explanation for this is: *Losing hurts more than winning feels good.* We are, it seems, exquisitely wired to avoid taking risks, and we would prefer to preserve the pleasant status quo at all times rather than take a risk that could make our circumstances worse.

Despite the pain of short-term loss, economists have said that there is a tipping point, after a few years, where we stop feeling regrets about what hasn't worked, and instead have more regrets about the choices we haven't had the courage to pursue! This point occurs somewhere between the third and seventh year after we've taken a risk that didn't work out, and instead of being sad about the outcome, we become grateful that we had the nerve to go after something meaningful or hard.

Kevin Clements, one of the best swimmers in the world in the grueling four-hundred-meter individual medley, finished third in the Olympic trials in 2000 and fifth in 2004—missing his childhood goal of making the Olympic team by a fingernail (only the top two finishers make the team)—but his early sadness and regrets about his near misses have been transformed less than ten years later into passion as a college coach to help other swimmers set and achieve the goals that matter to them. With the perspective of hindsight, he is grateful that he fought as hard and as long as he did to get close to the Olympics, and has found that his initial regrets are a distant, albeit bittersweet, memory.

Fourth and Yards to Go—What's the Call, Coach?

Ships are safe in a harbor, but that's not what ships were built for.
—ANONYMOUS

The crowd is screaming. The score is tied. The stakes are high. What does a football coach do when the situation is fourth and long, and an unsuccessful gamble to go for the first down might result in the ball being turned over to the opposing team with a field position good enough for them to easily score and win the game? The most common play called by NFL coaches in situations like this is the safe play, in which the ball is punted down the field, as far as possible away from the opposing team, even though it means that no score is possible. But some of the winningest coaches in the NFL are the ones who take those fourth-down risks and have the quarterback throw a pass, regardless of the possible negative outcome.

Bill Belichick, the head coach of the dominant New England Patriots, who almost had the perfect season by going unbeaten in 2007, is infamous for taking the fourth-down risk and making it work. Data from a large number of NFL football games have shown that head coaches rarely do what Belichick does, and will overwhelmingly choose to protect field position. But David Romer, an economist at the University of California, has found that coaches who make those scary calls tend to win more often than coaches who play it safe, which could explain why the Patriots will go down in history as one of the best teams of all time.

Another sports analogy that proves the payoffs of risk taking involves baseball. Hitters who have slightly lower batting averages than their teammates are often those who are willing to fail more often at bat in the hopes of hitting the game-winning home runs.

The legendary New York Yankees slugger Reggie Jackson, also known as Mr. October for his renowned ability to perform under the pressures of postseason play-offs, epitomizes the risk-taking strategy that results in greatness. Jackson has a lifetime batting average of .262, which isn't particularly noteworthy, and he even logged more strikeouts than anyone else in history. But Jackson was handsomely rewarded financially and was inducted into the National Baseball Hall of Fame for his winner-take-all-approach at bat by hitting more home runs than almost any other player in the history of baseball. If he had decided to play it safe and simply hit a single or double to improve his batting average, not only would he have gone down in history as just another good player, but the teams he sparked with his gutsy play might never have won the World Series.

Risk Taking Pays Off Emotionally

To do an evil act is base. To do a good one without incurring danger is common enough. But it is part of a good man to do great and noble deeds though he risks everything in doing them.
—PLUTARCH

Not only is risk taking a solid strategy for scoring points in football games, hitting home runs in baseball games, and accomplishing other tough goals; it also seems to be a winning way to see yourself in a more positive and proactive light. People who study risk taking say that surviving risks teaches self-confidence and builds the belief that you can handle whatever life throws at you. In an uncertain world, this type of inner strength can be the difference between flourishing and floundering. Physical risks add the benefit of making you hyperfocused on what really matters in a life-and-death situation, too, which is a quality that we can bring to other types of decisions that require us to quickly separate priorities from nonpriorities.

Near-Death Regrets of Playing It Safe

Shayna, a young woman in her prime, performed her tenth skydive in October 2005 after falling in love with her new, daring hobby. Although the jump should have been routine, it turned into a life-and-death situation when her parachute failed to open and she plummeted eleven thousand feet to an almost-certain death, while her instructor, who had also become her boyfriend, helplessly filmed her descent from a camera on his helmet as he floated above her.

Shayna hit the ground headfirst and broke every bone in her face, shattered her eye sockets, broke her right leg, and knocked out five teeth. But she survived, and later she said that she'd expected to meet her dead relatives as she plummeted to the ground, because she'd always read that that was what happened at the end of your life.

Instead, to Shayna's surprise, she saw all her unfulfilled goals flashing before her eyes, reminding her of the things she'd never had the courage or passion to pursue while she was alive. Shayna not only survived, but she discovered that she was ten weeks pregnant with her boyfriend's child. Now she's not only an energetic mother; she is a woman transformed who goes after all of her goals instead of waiting for life to come to her.

The Toxicity of Regrets

There are two kinds of people in the world: the vulnerable and the dead.
Those who live only to avoid hurt are the living dead.
—EDWIN A. LOCKE, COFOUNDER OF GOAL-SETTING THEORY

Shayna was lucky enough to have gotten a second chance at making her dreams come true and smart enough to take advantage of it. The intensity of her near-death experience and the extent of her physical rehabilitation gave her the time and perspective to decide that taking risks to make her dreams come true was more than worth the regrets she'd have by not even trying.

But what happens if you never take risks, simply playing it safe in life? Researchers such as Abigail Stewart and Elizabeth Vandewater have actually studied what happens when people perform a midlife review and take stock of these regrets. The results are interesting, and certainly lend support to the idea that using the energy of regrets to set and pursue important goals instead of letting them go pays off.

Here are the highlights of their findings:

- Regrets are normal. We all have them, and they usually begin to accumulate in our early twenties after we have made decisions about passing up various opportunities, such as pursuing one relationship over another, or choosing one college major over another that was just as desirable.
- Regrets about unexplored avenues can feel most painful, however, at midlife, when we ask ourselves if our goals are still viable.
- Women most often feel regrets around putting too many eggs into the domesticity basket, and wish they had pursued educational and career options at an earlier age. Traditional career women also feel regrets, particularly about missed bonding opportunities with their children, if they had them, but don't feel quite as sad about those choices as the first group feels about theirs.
- Setting goals to change your life is a common outcome of midlife review, but it simply isn't enough to change your well-being *or* your life if you stop right there.
- The only people who seem to fare well after using their midlife regrets as fuel for change are those who *set goals and then take action to go after what they want.*
- People who do not make changes are not stuck because of external obstacles, such as money and living conditions. The main obstacle to

change is a lack of confidence in themselves and their ability to bring about desired outcomes. This group is stuck in a permanent state of regrets, sadness, and what-ifs.

Amy, another coaching client, had a transformative moment when she realized that she hadn't even consciously known that she was sad about submerging her professional goals by being an endlessly attentive "helicopter" mother for her own child and her two stepchildren. "I have just been marking time until I'm too old to go after my goals," she said during one conversation. This lightbulb moment, and a clearly defined set of life list goals that she quickly penned, was all it took for her to become a student of handwriting analysis—her childhood goal—at the age of fifty-five, and to join a masters rowing team.

Shame-Attacking Exercises

What a man is ashamed of is always at bottom himself, and he is
ashamed of himself at bottom always for being afraid.
—ROBIN G. COLLINGWOOD, 1889-1943,
BRITISH HISTORIAN AND PHILOSOPHER

Albert Ellis, the founder of rational emotive behavior therapy, is seen as one of psychotherapy's most pivotal leaders because of his unique contribution to how humans can change their thinking to interpret upsetting situations more favorably, leading them to behave in more productive, and less fearful, ways. Ellis's plainspoken style and no-nonsense approach to not letting your feelings guide your life found a receptive audience beginning in the late 1960s, resulting in multiple best-selling books, including *A Guide to Rational Living* and *Feeling Better, Getting Better, Staying Better*. His approach, which is based on the thinking of the Stoic philosopher Epictetus, birthed the cognitive-behavioral movement—the primary approach used and taught by most psychologists.

Ellis's controversial but effective "shame-attacking" exercises help clients face their fears and take risks. The exercises are based on Ellis's observation that his own shame and fear kept him from going after what he wanted in life—dates with women, for example—and that the only way to deal with that fear was to attack it head-on. When he was nineteen and "painfully shy," Ellis set himself the task of initiating a conversation with every woman who sat down alone on a bench at the New York Botanical Garden. "Thirty walked away immediately," he recounted, but despite this setback and his own considerable anxiety, he talked to dozens of other women—for the first time in his life. "Nobody vomited and ran away. Nobody called the cops." The final outcome was that he got over his shyness "by thinking differently, feeling differently, and, in particular, acting differently."

Shame-attacking exercises for clients usually consist of doing something public and outrageous, such as singing a silly song at the top of your lungs, shouting the names of the stops while riding the subway, or wearing mismatched clothes to work. Clients inevitably find out that they are braver, happier people after they do something like this because they find out exactly what Ellis discovered, If you take a risk, nobody vomits or even dies, but you do learn new skills and face your fears, leaving you a much bolder and more proactive person.

> Dara feared taking the risk of doing anything out of the ordinary in public because her family had always valued a certain type of decorum, which included never being showy or drawing attention to oneself. As Dara got older, she found that this tendency prevented her from reaching out for friends or asking for promotions at work, so she devised a unique shame-attacking exercise that allowed her to try on an outgoing, extroverted personality for two hours. Dara applied for the job of college mascot for a local university, explaining that she wanted to do it only once so that she could have the experience of approaching strangers and giving them a hug, patting them on the head, or giving them a high five without worrying about the consequence. In exchange for wearing the mascot costume, she donated money to one of the college scholarship funds. Dara's reward was that she got to be a big fuzzy bird for several hours, and she said that her "butt shaking" at center court, dancing with the college band in front of thousands of spectators, and diving into the audience to pat men's bald spots unleashed the extrovert she'd always wanted to be. Taking the risk as a mascot led her to take other risks without hiding behind a costume, thus allowing her the freedom to pursue her life list goals in more fun and energetic ways.

What Kinds of Risks Do CEOs Take?

People who take risks are the people you'll lose against.

—JOHN SCULLEY

Taking a corporate approach to shame-attacking exercises, some businesses teach executives, and particularly CEOs, how to take physical risks that will encourage them to take risks in the boardroom. A chief financial officer from a British company said that learning "extreme skiing" opened her mind and made her a better person and worker. "I see people every day at work who are rigid in their approach. It's a huge barrier to success in a fast-moving world. Pushing your limits helps with being comfortable under pressure," she mused after her eye-opening experience.

Other business leaders who confess to regularly crossing their "freak-out point" said that skydiving, entering bodybuilding contests, playing ice hockey, riding motorcycles, and bungee jumping were just some of the ways they pushed themselves outside their comfort zone in order to learn that you can survive the things that frighten you. One of the many lessons these leaders say they learn from this type of risk taking is that you can learn how to concentrate and focus, even when you are scared. They all attest that knowing you can take a risk, accept the consequences of that risk, and not let fear rule you makes you a better person in multiple realms of life.

Interval Training for Risks

Take calculated risks. This is quite different from being rash.

—GEORGE S. PATTON

If you want to build your body's muscles and endurance quickly and effectively, there is no more tried-and-true method than interval training. Interval training is a method of pushing your body to approximately 85 percent of its limit for one to four minutes, interspersed with periods of less rigorous exercise. This type of workout has been shown to be incredibly effective for experienced athletes and less fit people, both of whom become stronger, quicker to recover, and able to burn more calories after incorporating this approach into their weekly workouts.

The same technique is useful if you want to expand your ability to take risks. By briefly going outside your emotional comfort zone, returning to a safe level, then going outside that zone again, then returning to your normal range, you will gradually adapt to the discomfort of fear and find yourself more and more able to withstand the stress of risks. As you do this more and more, you'll discover that occasionally being on the edge brings you the results you want.

Revving Up Your Risk-Taking Engine

There are a few more things you can do that might give you the courage to take risks that you never thought you could take before. One very effective method is called consciousness-raising, and it has been found to help move people who are contemplating change from inertia into action. An example of consciousness-raising for someone who wants to quit smoking is for him or her to see pictures of the damage done to the faces of longtime smokers. James Prochaska, the researcher who coined the stages-of-change approach, which has been widely accepted as a way to overcome addictive behaviors, says that consciousness-raising works because it helps to flood a person's body with powerful emotions that bring a desired goal into clearer focus.

Beth was a client who told us that her consciousness was raised by being a geriatric physician who observed in her work that the most frail, bedridden patients were those whose spines were the most inflexible. This observation was all it took for her to move her goal of attending a weekly yoga class from a dream to reality. As you can see from these two examples, consciousness-raising is sometimes quite painful because it exposes us to a future we don't want for ourselves, but consciousness-raising can also be done in a positive way that is equally effective.

Nick was floundering in his job as an investment counselor at a large firm, and when he was on the verge of quitting, he decided to spend a week shadowing one of his firm's top brokers. His goal was to learn everything that the broker did that might contribute to his own success, but he also wanted to motivate himself to work harder by seeing some of the fruits of success, such as leaving the office early to catch his child's school Christmas play.

That immersion week worked, and Nick returned to his home office in a more positive and proactive frame of mind. For example, he went back and knocked on the doors of people who had already told him they didn't want his services, and that persistence landed him the accounts he needed to stay in business. Now Nick is closing in on living the life of the man he once shadowed, and is grateful that he raised his consciousness around the potential fruits of hard work because instead of quitting, he hung in there and flourished.

Visualization

Another way you might be able to help yourself have the courage to do something a little bit scary is to actually see yourself in your mind's eye doing that very thing before you actually make the attempt. A study at Ohio State University in 2004 found that 90 percent of voters who pictured themselves from a third-person visual perspective as going through with voting actually did so, while only 72 percent of people who imagined themselves voting through their own eyes did so. Researchers explained that the possible reason for the enhanced success with the first type of visualization could come from the social pressure of imagining yourself as others might see you. "When participants saw themselves as others would, they were more motivated to actually get out and vote," the coauthor of the study explained, adding, "They saw themselves as more likely to vote and that translated into action."

So if you are considering entering a contest or speaking up at a local town hall meeting, but aren't feeling particularly courageous, try this tip: Close your eyes and see yourself doing the thing you fear, as if your best friend were watching you. Put yourself in clothes that you already own and look exactly as you appear to yourself in a mirror. You never know if this technique will be the one to help you get over the hump and give it a try.

Saying Good-bye to a "Lost Possible Self"

Sometimes we are afraid to take a risk in a new life direction because we are still clinging to an old goal that no longer suits our current life. We may not be aware of the energy this old goal is sucking from us, but researchers now know that this "lost possible self" not only is one of the ways we may be staying stuck and but also reduces our zest for other current goals.

Laura King of the University of Missouri is the premier researcher on this topic, and in her studies of women who got divorced or who gave birth to children with Down syndrome, she found that those who were able to bid farewell to an old image of "happily ever after" as a wife or mother were those who were able to reengage in life with goals that reflected their new circumstances. By doing this and being flexible in their thinking, they became happier and more successful in accomplishing their life list goals.

The same has been found true among teenagers who decided to move on from a goal that wasn't realistic anymore due to changed circumstances, and who instead set their sights a bit lower or in a different area. The teenagers who refused to accept reality and continued to stubbornly pursue a goal that simply wasn't workable showed greater susceptibility to illness and experienced lower moods, while those who accepted their "lost possible self" and moved on were happier, more resilient, and more successful.

However, in order to use Dr. King's research to your advantage, it is critical to understand the difference between quitting and being realistic about changed circumstances. Her work clearly identified the "lost possible selves" of the women she studied and showed that their now unrealistic goals were preventing them from making new goals and taking risks to accomplish them. To put this concept into another context, imagine holding on to a dream such as being a competitive female gymnast, for example, when your body sprouts to a height of five feet ten inches. Your height isn't going to help you succeed in your chosen sport and will probably make you miserable. Looking around for sports with tall women, like crew, swimming, and pole vaulting, however, will help you say good-bye to a "lost possible self" that is clouding your vision, and will give you the energy and tools to set a more realistic and current goal.

Where Your Life List Is Now

Now that you're in the habit of revising the goals on your life list, we'd like you to think of a scary risk that you can take in the near future that could help you accomplish a goal that is important to you. One of our clients, Jarred, took a fresh look at his life list after we discussed risk taking and decided to ask a well-known lawyer in his region to be his personal mentor. Within an hour of coming up with this goal during a coaching session, he had sent an e-mail introducing himself to the older man. By five o'clock the same day, he had not only received a return e-mail from the lawyer accepting the request to mentor Jarred, but he had earned the other man's respect for having the nerve to take the risk! "You're the kind of guy I want to know and help," he wrote back.

Life List Exercises and Worksheets

❑ Fill out the "Life Lists Are a Risky Business" worksheet on page 242. It will help you identify some of the risks you've already taken that have been useful in your life, and gives you space to identify more that might be helpful in accomplishing your goals.

❑ Ask yourself what the costs and benefits are of staying in a safe harbor instead of launching your ship on the open sea. Use the lines below to write about where your life could be in one year, five years, or ten years, if you continue on the same course you are on now:

_____

_____

_____

_____

_____

_____

_____

_____

_____

_____

8

THE COMPANY YOU KEEP

A man's friendships are one of the best measures of his worth.
—CHARLES DARWIN

I N THIS CHAPTER, we explore the nuances of how friendships can help or hurt us, how we unwittingly take on other people's good and bad moods, how to determine with mathematical precision which relationships contribute to our "flourishing" or "languishing," and how we can go about creating the vibrant support system that will enable us to be at our best and accomplish the goals that matter to us.

Obesity = Your Friends

In July 2007, the prestigious *New England Journal of Medicine* published the results of a study that sent shockwaves through the worlds of nutritionists, personal trainers, chronic dieters, and the weight-loss industry. After surveying the patterns of weight gain among more than twelve thousand people over thirty-two years, researchers at Harvard Medical School had determined that your chances of becoming obese are not necessarily closely tied to your sleep habits, your exercise regimen, or even what you eat, even though all of those things clearly play a role.

What these researchers determined was that the leading predictor of whether or not you will pack on the pounds and raise your chances of early death, as well as experience a long list of illnesses, is who your closest friends are. In fact, our friends are such a crucial determinant of our own behavior that the study found that we are 171 percent more likely to gain weight if our closest friends gain weight, *even if they live many miles away*, and that while family members' habits can and do impact us, that influence pales in comparison to what the friends in our social network do, think, and value.

Dr. Nicholas Christakis, the principal investigator in this study, explained his findings this way: "You change your idea of what is an acceptable body type by looking at the people around you," adding that if a close friend becomes obese, "it won't look that bad to you." Obesity researchers such as Dr. Rudolph L. Leibel at Columbia University said that Christakis's findings were groundbreaking and exciting because they examined an important subject in a way that had never been considered before. "It is an extraordinarily subtle and sophisticated way of getting a handle on aspects of the environment that are not normally considered," he noted.

While much of the world may have found the Harvard obesity study to be a front-page eye-opener, people in the goal-setting and psychology worlds were not surprised by this latest evidence of social and emotional "contagion," which shows the many ways that we adopt the attitudes of the people with whom we live, work, play, and socialize. We have long known that we "catch" moods from people who are in our environment, and even in our social networks, but it took the obesity findings for many to sit up and take notice that our friendships could be one of the biggest determinants of whether or not we actually set goals, and then whether or not we achieve them.

Emotional and Social Contagion Theories

The friendships of the world are oft confederacies in vice, or leagues of pleasures.
—JOSEPH ADDISON

The Harvard obesity study was just a drop in the bucket of emotional contagion theory, powerful research that shows the many ways we take on the moods of the people around us, and how we broaden that "contagion's" impact through the influence of the environments in which we find ourselves. Most people intuitively know that certain situations and people drain them, and that other relationships have the opposite effect of bringing out the best in them, but they are still astounded by the research around why and how this actually happens.

At the conclusion of this chapter, we'd like you to chart the web of people with whom you spend time and their values (see "My Web of Influence" on page 247) and then consider the ways that these friends have impacted your life already, as well as the ways you think that they might in the future, especially given your life list goals.

You will probably want to make some adjustments going forward, particularly in light of research that has shown how easy it is to take on the moods of the people around you. And if you have any questions about how to know whether or not certain relationships or situations are bringing out the best in you, we will show you a simple mathematical ratio that has been found to predict a "flourishing" friendship or workplace. [Knowing how to use the power of social support and recognize how the "right" friends and environments can maximize your happiness and success are keys to making your life list a success.]

Here are a few of the ways we are impacted by other people's moods, also known as "social contagion":

- **Contagion over the telephone.** In one study, college students who spoke to another student for just twenty minutes on the telephone found that if their mood was neutral at the start of the conversation, but the other person was depressed, their neutral mood shifted to depression by the end of the conversation, too.
- **Contagion without speaking.** A study at Uppsala University in Sweden found that people who were exposed to pictures of happy or angry faces for thirty milliseconds (not enough time for their minds to consciously register the image), followed by the image of a neutral face, moved their faces in the exact same expression as the face they'd just seen, triggering happy or angry emotions. A similar study exposed neutral subjects for several minutes to a happy or sad person, without any words being exchanged, and found that the neutral person left the room in the same mood as the more emotional person whose face they had just quietly looked at.
- **Contagion at work.** Professor Sigal Barsade at the University of Pennsylvania's Wharton School of Business has found that both positive and negative moods of our work colleagues impact us without our knowledge. Four groups of research subjects were given bonus money to distribute to employees while an actor sat among them, tapping his pencil in impatience or leaning forward in support. Depending on the actor's movements and expressions, the entire group "caught" his mood and made financial decisions based on the prevailing emotion in the room. Studies at insurance companies have also found that employees who experience burnout and depression pass those moods on to their colleagues, particularly when they discuss work-related stress.

Other studies have underscored the importance of a manager's mood on his or her department, finding that the people who work for upbeat managers are more productive and happy than the people who work for managers who are more pessimistic and cynical.

- ■ **Contagion in marriage.** A series of crossover studies has found that marriages also feature copycat emotions, with depressed, bored, and burned-out partners exerting a powerful pull on their mates' moods. For example, studies at the Arlene R. Gordon Research Institute in New York found that among elderly couples, when one spouse is depressed, the other one is more likely to report the same feelings, too.

- ■ **College contagion.** If you live with or date someone who expresses certain types of moods, your mood will "converge" with theirs, leading to less and less disparity between partners and roommates. In fact, a study at the University of Texas Medical Branch in Galveston showed that depression between roommates was particularly contagious if the more upbeat one sought reassurance or support from the depressed one on a regular basis.

- ■ **Suicide contagion.** It has even been found that reports of suicides in the news or among friends can cause suicide to "catch," particularly among people between the ages of fifteen and nineteen, when adolescents are most vulnerable to this copycat phenomenon. Interestingly, this phenomenon is not new, and has been called the "Werther effect" after Goethe's 1774 novel, *The Sorrows of Young Werther*, which triggered a spate of suicides in several European countries. At that time, the novel was actually banned in some countries in order to protect the vulnerable.

- ■ **Flow contagion.** A study of Dutch music teachers found that those who are more likely to experience a state of "flow" (a pleasurable state of doing an activity for the sheer joy it brings, particularly when one is challenged to use his or her talents) are more likely to have students who "catch" the flow and experience it themselves!

--- ⁂ ---

RESEARCHERS HAVE FOUND that immediate social bonding between strangers is dependent on one person's mimicry of the other person's actions and behaviors. When one individual mirrors a second individual's behavior—such as leg crossing, smiling, or nodding—the first individual not only likes the second; he or she behaves more altruistically toward the second individual, too.

Other People Matter

Today we are faced with the preeminent fact that, if civilization is to
survive, we must cultivate the science of human relationships.
—THEODORE ROOSEVELT

Chris Peterson is one of the leading researchers in the field of positive psychology, as well as a professor at the University of Michigan, where he has studied happiness and the qualities of well-being for decades, and has also published numerous studies and books pertaining to this topic. Peterson is fond of distilling positive psychology into a brief statement when he is asked to sum up his and others' findings.

"Other people matter," he intones, citing the reams of evidence showing that not only do other people impact our moods and behaviors, but they contribute in a powerful way to our health, longevity, and success in ways that we are just now learning more about.

In short, "other people matter" in the following areas of life and for the following reasons:

- **Happiness.** The happiest people have vibrant social networks, and they value and strengthen the power of their relationships as often as possible, which is partly why social scientists have said that strong social relationships are the leading indicator of our overall happiness. In several studies of people with self-reported high well-being, the number one strategy used to raise mood and combat depression was "social affiliation." People also report feeling happier when they are around others.

- **Health.** Large social networks and good family relationships appear to offer surgical patients protection from postoperative pain. A study of 605 people scheduled for chest or abdominal operations found that patients with small social networks reported almost twice as much postoperative pain as patients who had larger social networks. They also had longer hospital stays. Dr. Daniel B. Hinshaw, the senior author of the above study and a professor of surgery at the University of Michigan, noted, "The average physician, when he takes a social history, asks about smoking and drugs, and not the real social situation of the patient. And yet it looks like this is a real marker for problems." Lonely people age more quickly, according to two University of Chicago psychologists, Louise Hawkley and John Cacioppo, who found that lonely people had more epinephrine in their bodies, an indicator that they go through life in a heightened state of arousal—such as fear or hypervigilance—and are less likely to seek out social support when under stress. They also suffer from poor sleep, which is traditionally when the body regenerates itself.

■ **Weight loss.** People who embarked on a four-month weight-loss program were divided into two groups: One group did it alone and the other group had three acquaintances, family members, or friends do it with them. Only 76 percent of the people who went it alone completed the program, while 95 percent of the people who did it with others completed the program.

■ **New Year's resolutions.** People who set New Year's resolutions are much more likely to stick with their goals for at least two years, and up to six years, if they have the social support to do so.

The Science of Flourishing Relationships

Barbara Fredrickson is a friendly, middle-aged woman with an easy laugh, freckles, and pictures of her children all over her office in the leafy Chapel Hill suburb where she oversees the Positive Emotions Lab at the University of North Carolina. Although there is nothing flashy about Fredrickson in person, her work with mathematician Marcel Losada to take the "Losada Line" and apply it to her "broaden-and-build" theory has created a crucial breakthrough in the study of how we can identify or create flourishing relationships and environments, as well as understand what they can do for us now and in the future.

▶ THE LOSADA LINE

In 1999, Marcial Losada and trained speech coders studied sixty management work teams from behind a one-way mirror while they crafted their annual plans, and every time a member of the team spoke, his or her speech was catalogued as "positive," "negative," "inquiry," "self," or "other." Losada subsequently analyzed each team on three success indicators: profitability, customer satisfaction, and evaluations by superiors, peers, and subordinates. His analyses determined that fifteen teams were characterized by "high flourishing," with the rest having "mixed" or "low" results.

After running all of the speech coders' numbers against these performance results, Losada was able to determine that the highest-performing work teams were consistently characterized by being above the threshold of 2.9 positive comments to 1 negative—dubbed "the Losada Line"—with the highest-performing teams featuring closer to *six positive comments for every one negative!*

Tellingly, the work teams with the highest ratios of positive to negative featured interactions that appeared to build on one another, and that exhibited ever-increasing levels of creativity, resilience, social resources, optimal functioning, and flexibility. The worst ratios predicted the opposite: Low-functioning work teams were characterized by "self-absorbed" advocacy, narrow thinking, extreme negativity, and inflexibility. In contrast to the high-performing teams, which seemed to simply get better as the ratio improved, the lowest and most negative teams spiraled in the other direction, eventually "calcifying" and failing to thrive.

▶ THE POSITIVITY RATIO

Just one year before Losada's fascinating work, Fredrickson announced her groundbreaking "broaden-and-build" theory, which postulated that positive emotions in high-functioning environments did more than just make people happier, more creative, or more likely to have friends. Fredrickson went further, arguing that these fleeting moments of positivity allowed people to "broaden" and "build" their social and physical resources so that they could not just succeed in that moment, but be more likely to succeed in the future, too.

By matching Losada's mathematically precise line, which has now become known as the "positivity ratio," with her research, Fredrickson said that an extraordinary number of things occur when we are at or over this critical ratio. Specifically, Fredrickson said that our "thought-action" repertoire is expanded in the following positive ways:

- **We think more broadly.** The enhanced creativity elicited by positive emotions allows us to think of more and better solutions. We also fail to notice differences, such as racial bias, when we are in flourishing relationships and environments.
- **We approach the environment with curiosity and a sense of exploration.** Negative emotions including boredom and cynicism cause us to withdraw and avoid contact with the world, but positive emotions let us explore the world in a way that fosters experiential learning and allows us to learn from others. This enhanced knowledge of the world gives us more to draw upon when we are trying to accomplish our goals.
- **We make friends.** Fredrickson has argued that flourishing relationships have some of their greatest benefits in the future, because we "build enduring social resources," like friendships, that we lean on when we need support and ideas. She sees these resources as reserves that can be drawn on in the future, much like the deposits we put into a bank when money is plentiful.
- **We enter into an "upward spiral of well-being."** Being above the "positivity ratio" is an exciting place to be because it doesn't only help us build

all the emotional and behavioral resources that benefit us now and in the future; it also feeds on itself and spirals upward, creating a widening and expanding energy that brings us more and more benefits as time goes by.

The Love Lab

It is impossible to win the great prizes of life without running risks, and the greatest of all prizes are those connected with the home.
—THEODORE ROOSEVELT

At the University of Washington in Seattle, John Gottman and his wife, Julie Schwartz Gottman, have been studying married couples and the complex dynamics of flourishing and languishing relationships for well over twenty years. After observing thousands of hours of videotaped interactions, they have concluded that the "positivity ratio" of the best marriages is the same as that of the highest-functioning work teams—5 to 1 or 6 to 1.

In fact, after "thin slicing" relationships for years, the Gottmans can predict with more than 90 percent certainty who will divorce in the coming years, simply by counting the smiles, encouraging comments, playful swats on the rear end, defensive postures, and eye rolling of the couples he observes. The deal breakers in the relationships were expressions of contempt or disgust. But what really matters most to married couples, and what comprises the vast majority of overall satisfaction, is the quality of their day-to-day friendship. Seemingly mundane gestures, such as asking about your partner's day or folding laundry together, actually help buffer happy couples when hard times hit.

Surprisingly Bad Relationships

The great enemy of clear language is insincerity. When there is a gap between one's real and one's declared aims, one turns as it were instinctively to long words and exhausted idioms, like a cuttlefish squirting out ink.
—GEORGE ORWELL

There is more fascinating research to help you determine whether or not certain people or situations should stay in your life, and what you will need to do to optimize your own happiness and success with your life lists. The first surprise is that there is a limit to just how positive an environment can be for you to derive the social, emotional, and physical benefits that it can offer. Fredrickson and her colleagues have determined that *when the ratio of positive to negative is 11 to 1 or higher, the positive benefits disappear* and the environment becomes as damaging as if it were below the positivity ratio.

Why is this? One possible reason is because negativity does play an important role in our lives, since it makes us pull back from dangerous situations and analyze our behaviors in a more honest way. For example, if you are living in a praise-filled environment where there is never any criticism or sadness, you will instinctively know that this is "unreal" and will stop believing the praise and wonder if you are actually learning the truth about yourself. As the old saying goes, "Into every life a little rain must fall," and this breakdown in the science of flourishing is a perfect example.

RESEARCHERS HAVE DISCOVERED that when we receive phony "social" smiles from people who are insincere in their warmth, praise, or flattery, it actually injures our bodies. Subjects who wore sensitive monitoring equipment on their bodies in a study conducted by Barbara Fredrickson experienced microscopic collapses in their heart lining every time they received a phony "social" smile, which was undetectable on a conscious level, but constitutes a considerable risk factor in long-term heart health. On the other hand, a Duchenne smile, in which the muscles around the eyes and face contract in genuine warmth, has the opposite effect, but you may never see this type of expression at a cocktail party or networking meeting!

Killing Our Neurons through Social Stress

Although you may not need further evidence of the dangers of toxic relationships, it's worth noting that science gives us more data every year of what is happening inside our bodies when we think or behave in a certain way, or in this case when we encounter someone or something very negative or stressful. One study of animals has found that all it takes is a single terrifying incident for rats to obliterate two-thirds of the newly formed neurons in their hippocampus, the part of the brain that is involved in memory and emotion. Although it has long been known that chronic stress can contribute to depression by inhibiting the growth of neurons, it has now been found that damage can happen swiftly, and that we need to protect ourselves from such situations if we wish to flourish.

Below the Positivity Ratio

Thus far, we have presented evidence for the power of friendships, and how important it is to be in flourishing relationships and work environments that elicit emotions and behaviors that help you accomplish the goals on your life list now and in the future. We also now know how important it is to have at least three or more positive comments offsetting one negative comment if we are to experience the broadened "thought-action" repertoire Barbara Fredrickson has observed, and that John Gottman and Julie Schwartz Gottman see in even higher ratios in happy marriages. In addition, we've also shown you the research on how easy it is to "catch" the moods of positive and negative people and situations, and what can happen when you are unaware of the power of others to impact you, even when they don't speak.

This brings us to the very important question of what you can do if you suddenly realize that you are living or working in an environment where the positivity ratio is bad, and your thinking and behavior reflect that lack of vitality. Several of our clients made big decisions about their lives after they came to the realization that they were locked in difficult relationships and work environments that were making them depressed or even sick.

Cynthia is a prominent consultant who wrote a book that landed her on national talk shows and earned her a six-figure income for many years. Despite her apparent success, however, Cynthia wanted to try our approach to learn how to be happier, accomplish more of her goals (writing another book, for example), and in general create a better life for herself and her two young children.

Here is Cynthia's story in her own words:

I realized that I had been catching the emotions of my children's caregiver, who has arrived late or in a bad mood almost every morning that she has worked for me. She has her good points, but I suddenly realized how important her behavior is in terms of how I start my day, and how she must be impacting my children, too, even though they are very young. So I placed an ad for a new caregiver, and I had different criteria than I'd ever advertised before. I asked for someone who was good with children, but who also had an upbeat attitude toward life, who was more optimistic than pessimistic, and who started every day with a smile. It was amazing to see how different the interview process went, and who actually applied for the job this time. Because I approached the task in a different way, and with different criteria, I found someone who was perfect, and who is a genuinely happy person to be around. My daughters are happier, I start my workday in a different mood, and I think I've even been more productive than I was when I had the other babysitter. On top of that, I realized that my relationship with my book agent was way below the positivity ratio, and that I always felt awful when I got off the phone with him. I decided I deserved to work with someone who was more positive and complimentary of my work instead of being critical and too busy for my questions, so I changed agents and I'm working on a new book with someone who believes in me and makes me feel great.

Another client of ours decided to leave her job as a nurse and work in a different, more uplifting, environment after doing the math on positive versus negative at her workplace. Here is Janice's story:

When I was working as a nurse in a big hospital, I found that by the end of the day I was not only drained; I was depressed. Getting to my regular work-out class became impossible, since I never had the energy to get there, so I decided to evaluate the number of positive to negative comments I was receiving, on the floor of the hospital where I work, to see if a negative job environment was contributing to my mood. I made a simple scorecard, and every time I received a positive comment or had a good interaction with a colleague, a doctor, or a patient, I marked the card, and whenever the interaction was negative, I did the same. At the end of the week, it was clear that my work environment was not conducive to my happiness. I wasn't even at 1 to 1—I was below that. I actually saw that I had a ratio of three negative comments for every positive one. My husband and I decided that I could use my nursing training to work in a different way and be in a better environment, so after some research, I decided to become a traveling nurse and visit people in their homes. The money isn't quite as good, but I find that the quality of my life has improved dramatically, I'm happier at the end of every day, and I feel like I'm making a contribution to other people's lives. Using this research to help me see what was actually happening at work made all the difference, because I would never have known if I was exaggerating the negativity or not, but I now know that it was the right decision for me.

The Qualities of Positive Relationships

It's no mystery that positive relationships leave us feeling better about ourselves and more optimistic about our goals. Using a scorecard to help us evaluate how negative or positive our environment is can be hugely helpful, but most of us instinctively know when we have walked away from an encounter smiling, or have just had the life sucked out of us by an interaction with someone else, however brief. Researcher and psychologist Marty Seligman is in the early stages of identifying who these "black holes" are in our lives, and hopes to do a study in which subjects carry beepers and note whom they are with and how they feel whenever they are beeped. You can try this technique yourself, by setting a cell phone, computer, or watch timer to go off every two hours. At each interval, write down how positive or negative you feel, as well as the name of the person you are with.

Here are a few other positive qualities that researchers have discovered in happy, close relationships:

- **Active-constructive responding.** The people who are eager to hear about the good news in your life, and who encourage you to replay your successes and progress with them and others, are engaging in active-constructive responding. They are happy to talk to you, they are eager to draw out the details of your good fortune, and they never tire of being your cheerleaders. On the opposite end of the spectrum are "passive-destructive" and "active-destructive" responders, who ignore your good news, don't encourage you to "amplify" the telling of this news, and may even openly criticize you when good things happen to you.
- **Listening.** Good friends are good listeners. Dale Carnegie had it right long before research supported his best-selling book, *How to Win Friends and Influence People*, when he advised readers to become better listeners. Carnegie said—and it's still true now—"You can make more friends in two months by becoming genuinely interested in other people than you can in two years by trying to get other people interested in you."
- **Taking your time.** Good relationships don't just happen because you want them to. You need to take time out of your busy life to connect with other people, to care about what is happening in their lives, and to respond appropriately when sympathy, advice, and other support is needed. Although "face time" is always best, connecting in any way that fits your schedule and situation is better than not connecting at all.

Choose Your Friends Well

We like to ask our clients about who is on their "A-Team of Friends," and what it takes to make that particular cut. Not everyone who applies for this position ought to be accepted, so you need to be very thoughtful about which people deserve your time, support, and love. Some people simply wear us out and use up our emotions—and instead of being tolerant, we need to ask ourselves, "Does this relationship bring out the best in me? Does it uplift and energize me? Do I have a positive impact on this person?"

The Bible contains a parable about Jesus tossing seeds on rocky soil where they bear no fruit. We must remember that not all friendships will bear fruit, regardless of how much we want them to, or how much time and energy we put into them.

What Can You Do to Be a Better Friend?

Focus on other people, not on yourself.
—RANDY PAUSCH

There is no free lunch, even where friends are involved. Our friendships blossom the same way a well-tended garden brings abundance and joy. We tell our clients that there are many ways they can improve their friendship skills, including reading Dale Carnegie's *How to Win Friends and Influence People*, which is still relevant almost one hundred years after its original publication.

Some of our clients are particularly creative about making sure that their friends feel valued and appreciated. Here are some of the ways they have shown that they foster their best relationships:

- **Have a thank-you party once a year for your friends to express your gratitude for their friendship.** One cancer survivor felt so indebted to the people who drove her to medical appointments, cooked meals, and helped her children that she threw an annual party to give thanks to everyone who had supported her during her illness as well as introduce them to her neighbors, which in turn sparked new friendships.
- **Program your friends' phone numbers into your cell phone** so that you can easily call them to say hello when you are caught in a traffic jam or have extra time on your hands.
- **Be a good cheerleader.** Always remember to be positive for your friends who need support and encouragement.
- **Send one thank-you card a month to a friend who has made a difference in your life, and give specific examples of how he or she did this.** One of our clients makes a point of buying cards at drugstores and specialty paper stores so that she always has a plentiful supply of thank-you notes. Many e-card sites make it possible to send gratitude cards the moment you think of them, too, so have a few bookmarked for easy retrieval.
- **Start a mastermind group of your friends to share goals and support one another.** If you want to double or triple your goal progress on your life list, be sure to start a monthly meeting—even with a conference call—to help your friends articulate and accomplish their goals.
- **Go away once a year with at least one or two of your friends for bonding time.** Some of the best friendships we have heard about include getting away from the hustle and bustle of life to just connect and enjoy one another's company.

- **Take out an ad on Valentine's Day in the local newspaper to celebrate a valued friendship.** Although people are expected to go overboard with romantic relationships on Valentine's Day, it's a nice twist to let your friends know in a public way that they matter to you.

- **Remember their birthdays.** One of the best features of Internet social-networking sites like Facebook is that your friends can be notified of your birthday if you enter that information in your profile. One of our clients was struck by how overjoyed her son was when he received more than eighty birthday messages on Facebook, and how visibly moved he was that these contacts had all taken time to "poke" him, or remember him. This moved our client to do several things; one thing she did was to get herself a Facebook profile and invite all of her friends to join and to give her their birth dates so that she could send them electronic or paper greeting cards or take them out for a celebratory meal to honor them on their big day. Not only does she feel happier, but she has been struck by how much this gesture has mattered to her friends, too.

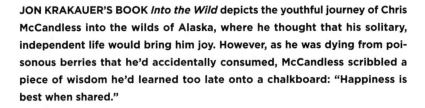

JON KRAKAUER'S BOOK *Into the Wild* depicts the youthful journey of Chris McCandless into the wilds of Alaska, where he thought that his solitary, independent life would bring him joy. However, as he was dying from poisonous berries that he'd accidentally consumed, McCandless scribbled a piece of wisdom he'd learned too late onto a chalkboard: "Happiness is best when shared."

Where Your Life List Is Now

You can now add the names of friends and situations that can help you accomplish the goals on your life list, and you might even make some of these goals more aggressive if you think of how a beefed-up support system can help you.

Life List Exercises and Worksheets

❏ "My Web of Influence." Make several copies of this form (see page 247) since you will want to update it from time to time, depending on a change of job or any other event that might cause changes in your closest sphere of influence. You want those who are closest to you in the web to always have the qualities and actions that you value and want for yourself, too.

❑ "Bright Lights and Black Holes." This worksheet (see page 237) is designed to help you identify just how positive or negative you are feeling every few hours, as well as whom you are with. This is a great tool to identify how people are influencing you on an hourly level, and how their actions, moods, or words are impacting you, whether they are consciously aware of what they are doing or not.

❑ Register at an Internet site that can send you reminders of birthdays and other special occasions, and that also allows you to send e-cards. One site that is devoted just to sending gratitude e-cards is www.gratitudeclub.com.

9

TATTOOS, LICENSE PLATES, AND CITRUSY SCENTS

We must always tell what we see. Above all, and this is more difficult, we must always see what we see.

—CHARLES PEGUY

I N THIS CHAPTER we teach you how to become a detective in your own life around the subject of "primes" (cues in your environment that prompt you to think or behave in a specific way) so that you can become aware of which ones are helping and which ones are hurting your goals. On the strength of your legwork, we will help you decide which connections you can encourage, and which ones you can remove, in order to energize your life list.

Acting Like a Superhero

What if you had a way to get something accomplished on your life list, and it didn't involve any real effort on your part? What if not only didn't it involve any effort, but you weren't even consciously aware of the fact that you were making progress on your goals while you were doing it, but you were? Well, have we got a deal for you! Some of the most powerful and convincing research in recent years involves the myriad ways our pursuit of goals is shaped, harmed, and helped by the "primes" in our everyday environment. These primes take many forms, including words, sounds, colors, smells, situations, and people that prompt us to behave in certain ways—sometimes without our knowledge or complicity. We encounter them from the moment we get up in the morning to the moment we go to bed at night, and as much as 80 percent of our day's activity is directed by our unthinking reactions to these cues.

If you don't believe it yet, consider the following scenarios:

You are an undergraduate at Princeton University, and you have been given an assignment to write about the qualities of superheroes, and how they would behave in a given situation. Another group of students is given the assignment to write about the items in their dorm rooms. You finish your superheroes assignment and go on with your life. Three months later you fill out a questionnaire about what you've been up to. Experimenters parse your daily life and they find that if you were part of the group that wrote about the qualities of superheroes, you were four times more likely to volunteer your time for a worthy cause than people who wrote about their dorm rooms.

———————

Students playing an imaginary one-on-one investment game with someone they couldn't see were exposed to two conditions during the game. The first group of students played the game with a backpack on the table. The second group played the game with a professional-looking attaché case and a leather portfolio on the table. Students who played in the presence of the backpack were generous with their money, while those who played in the presence of the briefcase were much stingier. Students were later surprised to learn that they had behaved differently under these two conditions, and that the group that had been primed with the professional items had competed more ruthlessly to win.

———————

Dutch psychologists asked undergraduate students to fill out a questionnaire in a solitary cubicle, and they then rewarded them with a crumbly biscuit. In the first experiment, the students filled out the questionnaire while a bucket of water sat nearby, giving off the odor of a lemon cleanser. The bucket was removed in the second experiment when another group of students filled out the same questionnaire. The psychologists filmed the areas where the students ate the crumbly biscuits and found that those who had smelled the citrusy cleanser were three times more likely to clean up after eating the biscuit than those who hadn't been exposed to the same odor.

Becoming a Detective

———————

You are probably scratching your head after reading the paragraphs above, wondering why we are so gullible or unaware of our own reactions that we'll either tidy up or volunteer to help others because of something we smelled or an essay we wrote ninety days earlier. But this type of cutting-edge research on how our surroundings alter our behavior and cause us to react in certain ways is nothing short of overwhelming, and once you understand how you are impacted, you can use this research to your advantage.

Our files are filled with stories of clients who changed a huge number of things in their lives, including e-mail addresses, the color of their car, their eating and reading habits, their iPod song lineup, the organization of their desk at work, and more after learning about primes. You'll undoubtedly want to make a few changes, as well.

You will also see how to pair your primes with a sophisticated technique called "implementation intentions," also called "if-then scenarios," that have been shown in multiple studies to triple your likelihood of success with difficult goals; they also make goal pursuit easier by allowing you to conserve your energy.

Very high achievers already know these secrets, as they have either stumbled upon this combination of techniques through trial and error, or worked with psychologists who are privy to this research. We have many clients who have used it successfully in sports and other important life domains where optimal results are key to surviving and flourishing.

Until now, this research has not been available in book form for those of you who want to get an edge in life, but if you use these techniques in the right way at the right time, you will have the tools to override many of the cues your subconscious mind is heeding, and you will instead take control of your life and make your life list goals come true.

Environmental Primes

First let's take a look at what is going on in your life right now, while you are reading this book. The color and design of the book jacket, the words you are taking in (and even the fonts) are having an impact on you, whether you know it or not. The room or location you are in is also impacting your mood, as are the clothes you're wearing. Look around where you are sitting or standing, particularly if you are at home. Are there pictures of loved ones nearby? Are there pictures of family members who have undermined you and not been supportive of your goals?

If you are at work, are there slogans on your desk—like "Think" or "Succeed"? If you glance at your computer, is your screensaver the company logo or a slideshow of your children's lives? And what is your e-mail address? Does it reflect a goal of yours or is it just a routine one like your name or your initials? Are there flowers nearby, or pictures of soothing scenes?

Look outside at your car. What color is it and what does the license plate say? Is it a routine string of numbers and letters, or is it a vanity plate you chose that says something like "Amen" or "Chaos"? Did you talk to anyone on the phone this morning? What type of mood was that person in? And did you read the newspaper, watch the morning news, or listen to the radio? What did you read, see, or hear?

Are you aware that every single one of these interactions and moments has the power to make you feel happier or sadder, and that your life list goals are either strengthened or undermined by them? Do you know what these influences do, and why?

Let's take a look at these ideas and scenarios, especially in light of the fact that our subconscious mind is as powerful as our conscious mind, and that if it is working against us because of the primes in our environment, we will be undercutting our efforts to achieve important goals without even being aware of it. Scientists are making daily progress in understanding the depth and breadth of how primes impact us, including our self-confidence and commitment to various goals, and even what parts of our brains are stimulated in response to what we see, smell, or hear.

The Hot Coffee Study

John A. Bargh, a professor of psychology at Yale University, has spent much of his professional life studying the role our subconscious mind plays on our behavior, and how this can be manipulated to decode how our brains work. In the following experiment, he and his colleagues demonstrated how an ordinary cup of coffee can influence whether we like or dislike another person.

This is how the experiment was set up: Students who were walking to a laboratory "ran into" a laboratory assistant who was juggling books, papers, textbooks, and a cup of iced or hot coffee. The students were asked to hold the cup briefly while the assistant regained control of the items. Later, the students who had held the cup of iced coffee rated a hypothetical person as cold, less social, and more selfish than people who had held the hot cup of coffee, who saw the hypothetical person in a more generous and kind light.

Bargh's experiment, and those of others who work in the field, underscores the fact that our subconscious mind is always whirring in the background, making rational and irrational decisions that impact our thoughts and actions. Bargh presented the coffee study at a 2007 psychology conference with his coauthor, Lawrence Williams, and explained its importance to people who want to accomplish important goals or behave in certain ways, but who don't always understand how or when they are thrown off course: "When it comes to our behavior from moment to moment," he said, "the big question is, 'What to do next?' Well, we're finding that we have these unconscious behavioral guidance systems that are continually furnishing suggestions through the day about what to do next, and the brain is considering and often acting on those, all before conscious aware-ness. . . . Sometimes those goals are in line with our conscious intentions and pur-poses, and sometimes they're not."

SOMETIMES WE FAIL at nonconscious goals (that is, goals we don't even know we have), prompting what researchers call "negative mystery moods." A nonconscious goal is one that you have consistently and fre-quently chosen in the past for a certain situation, and that becomes trig-gered the moment you encounter the same cue, whether you are aware of it or not. For example, a teenager might have the conscious goal of mak-ing friends and looking good when she goes to a party, and that goal might be triggered later in life, every time she goes to a party as an adult. When she fails at her nonconscious goal, she may be mystified, not knowing that her bad mood is a direct result of this failure.

Everyday Triggers

The implications of priming research are piling up quickly. A look at the com-pelling research, described below, will show you how much all of us are impacted every hour and every day by our surroundings, even when we are unaware of it. You may want to make some immediate changes in your life or the lives of your children after you've read this list.

- ■ **Hats and T-shirts with alcohol logos.** Middle school students who have been given logo wear and posters that depict alcohol products in a favor-able light are more likely to drink at an early age than their peers who do not possess or wear similar items.
- ■ **Sad movies.** A multidisciplinary team of researchers from Carnegie Mellon, Harvard, Stanford, and the University of Pittsburgh found that people who were shown sad movie clips spent 300 percent more money on a water bottle than a group of people who were shown neutral movie clips. In every case, the people who had seen the sad movie clips insisted that their purchase of water at a hugely inflated price had nothing to do with watching the sad movie clips.
- ■ **Anagrams and word images that promote altruism and cooperation.** Researchers at the University of British Columbia decided to find out if a belief in God influenced moral behavior among people who were

primed with religious words like "spirit," "divine," "sacred," and "prophet." In two studies, they found that both believers and nonbelievers were more likely to be altruistic when they solved anagrams containing these types of words instead of solving anagrams that included nonspiritual words, or even anagrams with words that pertained to social justice and civic involvement. Similarly, students who had words like "dependable" and "support" subliminally flashed in front of them on a computer screen were more likely to behave cooperatively, even if they had no awareness that the words had appeared in front of them.

■ **Words that make you act old or bold.** John Bargh was behind another priming experiment that became famous when it was cited in the bestseller *Blink* by Malcolm Gladwell. In this experiment, Bargh actually got his subjects to walk more slowly down a hallway after making four-word sentences out of word strings like "sunlight makes temperature wrinkle raisins." All of the word strings contained words that primed the brain to think about becoming older (other words used included "Florida" and "retired"), and that was all it took to influence youthful men and women to behave like old people. In another word experiment that Bargh was part of, students unscrambled one of two sentences and then were instructed to go down a hallway to get their next assignment, where an instructor was conveniently "too busy" to attend to them. Students who were primed with words like "disturb," "intrude," and "infringe" interrupted the instructor after about five minutes, but 82 percent of the people primed with words like "yield" and "courteous" never interrupted at all. (These were impatient New Yorkers, so the researchers were especially impressed!)

■ **Photographs and names of supportive people.** One study found that subjects who had subliminal images or the names of supportive people flashed in front of them had very powerful reactions when subsequently asked about their goals. Compared to a control group that had a random string of letters flashed in front of them, the subjects who were primed with names and images of significant others were:

1. More likely to believe that they could be successful with their goals
2. More likely to work hard at accomplishing their goals
3. More willing to spend time in the company of people who had similar goals
4. More likely to come up with creative solutions to accomplish those goals
5. More likely to have high standards for themselves if their romantic partner had very high standards, as well

- **Achievement pictures.** Although images and the mere mention of important people in our lives have an impact on our emotions and behavior, a picture of a runner crossing a finish line can produce even more zealous commitment to a goal such as fund-raising! In the first study of how priming can impact a conscious goal in a work setting, Gary Latham found that people who were given fund-raising guidelines raised more money when they had a picture of a runner crossing a finish line on the cover of the guidelines than they did if they were given the same guidelines without the picture.

- **Junk-food advertising.** A 2005 study by Indiana University for the Kaiser Family Foundation did the largest examination ever on the impact of television food marketing on young viewers. The study showed that the number one type of ad seen by viewers between the ages of eight and twelve was for high-fat, high-sugar foods—an average of twenty-one ads per day, or fifty-one hours per year. No commercials promoted fruit or vegetables, a finding that fuels support for the argument that kids are "brainwashed" by constant exposure to ads for unhealthy foods, contributing to the fact that this generation is the unhealthiest and most obese in the history of the United States, and the first generation that is unlikely to live longer than their parents.

- **Music.** Elizabeth Cady, a cognitive psychology doctoral student at Kansas State University, studied 124 college freshmen and sophomores, asking them to describe their strongest positive memory from a group of songs popular in their childhood and youth. She included artists such as Vanilla Ice, New Kids on the Block, and Queen. The students either heard a minute of the song, or they glimpsed the song title, the album cover, or a picture of the artist. When the cues were removed, the students wrote down all of their memories, including how vivid or pleasant they were.

  All of the students were able to record strong memories from their youth, both positive and negative, showing how the power of music is universal. Hearing the music clip wasn't the only way to create their powerful feelings and thoughts, though; Cady was surprised to find that seeing the lyric or a picture of the artist was just as strong a prime as actually hearing the song for changing mood and evoking nostalgia.

The Primes of Your Life

If researchers have found over and over that we are swayed emotionally and behaviorally by subconscious primes, and that these cues can cause us, in some instances, to become happier and more energetic, and in others, more depressed or angry, we owe it to ourselves to become our own detectives and pay close attention to the types of visual, emotional, physical, musical, and situational cues that we may be reacting to in our lives. Take a moment right now to look at your immediate environment and make a list of some of the objects, sights, smells, sounds, and people around you. Then write down how they make you feel.

POSITIVE PRIMES

1. _____

2. _____

3. _____

NEGATIVE PRIMES

1. _____

2. _____

3. _____

How to Overcome Negative Primes

Here are real-life examples from some of our clients who took proactive steps to create positive environments and situations after they realized that certain primes were eliciting behavior that didn't help them accomplish their life list goals.

Andrea grew up in a household where her parents were mean and always at war, and they seldom paid attention to their children's goals or lives. Whenever Andrea did accomplish something, her mother, who always compared her unfavorably to her friends, devalued it. Andrea decided that she was under no obligation to have family pictures around her house that reminded her of her miserable childhood and the negative messages she'd gotten all her life. So when she was in her mid-forties, Andrea went to an antiques store and bought a series of pictures from an estate sale that depicted someone else's family. Andrea gave all of the black-and-white images names, and she hung them on her walls. This new "family" is her daily reminder that she doesn't need to be held hostage by her family's negative messages. Pretending that strangers are her family also makes her smile and gives Andrea a feeling of empowerment that carries over into other areas of her life.

Linda read in an alternative health newsletter that going on a "news fast" would be a good way for her to eliminate unnecessary negative emotions from her life. She thought it was a good idea but wasn't sure why or how it might work for her, especially because she had a job that demanded that she be up-to-date on current events in Washington, D.C. After working with her life coach, she understood that she was probably taking on negative moods from more than just her morning newspaper, so she decided to do several different things that would ensure that she was both upbeat and knowledge-able about the news when she arrived at work. First, she changed her morn-ing alarm to a song that elicited the happiest memory she could think of, and she even made it her cell phone ring tone so that she could hear the song multiple times every day. Next, she created a Google desktop for her home page, and customized the content to reflect the news that she needed for her job. She also added feeds from blogs and Web sites that were devoted to publishing upbeat, happy news. Next, she signed up for a satellite radio network that had a channel that not only featured positive tips of the day during drive time, but also allowed her to listen to the news in a way that gave her more control. The morning newspaper and television shows were eliminated from her life, but instead of performing the recommended whole-sale "news fast," she came up with a solution that made sense to her on an intellectual level, and that still met the needs of her job and life.

Clever Primes

The number of new primes you can create in your life to elicit better goal-directed behavior is limited only by your imagination, and we hope the following ideas can help elicit positive results in your life right away.

- **Fantazein clock.** This ingenious little clock has a floating liquid crystal display that gives you to the power to program up to twenty messages that can flash all day in blue or red. One athlete who purchased this clock and programmed it to flash his time goals swears that he has achieved every single goal he has ever put into the clock, which flashes new and different messages from his bedroom desk all day and all night, depending on what he is trying to accomplish.
- **New e-mail address.** Although you might be limited by company rules about the type of e-mail address you can have at work, it's always possi-ble to get a free e-mail account that has an address of your own creation,

and that primes you to think about your goals. One investment broker we worked with, who wanted to remind himself that his slow, methodical approach to goal accomplishment would pay off, created an e-mail address that included the name "GrittyTurtle." Another client, a landscaper who wanted to remind herself of her mission to help others create gardens of beauty and grace, changed her e-mail address to "LuvYourGarden2Day."

■ **Vanity license plates.** Imagine driving down the highway and seeing a car in front of you that has a vanity plate that reads "SPDRCER." Would you want to get any closer? Probably not. But what do you think the impact is of seeing the following (real!) license plates on either your own car or someone else's?: "ALELUIA," "BLESSED," "THANKS," "AQWAMAN," "WEHVFUN," "PEGHAPY," or "LUV4KDZ"? And what would be the impact on your mood if you had these plates, or you saw them on someone else's car?: "BADKIDS," "MAGNATE," "RUTHLES," or "F-IRAC"?

CAR MAGNETS MAKE terrific primes, and instead of being permanently affixed like bumper stickers, they can be moved around on a car, or put anywhere they can stick, like a filing cabinet or a refrigerator door.

■ **Tattoos.** Athletes love to prime their bodies with tattoos reminding themselves of their aspirations, so it's not uncommon to see the Olympic rings permanently emblazoned somewhere, whether its on the hip of swimmer Michael Phelps or on the hand of Maurice Greene, one of the top sprinters in the world, whose "GOAT" tattoo reminds himself to train as hard as possible so that he will become the "Greatest of All Time." Unfortunately, tattoos can remind people to have violent and self-destructive goals, too, as in the case of gunman Steven Kazmierczak, who opened fire in a Northern Illinois University lecture hall where he killed several innocent students in 2008. Just six months earlier, he had an angel of death surrounded by drops of blood tattooed on his arm in a prominent place.

■ **Cell phone ring tones.** Music has been found to make people more energetic and happy, as well as to elicit memories and images that can support goal pursuit, so a large number of our clients now use their cell phone ring tones strategically. For example, one client wakes up in the morning to the theme song from sitcom *Happy Days*, which makes her think the word "happy" for hours after hearing it. Many people have the ability to create their own ring tones, which opens up a world of possibilities from the spoken word to a favorite song on the radio. Don't overlook the opportunity to create a banner on your cell phone face-plate that states your goals!

- **Charm bracelets.** For women, wearing charms on a bracelet can serve as a reminder of such things as a child's birth, a vacation they loved, an honor they achieved, or a hobby they love—all things that make them proud and happy.
- **Happy pictures.** The power of pictures to change our mood is so well documented that this is one of the easiest primes you can institute in your life. Pictures that make you think happy thoughts can be used on computer screensavers, digital photo frames, computer-generated calendars, photo mugs, key chains, refrigerator magnets, T-shirts, and so much more. One woman even decided to ditch her designer handbag in favor of one that featured a photo collage of her three children. "Why would I carry a purse with a designer's name on it when I can look at my children's faces all day, and even explain the purse to people who admire it whenever I carry it?" one of our clients marveled.
- **Vision boards.** Vision boards are an old favorite of goal-setting specialists, even if you're unaware of why the research about primes makes them such effective tools. Vision boards that reflect short-term and long-term goals are very powerful ways to remind yourself of your goals, particularly if you sprinkle them with inspiring words, phrases, and pictures of people who believe in you.

YOU CAN MAKE your own vision board with poster board, a selection of pictures, newspaper headlines, or anything else that inspires you to think and behave in a goal-directed way. You can choose a specific goal or a set of goals to accomplish over a specific time and put it on your vision board, or you can make a collage of these items, including pictures of people who are role models, or who believe in you. Use color as much as you like, including stickers, Magic Markers, and anything else that enlivens the board. Priming words can include "Joy!" or "Smile!" or "Win!" Put your vision board in a place where you can see it every day, at the office, in your kitchen, or on your closet door.

Not Tonight, Honey

Sandra drives home from her job, anticipating the night of warm showers and enjoyable sex that she has planned with her husband via e-mail during the day.

They have taken turns adding things that they both are looking forward to, and it reminds Sandra of how excited they were when they were just newlyweds, before they had bills, professional obligations, children, or worries about their elderly parents.

Sandra's mood changes a tiny bit as she pulls up to her house, but it's not particularly noticeable on a conscious level. As she walks into the house, though, and sees a mess in the kitchen, the children's homework on various tables, and no signs of dinner being prepared, her mood changes from anticipation to anger. Then her husband, Roger, who has come home early in excitement, bounds down the stairs to greet her with a big kiss, and instead of joy, she experiences a surge of anxiety.

Needless to say, an anticipated evening of mutual pleasure and connection fizzles again, just like countless other nights, despite a day of imaginative planning on both Sandra's and Roger's parts. Her reaction to his greeting is "Not tonight, honey," causing Sandra to doubt her real love for her husband. "What's wrong with me?" she wonders as she stomps around the kitchen, cleaning up from breakfast, starting a hurried dinner, consulting the calendar for carpooling duties, and wondering if she should get an estimate on repainting the front of the house.

"Do I need a workshop on Tantric sex? Isn't that what they said on that talk show the other day?" She suddenly worries that she's "cold," like her mother, which is what Roger has muttered in disappointment on numerous occasions when this has happened. This is Sandra's worst fear, so it hurts and scares her every time Roger dumps his anger on her when he is disappointed about not getting his sexual needs met. Or maybe it's menopause . . . She doesn't know, but she wants an answer that doesn't smack of drugstore therapy.

The hardest thing for Sandra to understand is why her excitement melted the minute she walked into her house and saw and smelled evidence that she had a number of important jobs to do immediately while everyone else languished in their bedrooms. Why couldn't she just walk away from these messes and hold on to her good mood? Would intimacy never be a part of her married life again? On that night, like so many others, Sandra cried herself to sleep while Roger read his book quietly, thinking his own dark thoughts. Can this marriage be saved?

Shielding Your Goals

The all-too-common scenario described above, which ended in disappointment for both Sandra and Roger, has nothing to do with physical problems, hormones, stale sex routines, or even irresponsible kids. In fact, it is an example of what goal-setting experts call a classic case of "conflicting primes," and it's one that you will need to learn to solve if you want to accomplish all of your goals in every realm of your life, and not just the bedroom.

Researchers have studied what happens when you enter an environment and receive stimuli that prime a number of thoughts and behaviors that are unrelated, but that pertain to goals that are meaningful to you. If you are completely unaware of what is happening to you, your "focal" goal—in Sandra's case having a night of fun sex after the kids go to bed—is undermined because other primes—a mess to clean up, food to prepare, homework to check, none of which have anything to do with the desired intimacy—have taken over. As Sandra mindlessly attends to these tasks while angrily stewing over them all the while, not only will she do all of them poorly in all likelihood, but she will continue to be in the mood that her husband interprets as "inhibited."

What could Sandra have done differently? Experts who have studied situations like this one have come up with two effective solutions to shield your goals when you are primed in a variety of ways, against your will:

- **Remove all distractions.** If you are not derailed by conflicting primes, you will not have to deal with any conscious or subconscious distractions. This is why Sandra and Roger have great sex whenever they are away on vacation or outside the house, and why marriage counselors often suggest "spicing up" your sex life with different locations, outfits, and behaviors. All primes that conflict with the focal goal are gone, leaving a clear path to goal accomplishment, and no emotional or physical distractions.

ONE OF THE ways single-sex schools shield the goal of maximizing educational opportunities is by keeping the distraction of the opposite sex out of the classroom. NFL football coaches are infamous for banning wives and children from the hotel rooms of their players before big games so that they will keep their focus on the upcoming football game.

- **Remind yourself repeatedly of the focal goal, despite conflicting primes.** This step requires that you have an exquisite understanding of yourself and the ways in which every person, situation, and cue changes your mood and makes you behave differently. Sandra could have left the dishes in the sink and ignored the homework mess and focused only on how she wanted her night to unfold, but she allowed herself to get caught up in the drama of family life, instead. A few extra stern reminders to herself might have allowed her to enjoy her night of intimacy.

SPECIAL FORCES TRAINING involves teaching members to "focus on the mission" when they face distractions like bad weather, enemy maneuvers, and other activities that could jeopardize what they have set out to do. One Green Beret said he used the mantra "The mission is all that matters" whenever he needed to remind himself of what he needed to accomplish. You can use this same statement when you notice that your focus has fallen away from your goal because of conflicting primes.

If-Then Scenarios That Triple Your Chances of Success

There's many a slip 'twixt the cup and the lip.
—ANONYMOUS

As researchers have increasingly dug into the topic of goal accomplishment and the various ways we can make ourselves more or less likely to fail, a unique and very successful theory has emerged from the University of Konstanz in Germany, where a professor named Peter Gollwitzer has found a simple way to triple your likelihood of success.

Gollwitzer started with the observation that of the four phases of goal pursuit—predecisional, preactional, actional, and postactional—the hardest step is between preactional and actional. This is the critical moment when someone takes a goal and then chooses to move forward with a specific activity that makes the accomplishment more likely. For example, if Mary has the goal of learning how to play the piano (preactional), but she never carves out the time to look for a teacher (actional), her goal will remain a pipe dream.

Gollwitzer decided to test his hypothesis by using environmental primes—like seeing a coffeepot or walking into a certain building—to prompt a person with a conscious goal to take a specific action that would help him or her make progress and go from preactional to actional.

An example of a statement attaching an action to a prime is "When I see the lawn mower on Sunday morning, I will fill it with gasoline." Another example is "When I see the candy dish on Jane's desk, I will keep walking so that I don't stop and help myself to sweets that I don't need."

Gollwitzer calls these scenarios "if-then" situations, also known as "implementation intentions." He thought that not only would they help people stay focused on their mission, but they would also allow them to notice and take action on things that they might have missed because they were engrossed in another task.

Here is the "implementation intention" sentence we use with our clients for our life list approach:

When I encounter a specific situation [thought, person, visual cue, etc.], I will do the following thing [behave a certain way, say a certain thing, think a certain thought] so that I can achieve [the goal].

Gollwitzer has shown over and over, along with other researchers in this field, just how important this if-then step is if you want to maximize your chances of succeeding. Because these steps are so powerful when they are taken, Gollwitzer calls them "instant habits."

Here is just a sample of the studies that demonstrate the effectiveness of "instant habits."

Almost one hundred college students were asked to select a project that they wanted to complete during their Christmas break. Because this is a notoriously hard time of year to work, the students were unlikely to select and complete any work, according to them. But of the students who were asked to specify exactly what they were going to do, what situation they would use to prompt them to initiate goal-directed activity, and when they wanted to be done, 62 percent of the students who furnished their if-then scenarios were successful versus 22 percent who had not taken that extra step. Accomplished goals included writing a report, finishing a novel, and buying career-related textbooks.

Sixty male college students were recruited to watch videotaped statements that were hostile and racist. The students who were told to form implementation intentions about when they would speak up with their point of view ("When two minutes of the video have gone by, I will state my counterargument") were three times more likely to present their opinions than students who were simply told to speak up whenever it felt appropriate to challenge the racist views.

Women who were told to make an appointment for a cervical cancer screening were divided into two groups. One group simply said that they would get an appointment, and 69 percent of them followed through. But more than 90 percent of the women who said that they had formed an if-then scenario ("I will call for my appointment after lunch on Tuesday," for example) made the appointment.

Why Do Implementation Intentions Work So Effectively?

It's indisputable that attaching if-then statements to goals has a massive impact on follow-through, particularly with hard goals. Regardless of whether the goal was a health screening, dieting, or studying a certain number of hours for an independent study project, subjects who said that they would take a specific action at a certain time or in response to another cue usually enjoyed triple the success of their peers.

Gollwitzer and others believe that this little-understood technique gives goal setters several significant advantages over just going through the process of setting a goal:

- **Removes ambivalence.** Creating an implementation intention removes all questions about whether or not you will pursue a goal. When you decide that you will take action at a specific time and in a specific way, you have removed the question of "Will I?" or "Won't I?" from the equation, making forward motion inevitable.

- **Turns a negative situation into a positive one.** An antagonistic situation can be used to make a goal more likely instead of undercutting it. For example, if encountering a work colleague usually results in low self-confidence, an implementation intention can use the same person to stimulate a positive step forward. For example: "When I see Marcia in the meeting, I will be sure to make eye contact with her and state my views in a clear way, without getting rattled."

- **Saves energy.** People who take preprogrammed automatic actions conserve energy and willpower. Researchers studying self-regulation have repeatedly showed that controlling our behavior on the spur of the moment not only depletes glucose levels; it lowers our daily store of willpower. Actions that are familiar, or that rely on the environment to direct us to do something (like a street sign instructing us to turn right), are less tiring.

- **Fosters habits.** When you follow through often enough on your implementation intentions, you create habits that become ingrained behaviors that will serve you well. For example, if you condition yourself to automatically get on your treadmill and walk five miles whenever you wear a certain exercise outfit or strap on a pedometer, you will vastly improve your chances of becoming a regular exerciser.

**IMPLEMENTATION INTENTIONS (if-then scenarios) not only triple the like-
lihood of taking important actions toward accomplishing goals; they are
most effective when used on hard-to-accomplish goals.**

Clocks and Chickens

Habit is the enormous fly-wheel of society, its most precious conservative agent.
—WILLIAM JAMES

Once again, we can learn a lot from watching how elite athletes perform. With
so much on the line, most of them have discovered how to avoid expending
unnecessary energy and how to make it as easy as possible to accomplish heroic
feats on a regular basis. Some of the athletes call their rituals "superstitions,"
although they definitely fit the definition of primes. Swimming legend and
Olympic gold medalist Mike Barrowman began his prerace ritual the night before
big meets by eating a Big Mac sandwich. This familiar prime always started a chain
of thoughts and predictable behaviors that he told people were partly responsible for putting him "in the zone" and leading to accomplishments including a
world record that stood for a decade.

Baseball superstar Wade Boggs has been lampooned for the exceptional number of rituals that he follows to keep his body and brain always geared up and
ready to perform on the baseball diamond. But a few of his rituals are worth noting because they are classic examples of how to make your environment work
on your behalf so that you are constantly cued for optimal and specific outcomes.
Here is just a sample of what Boggs does on a regular basis:

- When he is training or it is a game day in St. Petersburg, Florida, Boggs
  leaves for Tropicana Field at precisely 1:47 p.m.—not a moment before
  or moment later. (He has made the time on the clock the "if" condition, and leaving immediately to prepare for the game or practice is the
  "then.")
- When the center-field clock at Tropicana Field strikes 4:37 p.m., Boggs
  sprints toward third base, making sure to touch second base on the way.
- Between pitches, Boggs swipes the dirt in front of him with his left foot,
  taps his glove two or three times, and adjusts his hat. (Between pitches
  is the "if," and the "then" is made up of the actions that Boggs has
  learned will settle his mind and enhance his focus for the next pitch.)
- When he comes to the plate to hit, Boggs draws letters denoting the

word "*chai*"—Hebrew for "life"—in the dirt with his cleat for luck. (Again, like Barrowman's ritual, this is an action that triggers certain things in Boggs's behavior—possibly a certain batting stance—that he has learned will help him the most.)

Winning If-Then Statements

Since implementation intentions have been found to be particularly effective with difficult goals, this is your chance to apply the science to your life list. Take a look at some of the goals that you want badly but that scare you. Perhaps these are the goals that truly excite you, but you can't seem to move forward with them. We love to see how our clients use if-then statements to help them initiate behaviors that will take them closer to creating the life they want. Here are just a few of the ones they have created to successfully accomplish their life list goals:

- When I arrive at the Christmas party and see Peter, I will get something to eat and ask him if he'll go out to lunch with me this week.
- When my alarm goes off in the morning, I will immediately turn on the light and get ready to leave for swim practice.
- When I see my gym bag in the car, I will immediately drive to the workout facility for my class.
- When I wear my red power tie, I will make three sales calls before 10 a.m. that day.

Where Your Life List Is Now

You can now select some goals, or add new ones that have come to mind, and think of implementation intentions that will help you stay focused on your successes, both in initiating goals and in avoiding the problem of conflicting primes.

Life List Exercises and Worksheets

The following two worksheets are designed to help you identify the positive and negative primes in your life so that you can begin to chart what impact they have on you, and then remove the ones that are not beneficial, and add more of the ones that make goal pursuit and contentment easier.

❏ "Not Ready for Prime Time" worksheet (see page 248).

❑ "The Primes of Your Life" worksheet (see page 253). This worksheet walks you through the process of creating effective implementation intentions so that you can triple your chances of accomplishing your goals by using "if-then" statements.

❑ "Ifs, Ands, and Buts" worksheet (see page 240).

10

YOU GOTTA HAVE GRIT

Don't complain; just work harder.

—RANDY PAUSCH

How did "grit"—which is defined as "perseverance and passion for long-term goals"—suddenly rise to the top of the list of qualities that matter so much in accomplishing our life list goals, and how does it differ from other important personality traits that make such a difference in long-term success? This chapter reveals all the secrets of grit and how you can measure, foster, and build it into each of the goals on your life list.

Spelling Bees and Beast Barracks

A young boy stepped hesitantly to the microphone at the 2005 Scripps National Spelling Bee in Washington, D.C., as dozens of nervous parents and tens of thousands of viewers watched on live television.

"Trichotillomania," the judges intoned.

"Trichotillomania," the boy repeated to himself several times, tracing letters on the back of his hand before he confidently spelled it correctly and to great applause. With relief, the perspiring youth in braces returned to his seat, saved until he had to spell another word that he might never hear or use in a sentence for the rest of his life.

The Scripps National Spelling Bee is not just a classically American experience featuring the best and brightest spellers from many corners of the United States,

Puerto Rico, Guam, and elsewhere, all of whom are vying for a healthy chunk of change to help pay for college. It was also one of the laboratories used in 2005 to help quantify a quality that is now being cited as a key determinant in accomplishing long-term goals on your life list: grit.

Grit is increasingly considered so critical in life success that places like the U.S. Military Academy at West Point are using it instead of traditional intelligence measures to see which cadets have what it takes to gut out the first brutal summer of training, known as "Beast Barracks." If West Point admissions staff can better predict who will drop out of the academy in that first hellish summer and beyond, they will not only save hundreds of thousands of dollars on grooming these cadets for future leadership, but they will also be better able to spot leaders who have what it takes to hang in there when the going gets tough.

Underperformers versus Overachievers

In the mid-1990s, a young teacher in the Boston area, who had taught in a variety of public school systems, was puzzled by the lack of success she noted among some of her students, who seemed to have all of the advantages over their less intelligent peers, but who were consistently outperformed by their less gifted classmates. Angela Duckworth, a Harvard graduate and former Marshall Scholar, was so intrigued by this discrepancy that she uprooted her family to move to Philadelphia, where she could study and understand this phenomenon in a PhD program. At the University of Pennsylvania, under the tutelage of Marty Seligman, Duckworth has spent more than a decade working on this question, and her findings are extremely important to anyone who wants to achieve long-range, lofty goals.

Seligman and Duckworth decided to study people who were high achievers across many disciplines to discover what separated the successful from the unsuccessful. By interviewing composers, athletes, investment bankers, inventors, and others who had distinguished themselves in their chosen fields, they found that high achievers were always described as people who were not just talented; they were just as frequently called "tenacious," "hardworking," "passionate," and "stubborn in the face of obstacles." They also had accumulated more hours learning their craft and practicing those skills than people with equal or superior talent who had dropped out of that field.

Sifting through these interviews and reviewing the literature on giftedness led them to the conclusion that high achievers share an all-important quality that is independent of self-discipline, intelligence, and ambition. They gave this quality a catch name: grit. Then they set about finding a way to measure it in others. The former teacher in Duckworth knew that isolating and quantifying grit would help make a difference in other people's lives, particularly in light of the fact that she often heard people lamenting that they couldn't achieve an important goal because they couldn't "stick with it" when the going got tough. Understanding grit and how to foster it in others became her mission.

The History of Grit

Duckworth and Seligman were not the first to study this indefinable quality that had intrigued sociologists and researchers for well over a hundred years. In the early 1890s, Sir Francis Galton studied biographies of successful poets, judges, politicians, wrestlers, and others and concluded that talent was just one piece of high achievement. He saw that the most defining quality of success was "ability combined with zeal and with capacity for hard labour." Another researcher added decades later that childhood traits of "persistence of motive and effort, confidence in their abilities, and great strength or force of character" were essential to long-term life success.

Grit Includes "Task Commitment"

Joseph Renzulli wrote one of the most cited papers on the qualities of giftedness, which he had studied at the University of Connecticut and in his role as the director of the National Research Center on the Gifted and Talented. His observation that "task commitment" (perseverance, endurance, and hard work) is one of the three essential components of giftedness and is "nothing short of overwhelming." This was a bold statement because task commitment had nothing to do with inborn intellectual traits of ability and creativity, which were the other two legs of the giftedness stool.

Follow-Through Bests All Variables

In the 1980s, nine American colleges participated in the Personal Qualities Project to examine the effect on success in college of more than one hundred preadmission variables including athletic achievement, musical talent, leadership, and community involvement. One of these variables was follow-through, which was defined as "evidence of purposeful, continuous commitment to certain types of activities versus sporadic efforts in diverse areas." Students could receive anywhere from one to five stars on their follow-through ratings from expert panels reviewing the data on their applications and personal lives.

For the more than thirty-five hundred participants in the colleges involved in the Personal Qualities Project, *follow-through bested every other variable*, including SAT scores and high school rank, as a predictor of "significant accomplishment in science, art, sports, communications, organization or some other endeavor." Also, ratings of follow-through were better predictors of overall success than overall high school extracurricular involvement.

———————— ⁂ ————————

CHRIS COSTE IS a perfect example of a gritty person who pursued his passion long after others would have given up. For eleven long years, Coste played minor league baseball, bouncing from one team to another while continuing to refine his skills at different positions. After more than a decade of bad luck, low pay, and physical setbacks, Coste was called up by the majors on May 21, 2006, at the age of thirty-three, to be the backup catcher for the Philadelphia Phillies. That season was amazing for Coste, and he ended with a batting average of .328, with seven home runs and thirty-two RBIs in sixty-five games.

The Secrets of Greatness

In the late 1990s, an exhaustive review of expertise in fields like chess, music, sports, and the visual arts came to a similar conclusion involving long-term effort and greatness. K. Anders Ericsson of Florida State University and his colleagues postulated that the main differences that separated good, great, and elite individuals in their fields was daily "deliberate practice" spanning a minimum of ten years, with twenty years of this type of effort being an even better predictor of world-class achievement. Again, these researchers concluded that inborn genetic determinants like intelligence or talent were even less important than commonly thought, and that hard work over many years was the deciding factor in greatness.

The Grit Scale

What Seligman and Duckworth did to dramatically advance the field of human endeavor was to create a comprehensive definition of grit and then find a way to measure it among children and adults. The Grit Scale was developed through multiple iterations and rigorous validity checks, and this simple seventeen-question test has now been found to be the best predictor of myriad outcomes, whether it's determining which cadets will most likely drop out in the first summer of West Point to who will be the finalist at the National Spelling Bee. Another recent study found that undergraduate students at the University of Pennsylvania who had high grit scores had higher grade point averages than students of equal ability who were tested and found to be less gritty.

Grit, we now know, is that special something that can make all the difference between being talented and being great, or being smart and being successful. Grit has earmarks that can be glimpsed in childhood, but it's also something that can be fostered and fanned into a strength in the right settings and with the right role models.

Before we take a look at some real-life examples of grit, let's emphasize what grit is *not*:

- **Self-discipline.** Self-discipline, also known as self-regulation, is a necessary component of reaching goals, as experts like Roy Baumeister have repeatedly said. But self-discipline implies the ability to refrain from doing something you shouldn't do, and lacks the quality of enthusiasm and passion for long-term persistence. For example, West Point cadets who were high in self-discipline had high GPAs because they were able to withstand short-term temptations that would prevent them from studying, but grit is a more necessary commodity under the unrelenting pressures of Beast Barracks. As Duckworth noted, "Self-discipline is probably necessary for grit, but it's not sufficient."

- **Perseverance.** Perseverance is also a part of grit, but simple perseverance is just the ability to keep doing something, regardless of how long you do it or how well you are doing it. We can easily persevere at the wrong goals if we're not careful, mistaking activity for productivity.

- **Conscientiousness.** Again, being conscientious overlaps with being gritty, but conscientious, achievement-oriented individuals may be short-term sprinters instead of long-term marathoners. A gritty person is conscientious over exceptionally long periods of time.

- **Ambition.** Ambition is also a part of grit, but ambition is simply the desire to achieve a goal, whether you actually achieve it or not. Dean Simonton of the University of California at Davis has observed, "Ambition isn't enough to achieve greatness when it isn't combined with effort." Also, ambition comes in all shapes and sizes, and can involve "low goals" that don't necessarily stretch you outside of your comfort zone. Getting your dog trained or cleaning your closet might be your ambitions, but these efforts don't involve a long-term passionate pursuit of something that will elevate you.

- **Passion.** Gritty people have passion, but passionate people aren't necessarily gritty. Many passionate people lack self-discipline and can dissolve in the face of deadlines, or they might be the life of the party at night, but the jack-of-all-trades and master of none during the day.

■ **Optimism.** Optimistic people can be gritty, but they are not always. You must have optimism in your own abilities, however, to hang in there when no one else believes in you, particularly because gritty people often pursue their goals in the absence of positive feedback.

Some Gritty Greats

Brainy Princeton professor Andrew Wiles first heard about Fermat's last theorem when he was just ten years old. This problem had stumped the greatest mathematicians for 350 years, and it went like this:

Fermat's Last Theorem

$$x^2 + y^2 = z^2$$

There is no corresponding solution if the numbers are cubed instead of squared.

Intrigued, Wiles never forgot about this unsolved puzzle, and kept returning to it and tinkering with solutions, even as he went to college, launched his academic career, got married, and had children. Laboring quietly for thousands of hours in obscurity, he kept at it—including seven intensive years just prior to solving it when he limited his academic work—until he delivered three historic lectures in 1993 in England in which he presented his proof, prompting a media frenzy. Because fewer than one in one thousand mathematicians even had the ability to understand what Wiles had done, it took a few months for some tiny glitches in the proof to be discovered, but Wiles returned to the drawing board and solved them, too.

In 1995, Wiles joined the likes of Princess Diana as one of *People* magazine's "Most Intriguing People of the Year," but he downplayed the rock-star status that had been foisted upon him. Instead, when asked how he'd actually done what no one else had ever managed to do, Wiles didn't cite his talent or brains; he talked about perseverance. "That was the main thing," he said simply.

J. K. Rowling was once a poor, divorced, severely depressed single mother of an infant, who was struggling to make ends meet when she decided to try to make good on her goal of becoming a published author. While baby Jessica napped in a stroller, Rowling scribbled notes at cafés about characters named

Harry Potter and Hermione, and a game called Quidditch. Ten years, many movies, and seven mega-sellers later, Rowling is said to be richer than the queen of England.

Leon Fleisher was at the height of his recording and performing career as a pianist in 1965 when two of his fingers curled as a result of a medical disorder called focal dystonia. Although he was only thirty-five years old, Fleisher's career took a nosedive and he became unable to perform or use his right hand at all. Fleisher channeled his musical passion into teaching and conducting but never stopped looking for a cure, which he finally found after forty years of persistently trying everything from Rolfing to aromatherapy.

Shots of Botox in his hand freed up his clenched muscles, and Fleisher became a born-again star in 2004 when he released a comeback album entitled *Two Hands*. Although he could have given up on his forty-year search for a cure, Fleisher's ambition, optimism, perseverance, and tenacity gave him the "lucky" break-through in his seventies that triumphantly returned him to the keyboard.

Are the Millennials Gritty Enough?

We all know who they are. They balk at putting in long hours at work and would prefer to start at or near the top of their chosen profession, despite being only twenty-two years old. They are absorbed in themselves and are accustomed to posting continuous updates of their relationship status and appearance on MySpace and Facebook. They resent getting cell phone messages because text messages require less effort than actually punching a few extra buttons and listening to someone's voice. They were raised in the self-esteem movement and were told that they were great simply because they existed. They won trophies and honors for simply showing up on a soccer field. In many of their schools, competitive games and contests were banned so that no one could be declared the winner. After all, if there was a real winner, people might get their feelings hurt, school administrators earnestly explained.

Consultants, psychologists, motivational experts, and corporations are already concerned about what they are seeing in this generation of adults who tend to be self-absorbed, allergic to punching a time clock, and unfamiliar with delayed gratification. The dot-com bubble of millionaires in the 1990s led many to think that riches were easy to come by in a short period of time, and they also entered the workforce with résumés featuring wilderness experiences and expensive adventure trips instead of paid jobs or summer internships.

Mary Crane is just one consultant who has warned that the self-esteem movement that many were exposed to as children and young adults has left them unprepared for the realities of hard work and perseverance. "You now have a generation coming into the workplace that has grown up with the expectation that they will automatically win, and they'll always be rewarded, even for just showing up," Crane has said. She added that employers are now being told that working with these young people means coaching them gently instead of bossing them. "If you tell them 'You have got to do this,' they truly will walk. And every major law firm, every major company knows this is the future," she explained.

THE VAST MAJORITY of childhood prodigies never achieve greatness as adults because their early successes fail to teach them perseverance. "When success comes too easily, prodigies are ill prepared for what happens when the adoration goes away, their competitors start to catch up and the going gets rough," said Robert Root-Bernstein of Michigan State University. Jonathan Plucker, an Indiana University psychologist added, "I don't see anyone teaching these kids about task commitment, about perseverance in the face of social pressures, about how to handle criticism. We say, 'Boy, you're really talented.' We don't say, 'Yeah, but you're still going to have to put in those 60-hour work weeks before you can make major contributions to your field.'"

Building Grit

It's apparent that grit is a quality that people from all walks of life possess. It takes as much grit to rise from homelessness to job stability and home ownership as it does to be a concert-level pianist. Being gritty is applicable to accomplishing many important goals in our lives, particularly if we have long-term ambitions for ourselves that will involve years of hard work, persistence, setbacks, lack of family support, and other difficult conditions. We may even need grit to overcome an affluent childhood during which we were never criticized or asked to do something hard.

There are many ways you can build grit. Here are some of the best ideas from top researchers in the field:

- **Don't be a quitter.** It's tempting to fold your hands when you are tired or discouraged about the progress you're making toward a big goal. But when you fail to follow through, you destroy all chances of becoming the achiever you want to be.
- **Be around gritty people.** Duckworth is often asked how people can amplify this quality in themselves, and her response is that West Point

seems to take gritty individuals and make them grittier. So find a culture of mental and physical toughness, and spend time with people who demand the best of themselves and you, too. Even a sergeant's boot-camp program for weight loss will give you a taste of the type of grit required to be military-grade fit.

- **Work on optimism.** Although optimism doesn't necessarily make you gritty, as noted above, it *is* a learnable quality that allows you to hang in there and believe in yourself.

- **Read biographies or stories about gritty people.** The newspapers and media are filled with tales of people who offer real-life stories of not taking no for an answer, and persisting in their pursuit of a goal. Michael Jordan, for example, was cut from his high school basketball team and became infamous for his work ethic, which resulted in greatness in the same sport when he was an adult; Walt Disney went bankrupt several times before he succeeded with his lovable mouse character, Mickey Mouse. Cut out these stories and post them on an office or bedroom wall to remind you of what it takes to be a success.

- **Pursue something with passion.** Gritty people are passionate about what they do, and they don't often worry about "life balance" as they claw their way to greatness. Although this may be an extreme way to live, at least be sure that your long-term, challenging life list goals are things you are passionate about, because that will give you the edge that keeps you trucking in hard times.

- **Don't shrink from challenges.** Many of the grittiest people say that they pursued their goals because someone at one point told them that they couldn't do what they wanted to do. The only way to develop grit is to take on challenges and go outside your comfort zone regularly, because shrinking from challenges is the antithesis of grit.

- **Don't allow failure or criticism to define you**. Gritty people seek out and learn from criticism and failure, and they create emotional strategies to handle it and bounce back. This type of resilience is also part of being self-efficacious, or self-confident, so look for people who do this well, and ask for their assistance.

Where Your Life List Is Now

Take some time to focus on the harder and longer-term goals on your life list that will require more effort and persistence than others. Separate some of these into a list—your "superstar" roster—and share them with people who can be your cheerleaders when times are tough.

Life List Exercises and Worksheets

❏ Take the Grit Scale test. You can sign up for a free account at www.authentichappiness.com and get your score.

❏ Find a newspaper or Internet story every day about someone whose grittiness impresses you and make that person into your role model for the day. Put his or her story into your life list journal and refer to it for inspiration whenever you are tempted to quit. One easy way to do this would be to have an "alert" created from one of your favorite news sources, like Google, with a search phrase like "role model."

❏ Fill out the "All but Dissertation Goals" checklist on page 235 to see if you need to revisit an unfinished goal that you quit before, but want to add to your life list now.

PERSONALIZING YOUR GOALS IN SIXTEEN LIFE SPHERES

In the following six chapters, we have grouped the different areas of life that contribute to overall contentment into related clusters. After doing the Happiness House exercise, you may have specific goals in mind for the areas of life that matter most to you—like relationships with children or health—but if not, we'd like to present some specific research about all of these areas and their connection with overall quality of life for you to consider. Each section ends with specific takeaways that will help you look at your life list with a fresh eye, as well as some ideas about goals others have set in all of these areas that you might want to consider for yourself.

▼

11

MISSION STATEMENTS AND MORALS

It's not hard to make decisions when you know what your values are.
—ROY DISNEY

I N THIS CHAPTER, we examine the areas of life that give meaning to our goals, and that help define what we believe our purpose is. These are goals and values, which are your beliefs about what matters most in life and the goals that you set as a result, and spirituality, which are the spiritual or religious practices that you practice and hold dear. Because some people find that their spiritual beliefs create their values, these areas are often bunched together, but others separate them into distinct categories. Please do what feels right and authentic for you as you read about how others have enriched their lives by setting and pursuing these types of goals through our life list approach.

Goals and Values

In Chapter 4, you saw that the goals that emerge from your deepest values are the ones you're most likely to pursue, more than goals that are imposed on you, or that you adopt because you think you should. Values that help you set goals and bring your best efforts to the table include a desire for honesty, integrity, excellence, and kindness.

Now we'd like to ask you to spend some time thinking about something that is fundamental to the setting and accomplishment of all of the goals on your life list, and that ties these two concepts together in a simple way, goes even deeper than simply identifying your values.

Crafting a Mission Statement

Thoughts lead on to purposes; purposes go forth in action; actions form habits;
habits decide character; and character fixes our destiny.
—TRYON EDWARDS

One of the most enjoyable ways to examine your purpose in life is to craft a mission statement, which will help guide you in goal setting, how you approach life, and how you make decisions. At high-level corporate retreats, such as Dr. Jim Loehr's three-day Full Engagement Program in Orlando, Florida, which draws thousands of the world's top executives and athletes each year, one of the primary themes is to come up with a mission statement that defines your personal life philosophy. We believe that a mission statement, when phrased in a compelling way, not only will telegraph your values, but can act like a magnet, pulling your goals toward you, and shaping your behavior in desired ways. A mission statement, which can be one word, sentence, or phrase, has the power to become your ethical and behavioral touchstone.

One religious school, for example, came up with "Play hard. Work hard. Be a good guy." One mom decided that hers was, "Leave them laughing." The mission statement for 3M, the company that produces the ever-popular Post-it notes, is "To solve unsolved problems innovatively." The Green Berets live by "To free the oppressed." The mission statement of one of our clients, "To make everyone feel a little bit better for having encountered me," is emblazoned in big letters on the front of her journal. As her personal statement, another mom thought up "Be the mirror I want my son to see." And the personal mission statement of Marty Seligman is "To increase the tonnage of happiness in the world."

We've found the following six steps—or prompts—to be helpful in customizing an individual mission statement:

1. Ask yourself what your most cherished values are.
2. Ask yourself how you want others, including your children, to remember you after you're gone.
3. Ask yourself what words or phrases inspire you most from history, current events, politics, humanism, or religious work. Peruse a quote book or Internet site to get ideas if you need them.
4. Look at the mission statements of successful companies on their Web sites, delivery trucks, or letterhead, and ask yourself if those phrases elicit a feeling in you that matches what the product actually delivers.
5. Be sure that your final mission statement is compelling, action oriented, inspirational, simple, and easy to understand. It should at once state your goals while eliciting your best self and most authentic behavior.

6. Don't worry if you don't get it right the first time. Keep trying until you feel the "fit."

Team Hoyt

When Rick Hoyt was born in 1962, he was diagnosed with cerebral palsy and declared a spastic quadriplegic, and it was not expected that he'd learn to speak. Although many doctors gave up on him and advised his parents to institutionalize Rick, his parents refused, treating him just like they treated his siblings. Later, teachers discouraged Rick from getting an education; however, not only did he do so, communicating through a special computer, but he eventually graduated from Boston University with a degree in special education. One day, Rick typed out a message to his father, Dick, saying he wanted to enter a foot race. His father agreed to do it by pushing his son's wheelchair the entire way, resulting in "the biggest smile" Rick's parents had ever seen on his face when they crossed the finish line. After the race, Rick Hoyt told his father that he felt like his disability had "disappeared" while his wheelchair was flying along the course, which led his father to decide to train for, and enter, as many athletic contests as he could with Rick along for the ride (pushed in the running, pulled in the swimming, and connected in the cycling). Since 1992, they have completed more than two hundred triathlons, including six Ironman competitions, as well as sixty-five marathons. As a result of the joy that came to Rick from feeling like a participant in athletic events, Dick Hoyt's mission statement is magnificent: "To integrate the physically challenged into everyday life," and he thanks his disabled son for giving him this worthy purpose.

TAKEAWAYS FOR YOUR LIFE LIST

- A purpose in life guides our behavior and thoughts. It starts with our values, it shapes the goals we set and our reactions to setbacks, and it clarifies our future endeavors.
- A mission statement is a rich, specific way to compellingly telegraph your beliefs and inspires you to be your best self every day.

Spiritual and Religious Goals

Spiritual energy flows in and produces effects in the phenomenal world.
—WILLIAM JAMES

Almost every life list we've ever seen has had spiritual or religious goals, or both. Most often we see a sincere longing to have more time to seek out spiritual teachings, practice a form of worship that feels positive, and join a group of like-minded people who share that individual's beliefs and goals. One of the reasons why we long for these types of connections is because they feel good, partly because they offer a way for us to strengthen social relationships and demonstrate our gratitude for the blessings in our lives In fact, David G. Myers of Hope College says that research into more traditions has consistently found an association between having an active spiritual life and greater contentment, happiness, stronger marriages, and reduced risk for drug or alcohol abuse.

As strong as the link is for adults between happiness and having a strong spiritual belief system, it's even stronger for children. A study of 315 children between the ages of nine and fifteen at the University of British Columbia found that spirituality accounted for 16.5 percent of happiness among children, as opposed to 5 percent of happiness among adults. "From our perspective, it's a whopping big effect," said Mark Holder, associate professor of psychology at the University of British Columbia. "I thought their spirituality would be too immature to account for their well-being."

A 2007 TELEPHONE survey of thirty-five thousand Americans found that more than a quarter of those surveyed had left their childhood faith to join another religion or to pursue no religion. Nearly 20 percent of men stated that they had no formal religious affiliation, compared with 13 percent of women. The Catholic Church showed the greatest net losses to membership, while those who considered themselves "unaffiliated," or "nothing in particular," showed the greatest increase. Experts looking at the results cautioned that the rise in unaffiliated Americans doesn't mean that they are also becoming less religious. "The trend is towards more personal religion, and evangelicals offer that," said Professor Stephen Protethero, chairman of the religion department at Boston University, noting that evangelical churches offer small ministries that cater to teens, for example.

The Impact of 9/11

After 9/11, many life coaches found their practices bulging with new clients who wanted to get more out of life in the present, instead of waiting for the "someday" that may never come. The extraordinary number of deaths that were covered by the media around the clock, for many weeks, and the images of people jumping from the burning towers to their deaths also prompted a spiritual crisis among many who couldn't understand how a loving God could allow so many ugly actions, motivated by religious reasons, to occur.

While some people's spiritual beliefs were set adrift by the events of 9/11, others experienced a deepening of their faith, despite having lost what was most precious to them. The stories of Gila Barzvi and Travis Holmes illustrate this polarity:

> Guy Barzvi was killed in the World Trade Center at the age of twenty-nine, and his mother, Gila Barzvi, said, "Whatever faith was left to me, I lost when they took my son away." Gila's husband died several years after their son was killed on 9/11, probably from "a broken heart," his widow notes. Now she says that she lives "day to day," without a spiritual framework to sustain her, although she wishes she had something to help her understand the complexities of loss and grief.

> Liz Holmes, a single mom, died at the World Trade Center, too, and her twelve-year-old son, Travis, went from hospital to hospital searching for her until his prayers changed from asking God to find his mother to asking God to help take care of him in her absence. "I knew God does things for a reason, not just when and how we want them," he said later. "Things don't happen on our time; they happen on God's time."

A GALLUP SURVEY reported that 54 percent of adults and 37 percent of teens said they express thanks to a god or creator "all the time," and people who describe themselves as religious or spiritual are more likely to be grateful than those who describe themselves as neither.

TAKEAWAYS FOR YOUR LIFE LIST

- Spiritual and religious goals often spring from a desire to deepen one's faith, or to search for a faith that fills a need.
- People with spiritual lives are often happier than people who don't have a specific type of belief.

A Few Goals to Consider

Here are some spiritual, religious, and value-driven goals that we've seen on other people's life lists that you might want to consider:

❏ Create a mission statement for my family, with input from all of my children, and post it in the kitchen.

❏ Pray for guidance daily, and listen for the answers.

❏ Leave the world a better place through my actions.

❏ Teach my children the differences between right and wrong, and be a good example of this.

❏ Tell the truth whenever it won't hurt someone else.

❏ Get a meditation or spiritual guide.

❏ Join a Bible study group or read a verse from the Bible before beginning my workday.

❏ Make a sincere apology when I have wronged someone.

12

THE HOLY GRAIL OF HAPPINESS

One friend is worth a thousand relatives.

—ITALIAN PROVERB

RELATIONSHIPS WITH OTHER people have a powerful impact on your health, well-being, and quality of life, so life list goals around building and strengthening these bonds will always pay good dividends. People who have strong, positive relationships with family, friends, and coworkers have more fulfilling lives they are more likely to both set and achieve goals that are important to them, and they report being happier than their peers who have fewer friends or less positive connections to others. Also, when people are surveyed about what makes their life meaningful, most immediately cite their need for close relationships with family, friends, or romantic partners.

In this chapter, we examine the spheres of life pertaining to relationships, such as friendships, love relationships, and family relationships, and why fostering and improving these bonds can dramatically impact your life and enrich it in multiple ways.

Friends

A man's friendships are one
of the best measures of his worth.

—CHARLES DARWIN

The quality of one's friendships is very important when it comes to feeling satisfied with one's life, and because this is one of the most rewarding of the sixteen areas, we'd like you to take a special look at how to make this a meaningful part of your life list. For example, our friends—whom we define as people we know well and care about—can participate in some of our goals, as well as give us comfort when we need it most. The case studies below give examples of how important it is to always foster and nurture relationships like these.

On the morning of 9/11, Elizabeth was with her three young children when she heard that terrorists had taken over several U.S. commercial airplanes and were wreaking havoc on American soil. Elizabeth's mother, a flight attendant with one of the major airlines that had been hijacked, was unreachable, and Elizabeth was gripped with fear and grief. Without a second thought, she gathered her children and drove immediately to her closest friend's house, where she sat all day, glued to the television, just taking comfort in the presence of her friend's warmth, proximity, and compassion. Later, Elizabeth heard that her mother had been on call for the next flight out of Dulles Airport in suburban Washington, and had narrowly missed being on the ill-fated flight that crashed in Pennsylvania. She says that she could not have survived that day without her friend, who made one of the hardest moments of her life more bearable.

Tend and Befriend

Life is to be fortified by many friendships. To love and
to be loved is the greatest happiness of existence.
—SYDNEY SMITH

A landmark study out of UCLA showed that Elizabeth's response to stress—an immediate pull to go with her children to her friend's house—is the result of the cascade of chemicals that are evoked when the fight-or-flight response is activated. Unlike men, stressed-out women don't just get flooded with stress-induced chemicals like cortisol and adrenaline; they also secrete oxytocin, which promotes bonding with others (oxytocin is also released when a mother nurses her child).

THE HUG DRUG

A BRITISH STUDY has found that 72 percent of chronically depressed women in London reduced their depression symptoms by simply meeting volunteer "befrienders" for a chat, an outing, or a cup of coffee over the course of a year.

Researchers have concluded that the female urge to "tend and befriend," which was borne out in the landmark UCLA study of 2002, is one of the ways that women calm themselves and also strengthen their relationships with others. The importance of female friendships can't be overstated. In the famed Nurses' Health Study from Harvard Medical School, it was found that the more friends women had, the less likely they were to develop physical impairments as they aged, and the more likely they were to lead a joyful life.

Although men and women often respond differently to stress, friendships confer powerful benefits to both sexes. In a Duke University Medical Center study, researchers found that people with fewer than four friends were more than twice as likely to die from heart disease compared to those who had more friends. Having more than four friends didn't seem to make a difference in conferring additional health advantages, although it certainly didn't hurt.

ACCORDING TO BARBARA Israel and Toni Antonucci, "People report greater well-being if their friends and families support their goals by frequently expressing interest and offering help and encouragement."

Friendship Goals

Loneliness is the most terrible poverty.
—MOTHER TERESA

People often intuitively know the exquisite power of friendships without being told, and they like to have life list goals that involve strengthening these bonds. In the following stories, we see how even the busiest among us find time to nurture those relationships and reap the benefits they bring.

Julia's years of being a mom with an entrepreneurial streak had left her exhausted and depleted in the friendship department. When she wasn't taking care of her children, she was on the computer, building her business. The demands of both of these roles left her without time to see friends as regularly as she wanted, so she decided to set some aggressive goals to change things. First, she made a commitment to meet with her closest girlfriends from college once a year, and she volunteered to organize the gathering, which has become an annual hit. Julia always returns from these three-day trips with a renewed vigor and feeling of contentedness that is obvious to her family. She also now schedules time for a neighborhood bunco game every few weeks, and she asked one of her best friends to walk with her on a more regular basis in the mornings so that their friendship won't fade away.

While Sylvester does well with work friendships, he had let his hobbies slip away over the years, so he decided to set a joint play/friendship goal that revolved around getting back into shape while having fun with his friends. Now Sylvester goes away to mountain bike in Utah or Wyoming with his college friends once a year, and he is also setting goals around becoming better friends with some of the neighborhood dads whose children play regularly with his kids by scheduling pickup basketball and football games, and asking them to golf with him.

TAKEAWAYS FOR YOUR LIFE LIST

- Friendships are powerful drugs for well-being and life satisfaction.
- Friendships need to be tended, much like a garden; regular connection requires special care and planning.
- Four basic behaviors govern whether or not a friendship is maintained: communication, extending oneself, interacting (by phone or in person), and being positive, according to Marquette University psychologist Debra Oswald.

SOCIAL NETWORKING TOOLS have made it easier and easier to connect online and make new friendships with people who share similar interests. Some people add goals like "Get a profile on Facebook" or "Add three people to my LinkedIn profile" to their life lists.

Lovers and Love Relationships

"I want to find my soul mate and marry her"; "I want to make love on the beach with my partner while the sun comes up"; "I want to be as happy with my husband in twenty years as I am now." These are all life list goals that we've seen over the years from people who urgently desire to find love and contentment with the person of their dreams, or with someone who can be a meaningful partner. In fact, when we ask clients to enumerate their most cherished desires, we almost always see love goals listed in the top ten goals of "One Hundred Things to Do before I Die," or on the "ground floor" of the "Happiness House" exercise (see page 67).

----------- ⁂ -----------

RESEARCH FROM THE University of Warwick has found that a married man or woman is significantly happier with life when his or her partner is satisfied with life. For example, when your spouse has a 30 percent increase in his or her life satisfaction score, it completely negates your own experience of something as difficult as unemployment. The same effect did not hold true for couples that prefer cohabitation to marriage.

We have found many creative ways to help our clients make progress on their goals in the area of love and relationships, and are always excited to see how their quality of life is positively impacted when they find happiness in love.

Here are some of our clients' life list love goals that they actually achieved:

Stephanie wanted to marry a man who excited her physically and emotionally, and she even described in her journals how she hoped he'd look. After writing her wish list in great detail, including the fact that she wanted to get married in the romantic city of Paris before she turned forty, she shared her dreams with her friends to see if they knew anyone suitable. One of her friends' husbands set her up on a blind date with his brother, who eerily matched the physical description of Stephanie's ideal guy. Not only did she hit it off with Bill, but he got along well with her son from her first marriage, too, which had always been a concern. As their courtship progressed, Stephanie added some of his favorite activities, like softball, to her life, while he took her son out to basketball games and on long drives. On the eve of her fortieth birthday, Stephanie sent a postcard to her coach as she got ready to depart for her wedding in Paris, thanking her for the assignment of writing down what she wanted in a man, because she believed that putting her dreams on paper, and in great detail, allowed her to screen out everyone who didn't match, and brought other people's brainstorming to the subject in the most positive and powerful way imaginable.

Harry felt that his wife wasn't treating him with the love and affection she had once shown him, so he set the goal of bringing the romance back into his marriage by finding out what made her feel good. Surprisingly, she didn't want roses, trips, or new clothes. She wanted more free time by herself, free from work and family obligations, and she also wanted to reinstate the "date night" that they'd had much earlier in their marriage. Harry quickly found that when he gave his wife more "time off" to do what she loved while he watched the children, she was more grateful and affectionate in return. Instead of leaving it up to her to find a babysitter for their night out, he also took that upon himself, further enriching their time together, and helping Harry to meet his own goal of getting more romance and caring back in his life.

———— ⁂ ————

NOVELTY IS THE spice of life when it comes to date nights for long-married couples. Several experiments have found that middle-aged couples can rekindle their love life by having regular date nights that involve new activities and settings that they both enjoy. Couples who just added "pleasant" date nights to their romance revival plans didn't show the same relationship improvements as risk-taking couples that ventured outside their comfort zone and did more novel things.

TAKEAWAYS FOR YOUR LIFE LIST

- A good love relationship can improve the quality of your life across many realms.
- Long-term love relationships respond well to novel approaches to eating, socializing, and playing.

Family

My family tree is full of nuts.
—ANONYMOUS

Family harmony is an important goal for many people, but it is elusive for some, which is why we see so many life lists sprinkled with goals that have to do with making peace with an estranged sister, taking an annual family vacation without friends or outside interruptions, or being on good footing with in-laws. The jokes about mothers-in-law are funny but only to a point; many of our clients feel that the quality of their lives is less than ideal because of their relationships with in-laws, who manage to undermine every family gathering with a pointed remark about how their daughter-in-law or son-in-law can't seem to learn how to cook a decent stuffed pepper or fix a broken toilet.

We are pleased that so many people value positive relationships with their relatives and children, which are two of the sixteen areas of life, because studies have found that happy families promote children who flourish. In these families, you often find nutty uncles and eccentric grannies, but everyone seems to have a place at the table. Researchers say that children who grow up seeing that there is room in their family for "strange" relatives, and that disagreements between people are eventually solved, feel more comfortable about expressing their own differences—and have a happier and more open attitude about life as a result.

Many of our clients prioritize their families on their life lists and focus goals on improving these vital relationships. As a result, they are handsomely rewarded.

Colette became one of the top salespeople in her company; as a result, her husband left his job to become her assistant. The success of the business was good news, but it came at the expense of their relationship with their oldest daughter, who grew up with babysitters and television after school instead of a parent. When Colette first started working with a life coach, she made it her top mission to improve the situation by going on a mother-daughter getaway weekend. The rules for the weekend were that Colette couldn't bring her BlackBerry or do any work, and her daughter was allowed to pick anyplace to go within three to six hours' driving distance by car, and could also choose the activities for the weekend. Colette said that her daughter was so moved by her mother's undivided attention that she begged her mom to schedule another getaway for six months later. Colette returned home humbled by how important it was for her daughter to see her more, and resolved to hire another assistant so that she and her husband could have family dinners five nights a week.

Doug wanted to tell his father he loved him before his father died. Although they had had a strained relationship throughout Doug's life, he knew that his father loved him but couldn't express it, and he didn't want to let his father's behavior color his own willingness to reach out. He put this life list goal in the number one spot, and when his coach challenged him to make that call right after the coaching session, Doug hesitated but agreed. Later, he said it was the scariest, and best, goal he'd ever taken on, and that it had given him a feeling of release that he'd unconsciously desired for years.

A UNIVERSITY OF Colorado researcher has found that people receive more enduring pleasure and satisfaction from investing in life experiences than in material possessions. Leaf Van Boven has said that his research shows that having experiences helps shape an individual's personal identity, while also contributing to building successful social relationships. Possessions, he noted, are always "out there," and separate from who we are, which makes them harder to identify with and feel proud of, while experiences become part of us.

TAKEAWAYS FOR YOUR LIFE LIST

- Family relationships can be tricky, but life list goals about strengthening bonds and creating harmony can be life changing.
- Happy families have regular playtimes, like backyard football games or basement jazz jams, so aiming for fun togetherness is a good idea.

A Few Goals to Consider

Here are some interesting goals we've seen on life lists that apply to relationships of all kinds and that might inspire you to add new goals or change some of the goals on your list:

- ❑ Read a book to my children every night.
- ❑ Instant message my son at college every day, just to say hi.
- ❑ Make a scrapbook for my in-laws' fiftieth anniversary by collecting stories and pictures from all of their children.
- ❑ Tell my partner one thing I'm grateful for every day.
- ❑ Take my children to visit their ancestors' graves in Ireland.
- ❑ Participate in a monthly women's gathering on a topic that is interesting to me.
- ❑ Spend one afternoon each weekend with one of my children.
- ❑ Make Sunday a day of rest for the entire family, without sporting events or outside socializing.

13

YOUR BODY, MIND, AND SOUL GOALS

A vigorous five-mile walk will do more good for an unhappy, but otherwise
healthy adult than all the medicine and psychology in the world.
—PAUL DUDLEY WHITE

I N THIS CHAPTER, we focus on how to strengthen and optimize what we call
the "body, mind, and soul" goals that pertain to the areas of life that include
health, self-esteem, and volunteering. These areas all promote growth in areas
that make us more resilient, empathic, and self-confident, and we have research
supporting the importance of each sphere. Every life list ought to contain goals
in these areas, so read the case histories below for ideas that might contribute
toward your own goals.

Health

It's the rare life list that isn't crammed with health goals such as "Lose ten
pounds," "Finish a triathlon," or "Complete a fund-raising walk for a cause that
matters to me." Most of us want to improve some aspect of our physical well-
being because exercising and eating well don't just feel good; they contribute to
keeping us out of the doctor's office and dramatically improve our mental health.

Dr. John Ratey of Harvard Medical School has said that exercise is the single
most important tool people have to maximize brain function, and his research
shows that when your body gets fitter, so does your mind. "Studies show that
exercise is as effective as antidepressants," Ratey said, adding that exercise "sparks"
the brain, giving it energy that he likens to Miracle-Gro.

AEROBIC ACTIVITIES THAT are combined with complex motor activity, such as the martial arts or ballroom dancing, are especially beneficial for one's happiness and brain fitness. When the exercise is complicated and involves new learning, the brain is optimized through the stimulation and creation of neural pathways.

Although there are myriad activities to choose from to add exercise to your life, experts say that you set yourself up for success when you select activities that suit your personality and add some form of accountability to your life to ensure that you follow through on what you intend to do. For example, introverts sometimes do best with solitary activities, like long-distance running, single sculling, or swimming, while extroverts may thrive in team-related settings, where they can talk and interact while exercising.

Accountability is an important aspect of improving your chances of success with any goal, and this is especially true of fitness because it usually involves conscious choices such as changing clothing, uncomfortable physical exertion, and actually going to a specific location in order to exercise. Many people find that clipping on an inexpensive pedometer to track their steps each day has a big impact on staying focused on walking as a goal. In fact, studies have found that people who wear a pedometer walk approximately two thousand more steps a day than people who don't wear one. Personal contact on a monthly basis with a weight-loss professional has also been found to help people keep off more weight than if they "go it alone." Even the persistent beeping of a PDA, asking you if you've finished your daily exercise routine, results in more than double the time spent exercising than if you track your goals on paper.

PEOPLE WHO RELY too heavily on the accountability of a personal trainer to help them lift weights or exercise may have low self-confidence about working out on their own. At some point, you must shift accountability from a trainer to yourself if you want to develop more self-confidence and self-regulation skills, and avoid becoming lazy when your trainer is away or unavailable.

Case Histories of Health-Related Goals

The health goals we've seen on most of our clients' life lists cover the whole spectrum of wellness and have helped them develop more zest and feel more optimistic about their futures. Here are some health-related goals that worked for two of our clients.

> Patricia wanted to do something unusual to rejuvenate her fitness routine, and she wanted to involve her daughter, too. So both enrolled in a local tae kwon do studio, where they made themselves accountable by paying for an entire black-belt curriculum ahead of time. Patricia not only got her black belt by the age of forty, along with her ten-year-old daughter; she also developed self-confidence about protecting herself, if necessary, and made a whole new circle of friends who shared her passion for the martial arts. She also lost weight and inches around her hips, and found that she carried herself with an air of newfound self-confidence that spilled into every other part of her life, as well.

> When Lucy started her life list, there were no fitness goals on it at all because she had no confidence that she could achieve any of them, given her long history of failed efforts in gym class and elsewhere. But with the encouragement of her coach, she set the goal of learning how to lift weights, and committed to working with a trainer once a week to simply get stronger and more flexible. The first time she did it, she felt like an "idiot" because she didn't feel comfortable sweating in public, but she persevered. A few months later, she added the goal of walking around the local high school track one time every day, and then she began to add more distance. Lucy then joined a group of mall walkers who had coffee after window shopping and walking briskly for an hour during cold months, and she made a new group of friends. Now Lucy feels like a new woman and swears she has more energy and better health than she has had in decades.

AT UNION PACIFIC Railroad, 75 percent of employees who participated in regular exercise reported improved concentration and overall productivity at work.

Self-Esteem

Everyone has won and all must have prizes.
—THE DODO IN ALICE IN WONDERLAND

In one of the funniest moments in the comedy *Meet the Fockers*, in which the overblown self-esteem movement of the 1980s is skewered, Bernie Focker shows off his adult son's trophies and ribbons to the parents of his son's fiancée, one of whom notes wonderingly, "I didn't know they made ninth-place ribbons." Bernie Focker replies happily, "They have them up to tenth place. There's a bunch on the A-for-effort shelf."

As we mentioned in Chapter 10, "You Gotta Have Grit," some American children who came of age in the early part of the twenty-first century were raised with the false idea that self-esteem comes from simply being alive and merely showing up on a soccer field, for example, avoiding the idea or pain of failure at all costs. The state of California even created a commission to study the pressing issue of how to raise children's self-esteem, while too many well-meaning parents and educators encouraged the use of affirmations and awards so that every child could "be a winner." In the most extreme versions of this trend, competitive games, elementary school "fun runs," and even national challenges like spelling and geography bees have been eliminated from children's lives because they are "too competitive" and might damage the self-esteem of children who don't win. Although we take the position that we're all worthwhile human beings, and that our actions don't necessarily dictate our basic self-worth, we don't endorse the idea of self-esteem goals that don't have specific and challenging parameters. Even the Girl Scouts now promote the growth of self-esteem by emphasizing strengths and skills that contribute to self-efficacy and well-being. "It used to be, 'Whatever you do is great,'" said Harriet Mosatche, senior director of research for the organization. "That old-fashioned misuse of the notion of self-esteem is not positive. It's unrealistic, and not helpful."

With that caveat in mind, let's take a look at some of the successful efforts our clients have made in the area of self-esteem:

Carolinda weighed more than two hundred pounds when she got involved with a man who had a stressful job in law enforcement. He was handsome, brave, and strong, or so she thought, until he began to push her around after he drank too much, harshly accusing her of having nonexistent affairs with some of their friends. Carolinda said she had "the self-esteem of a snail" when she walked into a fitness center and signed up for a weight-lifting class, but she somehow knew that becoming stronger physically would help her become stronger mentally. Carolinda set the goal of "standing up for myself when Paul is drunk and angry," and she found that this happened as she worked out more and liked seeing the results in the mirror. Paul got angrier as she got thinner and stronger, but the moment Carolinda hit her seventy-pound weight-loss goal, she moved out and got a restraining order. Carolinda's rise in self-esteem came from the pride she took in her efforts to control her life and body, resulting in a surge of well-being in other areas of her life, as well.

Anne didn't know why she always deferred to her two male business partners, who left her with most of the work in their government consulting business, particularly when she was the one writing the proposals, doing the research, and getting the clients. She sheepishly told her coach that she wanted to raise her self-esteem enough to renegotiate the division of profits in their business, and she decided to do it by setting the goal of taking a public-speaking class. Anne was so scared of speaking in public that she often clammed up in meetings with her partners, but she felt that public-speaking skills would help her overcome this hesitancy and feel better about herself. She was right. After completing a three-month community class, Anne had not only conquered her fear of speaking in public; she had given a trial speech in front of her class about how she planned to approach her partners and state her needs.

TAKEAWAYS FOR YOUR LIFE LIST

- Self-esteem is an important quality that is tied to happiness, but it is not achieved through affirmations or false praise.
- Self-esteem changes need to be tied to the accomplishment of challenging and specific goals that enable you to feel proud of your initiative and hard work.

Giving to Yourself by Giving to Others

We have yet to see a life list that doesn't include one or more "helping" or "service" goals—which can take many forms, including donating your money, time, or resources to a person or organization that needs your help. For example, we've seen people express the desire to donate a library in a parent's name, give away one million dollars by the age of sixty, and build homes for those who have lost everything in natural disasters. We've also seen giving goals that involve political service, such as running for a seat on the local school board, or helping the public school system by serving on the Parent-Teacher Association.

Giving to others is also seen in many spiritual traditions as one of the chief paths to enlightenment. Diverse contemplative spiritual traditions such as Sufism, Kabbalah, Buddhism, and Christian monasticism all encourage adherents to take time for this type of generosity. No less a venerated monk than Thomas Merton said that kindly and patient service to others is the embodiment of the Christian commandment to "love one's neighbor as oneself."

Happiness researchers such as Sonja Lyubomirsky have suggested that acts of helping and service to others may help us to appreciate our communities and neighbors more. Available research suggests that we flourish and prosper in communities where we act as if strangers and neighbors are our friends. Service also evokes feelings of gratitude because we realize how fortunate we are. Helping others also lets people foster and build social relationships.

SPENDING AS LITTLE as five dollars a day on someone else has the ability to significantly boost happiness levels, according to experiments on more than six hundred Americans. "Regardless of how much income each person made, those who spent money on others reported greater happiness, while those who spent more on themselves did not," Elizabeth Dunn, a psychologist at the University of British Columbia, noted about the results.

Helper's High Goals

There are countless ways for you to be creative about serving and giving to others, but perhaps these case histories will help spark some ideas:

Paul, a highly decorated war veteran, reached the pinnacle of his profession as a psychologist by the age of sixty and began to think of ways to give back to people who couldn't afford his fees, or who didn't have mental health insurance. He decided to give back by volunteering to counsel Iraq war veterans who were having trouble adjusting to their lives at home after deployment, and who were not receiving appropriate or timely care at the local VA center. The work he has done is the most enriching and satisfying he has ever done, Paul now says, because it has helped him see how his own experiences have given others hope that they can and will find ways to adjust to life after living and working in a war zone. His work has also deepened his appreciation of his own service and the impact it has had on his life, while helping to heal his wounds from his many years overseas.

Martha wanted to help integrate her family into a new church that they joined when they moved to a northeastern city, so she decided to sign up for casserole baking at a local soup kitchen. Her twelve-year-old son excitedly volunteered to be the one who made the tuna casserole every week, and he couldn't wait to wrap it and take it to the church's kitchen as his contribution. Not only did Martha feel more connected and happy about this volunteer work, but she saw that the biggest beneficiary was her son, who suddenly couldn't wait to get to church every week, where he felt like a valued member of the community.

TAKEAWAYS FOR YOUR LIFE LIST

- "Helper's high" is a real phenomenon that has been found to help the giver more than the givee, with profound health and emotional benefits.
- Volunteering takes many forms, whether it's serving your local school, becoming more involved in charitable works through your religion, bettering your community through political work, or giving a gift of your resources anonymously.

A Few Goals to Consider

We never cease to be amazed by how many wonderful and kind goals we see on life lists. Here are a few you might like to consider for your own list:

- ❏ Establish a nonprofit family foundation and give away money on a regular basis with family input.
- ❏ Take shut-ins to church.
- ❏ Take my friend who has a visual impairment anywhere she wants once a month so that she doesn't have to call a cab.
- ❏ Always keep energy bars with a dollar bill wrapped around them in the car to give homeless people.
- ❏ Tithe 10 percent of my income annually.

14

LIVE, LAUGH, LOVE!

It matters with life as with play; what matters is not how long it is,
but how good it is.

—SENECA, FIRST-CENTURY ROMAN PHILOSOPHER

T HE NEXT AREAS we will explore among the sixteen valued spheres of life are play, creativity, and learning. These areas are invaluable when it comes to enriching our lives with laughter, fun, and an appreciation for what is new and interesting in the world around us. In order to deepen our connection with others, we must include play and recreation goals, and by allowing our creative and curious sides to surface, we engage in passionate learning that keeps us young at heart and in our heads. We include research in this chapter on the importance of goals in these areas in the hopes that your life list becomes peppered with these types of meaningful and rewarding pursuits.

Play and Recreation

"I want to have more fun in life, and I want to play, but I don't know how anymore! I feel old!"

This is the type of lament we hear all too often when we ask people what they do to have fun on a daily basis. Frequently, they silently search their minds for the activities and friends with whom they play or joke around. Some people, however, have no trouble identifying their play partners because they regularly bike, swim, bird-watch, take cruises, go on short trips, and have game nights with their families. For the most part, though, these outgoing and fun people are not the norm, and most of us need some help thinking of ways to have regular fun, relaxation, or self-improvement in our lives.

A NUMBER OF recent studies show that there has been a steady decline in outdoor recreation, with lowered participation in outdoor sports such as golf, tennis, swimming, hiking, biking, and downhill skiing.

Children Naturally Know How to Play

We do not quit playing because we grow old;
we grow old because we quit playing.
—OLIVER WENDELL HOLMES

Play goals are important for a variety of reasons, not the least of which is that they give life a fun, zestful edge. Dr. George Vaillant, one of the leading researchers and authorities on the topic of aging gracefully, has said that including play in one's daily routine is one of the keys to being vibrant throughout life. Children, he and other researchers have found, are naturally energetic and full of enthusiasm and curiosity. The quality of zest, in fact, is almost always found among the top five strengths of children across all cultures, although alarmingly it drops to the bottom five as people age and they stop playing and having fun.

Vaillant feels that the majority of adults need "zest" or "play" interventions so that they can have more fun in their lives. He says that children are our role models, and encourages us to find inspiration in their behavior if we aren't sure how to start. For example, he points out that children never pause or worry about whether they'll look funny on park swings or whether they ought to wear Halloween costumes or not.

Valliant is adamant. "Do what they do! Skip down the street! Shoot baskets in your driveway! Act like a kid—you might feel like one, too!" He added that if acting like a kid doesn't work as a play intervention, hang around a lot of playful people to see if their enthusiasm rubs off on you. At least one of our clients swears that this works, because she found that adding young children to her piano classes instantly made her feel younger and livelier than when she teaches only older adults.

Why Play Matters

People are going to be most creative and productive when they're doing
something they're really interested in. So having fun isn't an
outrageous idea at all. It's a very sensible one.
—JOHN SCULLEY, FORMER CEO OF APPLE COMPUTERS

When children play, they acquire a number of lifetime skills such as how to get
along with others and how to learn new things. It has been found that imaginative play is particularly important to the development of self-regulation skills
such as impulse control. Experts say that when children take on different per-
sonas and remember what role they are playing in games like house, school, or
babysitter, the more imaginative and creative play, the greater their "executive
functioning" abilities, which include organizing a variety of goals and being mentally flexible about the variety of ways they can be accomplished

Adults also benefit greatly from play goals for these reasons and others. Playing
games and being spontaneous make us smile. Play goals also often involve learning new habits, making friends, getting fit, laughing, and exploring the world.
Psychologists note that humor is one of the most powerful antidotes to discouragement and pessimism. Play also often puts us in the state of "flow"—where
time stands still and we are completely engaged in the challenges in front of us—
and it helps us restore our equilibrium and simply unwind or recharge our batteries when we need it most.

DR. ALAN MARLATT of the University of Washington says that play activities ought to be "want" activities instead of "should" activities, lest we run
the risk of burnout and turn to alcohol and other chemical substances to
give us the relief that we can get from play.

Sample Play Goals

If I'm going to Hell, I'm going there playing the piano.
—JERRY LEE LEWIS

Once our clients begin to incorporate more play into their lives by setting specific
life list goals, they experience more well-being and feel better in other ways,
including improved health, stronger friendships, more creativity, and greater zest
for life.

Here are examples of some of our clients' play goals:

When Clare's children began to take piano lessons, she felt a familiar long-ing in her fingers to play again. Clare had played for many years in her childhood, but had stopped after college because she didn't have a piano any longer, and she didn't feel she had the time. She decided to ask around for a teacher who took on adult students, and she even found one who specialized in playing jazz, one of Clare's childhood dreams. "Although I appreciated classical music, I always wanted to play songs that might make people smile—like the people at Nordstrom department stores who play jazz and show tunes. So I put down the goal of playing the piano at Nordstrom on my life list. Now I'm taking weekly lessons and finding that my day is just so much happier when I put in twenty minutes of practice every day."

Linda decided to set the goal of playing April Fool's jokes on her coworkers when she realized that she had fallen for other people's pranks every year, without ever playing a joke of her own. Now Linda is renowned for the elab-orate schemes that she cooks up every year in time to surprise her husband, children, and coworkers. "I love seeing people crack up when they realize that I've gotten away with a great joke, and it builds great rapport at work. It also gives my kids years of stories to tell about their wacky mom!"

ANTHROPOLOGISTS SAY THAT pranks have served an important purpose for centuries because they are rituals designed to bring a person into a group, and to temper success with humility. Pranks that are well done, and that don't involve put-downs or bullying, can bring a group closer, and also stir self-reflection in the person who has been duped.

TAKEAWAYS FOR YOUR LIFE LIST

- Play activities often evoke a state of flow and enhance self-regulation skills because the happier moods we experience have the impact of replenishing our willpower muscles and reducing stress levels.
- Making physical activity fun or playful is a way to maximize your recre-ational pursuits.
- Play leaves us rested and recharged.
- Play is important for the good life, since it includes activities that are pleasant, but not necessarily meaningful.

A STUDY OF 737 chief executives of major corporations found that 98 percent said that they would hire an applicant with a good sense of humor
over someone who didn't seem to have one. In addition, *Harvard Business
Review* found that executives described by coworkers as having a good
sense of humor advance up the corporate ladder more quickly and earn
more money than their peers.

Creativity

*A creative approach to teaching, to cooking, to play, to study,
to bookkeeping, to gardening adds something valuable to life.*
—IRVING YALOM

We have great news for people who want to add more creativity to their lives
without having to be famous artists whose work is on display in every museum
and gallery. You can be just as creative by coming up with clever ways to solve
everyday problems or by pursuing hobbies that matter to you, whether it's landscape painting, photography, needlework, or rebuilding engines in vintage cars!

Instead of being daunted by the idea that creativity is something you are born
with and that manifests in elementary school art classes, we want you to look at
the practice of creativity as simply a new way to apply unique or out-of-the-box
thinking to any and all spheres of your life. This can include becoming more creative in the ways you stretch your budget, redecorate a room, create an e-mail signature, or give gifts to others.

Creative Problem Solving in Everyday Life

Creativity comes from trust. Trust your instincts.
—RITA MAE BROWN

Just as children are naturally playful, they are also quite creative and inven-
tive when it comes to making up games and passing time with friends. People
who have studied creativity say that this important quality begins to be stifled
as a child grows up and is instructed to think, dress, and behave in certain
ways. As a child begins to narrow his or her definition of what is acceptable,
unique and creative responses to life get lost while predictable, rote behaviors
become the norm.

However, people who continue to foster their creativity through the way they dress, for example, or through a unique lifestyle, or a commitment to independent thinking, exhibit many of the hallmarks of happy people: They are open to new experiences, they have a wide set of interests, and they are bolder in their behavior and thinking than their less playful peers.

Robert Sternberg of Yale University defines creativity as a skill that is brought to problem solving in any and all spheres of life. Allowing your creative side to blossom through a variety of pursuits, ranging from quilting to singing, is also good for your body. Dr. Gene D. Cohen, director of the George Washington University Center on Aging, Health and Humanities, says that creativity "has profound implications for maintaining health." His studies have found that people who attend art, poetry, painting, and jewelry-making classes spend more time socializing, are less likely to take prescription drugs, and are happier than people who are not engaged in creative pursuits.

RESEARCH ON CREATIVE and talented teenagers finds that the most talented teens say that some solitude and quiet time is necessary for their creativity to blossom.

Sample Creativity Goals

All people have the capacity to derive satisfaction from
artistic activity in some way, at some level.
—SEYMOUR SARASON

There are multiple ways to use your life list if you would like to be more creative. Some of our clients like to pursue visual media such as photography, painting, sculpture, and drawing, while others try their hands at woodworking and landscape design. Others have actually changed their careers and become Web site designers, seamstresses, and actors. Because there are so many ways to add creativity to your life and enjoy its benefits, it's a good idea to expose yourself to public access shows that depict many different types of creative pursuits, or visit local craft fairs where artisans display their handmade wares. One man we know was a computer-programming analyst until he went to a craft fair and got hooked on making huge metal sculptures, a passion that has now become his line of work. For those of you who are not artistically inclined (or for whom artistic expression is not an interest), but who are searching for other ideas to bring creativity into your life, take a look at the following case histories of clients who did just that.

Joy took a look at her closet one day and realized that everything she owned reflected another woman: her mother. Although Joy admired her mother, she had stifled her own longings for years, and had even forgotten what clothing styles she liked. Joy revised her life list to include this new goal: "Have a signature look that is mine and that makes me feel comfortable." Once Joy established this goal, she worked with her life list coach to come up with colors, styles, and even a new haircut that matched who she wanted to be. Now Joy is known as "the scarf woman" because she accessorizes her outfits with different scarves that bring her pleasure, and that allow her to feel creative every day.

Lars missed the creative outlet of playing the bagpipe when his children were young and their needs overtook his usual music practice time. So he decided to be creative in a different way that also helped his health goals. Instead of going on the same walking or running route in the mornings, he decided to set off in different directions, or drive to new locations, so that his routes were different almost every day. Although he still misses his music, he finds that being creative in an untraditional way has satisfied this urge for now.

Wendy felt like she was just going through the motions of her life, so she wanted to see if she could do her everyday activities with more flair and pizzazz. One of her life list goals read, "Make one creative meal every week for the kids." So, Wendy began to watch the Food Network while making her children's lunches in the morning, and she always saw at least one dish that she decided to cook for her family, much to their delight. Wendy also began to have more fun with cooking in general, and took great pleasure in making her children giggle as she pretended to be a Food Network chef while making peanut butter and jelly sandwiches, boosting her play skills at the same time.

TAKEAWAYS FOR YOUR LIFE LIST

- Creativity can be fostered and learned through experiments and the attitude "I'll try anything once!"
- Allow yourself time to brainstorm about problems with people who think differently than you do, because their input very often leads to "Aha!" breakthroughs.
- Travel to different places to expose yourself to other lifestyles.
- Devote one place in your home to expressive art, creative hobbies, or unhurried thinking.

- Visit art galleries or exhibits of creative work.
- Watch public access shows about music, art, creativity, science, and other areas that promote out-of-the-box thinking.

Learning

Just as creativity goals are not limited to traditional artistic avenues like painting, learning is not limited to reading textbooks, although this undoubtedly brings pleasure to some people who love being students. Learning can occur in any setting that teaches you something new, and that adds to your appreciation of life.

Carol Dweck, a noted researcher and professor at Stanford University, has discovered that people with a "growth" mind-set, who believe in challenging themselves through self-improvement and learning experiences, actually experience more success in life than people who believe that intelligence is "fixed." People with a "fixed" mind-set avoid putting themselves into situations in which they will be challenged and might fail, and they also avoid learning goals.

Sample Learning Goals

Learning goals can be set in any area of life that interests you. Some people enjoy learning new languages, and some enjoy cultivating new sports and hobbies. The Internet has opened up an extraordinary variety of avenues that people can use to learn in every possible way, and on any conceivable topic. Some of our clients have earned graduate degrees through virtual programs online, and we've seen stay-at-home moms learn how our political system works by becoming neighborhood and school advocates. Here are the case histories of two of our clients who have pursued life list learning goals:

> After all of his children left home, Mark's experience of the "empty nest" was acute, and he found hours of free time in his formerly jam-packed schedule. We urged him to write a "Portrait of Your Life" (see page 249) for himself, an exercise that helped Mark get in touch with his longing to join a band and reignite a childhood passion for drumming. Mark went onto Craig's List, found a high-quality drum set for sale, and then started to practice with a teacher from the local middle school. Instead of rock, Mark took up jazz drumming, and he often lost track of time while practicing. Now Mark is in a band of local dads who jam on several weekends every month, and they even play in local

arts festivals, an activity that has certainly added a new dimension to Mark's life when he most needed a new outlet.

Victoria worked in a nonprofit organization by day, but found herself drawn to shows on real estate "flipping" and interior design when she relaxed at night with the remote control in her hand. Victoria added the learning goal "Get a real estate license" to her life list so that she could open the door to a possible career shift while also educating herself about eventually finding an underpriced house and buying, restoring, decorating, and selling it for a profit.

TAKEAWAYS FOR YOUR LIFE LIST

- Learning goals can take the form of classes, travel, watching instructive television shows, listening to books on tape, or attending work-related seminars.
- Being a lifelong learner confers physical and emotional benefits, including better memory, improved immune system function, and passion for life.

A STUDY ON creativity and healthy aging found that music is one of the best all-around exercises for senior citizens because singing or playing an instrument can reduce the risk of dementia while also lessening the pain and stiffness of arthritis. Making music is also a potent cocktail of intellectual, physical, and social benefits that make it a healthy morale booster, too.

A Few Goals to Consider

Here are some other interesting goals we've seen on clients' life lists that include play, creativity, and learning, and that might inspire you to add or change some of the goals on your own life list:

- ❏ Type a question into a search engine every day, just to learn something new.
- ❏ Read a book a week every year.
- ❏ Play paintball with my kids.
- ❏ Have a blowout party when I'm fifty for all of my friends.
- ❏ Go to a book reading or join a book club.
- ❏ Sign up for a concert series.

15

CAN MONEY BUY HAPPINESS?

Money doesn't make you happy. I now have fifty million,
but I was just as happy when I had forty-eight million.
—ARNOLD SCHWARZENEGGER

T HE NEXT AREAS of life among the sixteen that we are exploring are some of
the most practical, but important, ones; they affect us every day, and they
pertain to money, work, and retirement. How much money we earn and save,
what we do for a living, and how we choose to fill our golden years are subjects
that can often vex us, but the newest research into these realms offers some surprising information that will help you set goals that will contribute to a happier
and more meaningful life.

Money

If you take a moment to scan people's life lists, you'll find that money goals are
always there in various forms, for example, "Make more money," "Pay off all
credit card debt," "Pay for children's college education," "Buy a new house or
build a new addition," "Turn a profit in an entrepreneurial business." In fact, it's
a safe bet that for most people the goal is to make more money rather than actually give it away.

The newest research on happiness does show that more money leads to
greater happiness, but it's also true that the happiness we derive from experiences with friends, lovers, work, recreation, and retirement pursuits dwarfs any
satisfaction we get from financial gains. In fact, research has shown that people

who emphasize the accumulation of money and possessions aren't as happy as people who do not.

TIM KASSER OF Knox College and Kirk Brown of Virginia Commonwealth University studied two hundred people who embrace the voluntary simplicity movement, which focuses less on materialistic goals like money, and more on intrinsic goals like being connected to family and friends, exploring one's interests or skills, and making the world a better place. They found that although the members of the movement make around twenty-six thousand dollars per year—fourteen thousand dollars less than the control group—they are much happier, healthier, and content than those in a higher tax bracket. The conclusion: Investing time in relationships and quality of life is better for you than pursuing financial goals that are not related to intrinsic values.

Sample Money Goals

Money is not required to buy one necessity of the soul.
—HENRY DAVID THOREAU

Although the pursuit of money for money's sake doesn't seem to bring lasting joy, striving to earn a better income so that you can provide for your family, pay off credit card debt, and become educated enough about stock investment that you can read an annual financial report are the types of life list goals that can bring feelings of empowerment and success, reduce anxiety, and increase joy.

Take a look at these examples of two of our clients' successful money goals and see if they fit into your life list:

Tammy wanted to stop leaning on her parents to support her lifestyle, but she was fairly ignorant about finance and didn't know anything about investment, saving, or money management. She knew she couldn't change what she didn't track, so she set two goals for herself. One was to write down each of her credit card purchases on a sticky note that was attached to her credit card, and the other was to create a budget using money management software. As Tammy became more skillful at tracking her spending, she became more aware of how much she'd need to earn to get off the dole with her parents. Her self-confidence grew, and she even asked for a raise because she knew exactly where she was heading and how she wanted to get there. Now Tammy is self-supporting and saving money to buy her first house.

Linda is a talented photographer whose gift is creating beautiful artwork, not doing spreadsheets or preparing business tax returns. Linda spent so much money buying new camera lenses, software programs, and marketing initiatives that went nowhere that she never made a profit. Linda worked with a coach to identify the most profitable types of photo shoots and products, created a price for that work, and then offered only those services to her clients. She refused to get sidetracked by requests that would take more time and earn less money than she needed until she began to make a profit. She also asked a successful photographer who lived in her city to help her set up a spreadsheet to track the categories that mattered the most in running her business so that tax time would be less stressful. Now Linda has a thriving Web site and a booming business in making posters, and she has learned not to spend marketing money she doesn't have. Setting targeted money goals helped her save her business and build it in a strategic, planned way so that she began to love what she does for a living, instead of resenting it.

RICHARD LAZARUS OF the University of California, Berkeley, says that wealth may be a necessary buffer against the inevitable ups and downs in life. A good standard of living gives us a sense of satisfaction and security by increasing the options we have for coping with problems, including the option of paying for qualified professional assistance, such as an accountant, when we need it.

TAKEAWAYS FOR YOUR LIFE LIST

■ Money goals are often focused on the attainment or management of money or other assets, but aspiring to money for money's sake doesn't necessarily bring joy.

■ Learning how to self-regulate in financial areas can be helpful in other parts of your life that require willpower and restraint.

ALTHOUGH LOTTERY WINNERS tend to be happier overall than they were prior to hitting the jackpot, researchers found that they tend to reward themselves with cost-free treats when they are stressed or sad, such as taking a long bath, playing games, enjoying a hobby, or being with people they love. People who said they were unhappy compared to people who had

won the lottery preferred treats that cost money, such as DVDs, meals, and clothing. The researchers' conclusion: "It appears that spending time relaxing is the secret to a happy life. Cost-free pleasures are the ones that make the difference, even when you can afford anything that you want."

Work

Happiness is loving what you do.
—DAVID G. MYERS

When you love your job, it shows. People who have a passionate calling enjoy and feel energized by their work, they feel challenged on a daily basis, and they are more likely to enter states of "flow" than people who report disengagement or dissatisfaction on the job. Unfortunately, most workers don't experience these optimal conditions. Many of our clients' life lists include the goal of finding an occupation or calling that earns them enough to get by, but that also brings them feelings of satisfaction and challenge. Research backs up the importance of this quest; an exhaustive review of the connection between work and well-being reveals that a satisfied worker has better physical and emotional health, as well as a higher quality of life!

Amy Wrzesniewski does research on the happiness you derive from your job when you view it as a calling. In one landmark study, she discovered that hospital orderlies who rearranged patients' rooms on their own initiative, simply because they felt it would create a more healing environment, were happier in their jobs than people who didn't think their jobs were meaningful. Here are a few tips we've learned from our clients to help you find a passionate calling in work or retirement:

- Find out what your passions, hobbies, and talents are, and research occupations that put them to use.
- Shadow someone who does the work you think you want to do, in order to get an up-close look at the field.
- Volunteer at night and on weekends to do work in areas that intrigue you.
- Know your salary and benefits requirements.
- Be prepared for the eventuality that changing jobs can create anxiety and involves risk taking, and know that each step you take will bring you closer to your ideal occupation.
- Sitting on the fence and remaining ambivalent about changing occupations will only make you feel regretful and stuck, so add accountability to your search by working with a buddy or coach.

There are many ways to pursue work goals on your life list that involve finding passion. Here are some case histories of people who did:

Morgan grew up poor, and never again wanted to feel the kind of deprivation she experienced every day as a child, so she set her sights on becoming a well-educated, self-sufficient woman who could give generously to those in need, including members of her family. Through focus, discipline, and hard work, Morgan earned a graduate degree in pharmacology and was hired by a large drug company, where she climbed the corporate ladder and made a lot of money. But Morgan also felt empty and unmotivated by her daily responsibilities As she approached forty, and received a performance review that indicated that she appeared to be unmotivated, Morgan hired a life coach to help guide her through the process of discovering a more engaging and enjoyable line of work. First, she made a list of all her hobbies, interests, and strengths. Next, she evaluated whether or not the company she currently worked for offered a position that fit her creative talents and extroverted personality. When Morgan discovered that the company did in fact offer a job that was a better fit for her, she asked her mentor at work to guide her through the process of changing departments. Instead of leaving the company and relinquishing a salary that gave her the means to buy her mother a new stove or a front door, Morgan redirected her energies and found that overseas travel and working with teams suited her better than one-on-one research. Now, instead of waking up and dreading the drive to work, she has different responsibilities, an opportunity to be more creative, and a chance to see parts of the world she's never seen before.

———

Lavinia hired a coach in her twenties when she realized that although she had a job with a Big Eight accounting firm and was making a great salary, she felt isolated in her cubicle and had no real passion for numbers. Her mother had always stopped and started career pursuits without ever finding a satisfying job when Lavinia was young, leaving her with the unconscious message that it was better to find and stick with a job you were good at, even if you didn't love it. Lavinia and her coach identified the times she felt passionate and in a state of flow, which happened, as it turned out, whenever Lavinia was involved in decorating and volunteering at a church-sponsored health clinic. Based on this feedback, Lavinia began to look for a career that would help her combine these two areas of interest. After "shadowing" an interior decorator for one week, she decided to pursue a degree in that field at night, a move that she believed would help her pursue her passion for design while also helping people create healthier, happier home environments.

TAKEAWAYS FOR YOUR LIFE LIST

- Work that feels like a "calling" as opposed to "just a job" will usually engage you in a state of flow throughout the day, and leave you energized and satisfied.
- Work that engages your talents and strengths also brings greater happiness than work that does neither.
- Jobs that you pursue for intrinsic reasons (you wanted the job because it fit your values and interests, and not someone else's) will enhance your life satisfaction more than jobs that you take because they are "safe" or because your parents thought they would be a good fit for you.

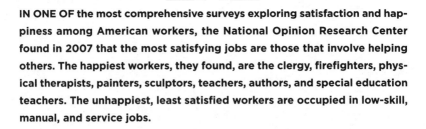

IN ONE OF the most comprehensive surveys exploring satisfaction and happiness among American workers, the National Opinion Research Center found in 2007 that the most satisfying jobs are those that involve helping others. The happiest workers, they found, are the clergy, firefighters, physical therapists, painters, sculptors, teachers, authors, and special education teachers. The unhappiest, least satisfied workers are occupied in low-skill, manual, and service jobs.

Retirement

The best work never was and never will be done for money.
—JOHN RUSKIN

Now that we are living longer than ever before, and have more time, money, and opportunities when we stop working, the old view of retirement as an endless bridge game played in the eternally warm Florida sunset has gone by the boards. Today, seniors are engaged in vigorous creative and educational pursuits, such as working in underprivileged communities, or becoming politically involved in causes that matter to them.

Louis Wray, founder and CEO of LiveAnew, is at the forefront of helping retirees reinvent themselves by using their money and time to leave the world a better place, while also matching their interests and talents to meaningful volunteer work and fun pastimes. Wray, who has combined a master's degree in applied positive psychology with knowledge accumulated through many years of working as a top executive with a major investment firm, says, "Life is meant to be lived fully alive. Retirement allows us the opportunity to replace the space left by our occupation with a renewed freedom to grow and express our inner passions."

It's never too early to have life list goals for your retirement years. Illinois psychologist Dr. Mark Frazier has worked on "graceful aging" with thousands of people between the ages of sixty-five and 105 and has found that those who spend time planning and anticipating their future are better able to accept old age and flourish emotionally.

"You have to continue to find things that are important to you. Without meaningful goals, you get into this whole attitude of 'Oh, my gosh, woe is me. . . .' If you don't have important things out in front of you, there's enough about the aging process that is not positive and you can get caught up in what you don't like about it," he cautioned.

Whether you are planning for your retirement years or are already retired, and you want to add more engagement, zest, and flow to your life, our approach can help. Here are some examples:

Carly worked in a "safe" job as a purchasing agent for three decades because it allowed her to provide for her children as a single mom without worrying about health insurance, a pension, or paying the bills every month. She worked with her coach to plan a satisfying retirement, however, because she felt that she would be able to fully enjoy her life and her passions, when she retired, by working with endangered wildlife. Starting in her late fifties, Carly researched where she wanted to live, which organizations would help her donate her time and energy most effectively, and how she wanted her days to unfold. Instead of dreading retirement, Carly now has a vibrant plan that she is anticipating for her "golden years." In fact, she has already begun to work on weekends with a wildlife rescue organization, which is giving her life even more enjoyment than she had thought it would. "I was put on this earth to help animals, and now I know I will really be able to do it," she enthuses.

―――――――

Robert retired from a busy life as a top manager at a global organization, and anticipated spending his retirement years sailing around the globe with his wife, Jane, who had always been his full partner in raising their children, running their home, and helping him manage his work-life balance. Then tragedy struck. Jane was diagnosed with Shy-Drager and was dead within one year of Robert's retirement. Shocked and in grief, Robert was left unprepared for the years of living alone that stretched in front of him. Fortunately, Robert's children lived nearby, and they quickly worked with him to help find ways to reengage in life by including him in every family gathering or outing they scheduled. In the midst of this, one of Robert's grandchildren was diagnosed with regressive autism, requiring special care, numerous therapy appointments, and expensive medical bills. Robert found his passion in life by bonding with his grandson in a new way. He volunteered to coordinate his grandson's appointments with specialists, keeping a careful spreadsheet that recorded the outcome of each visit, the costs, and whether or not reimbursement had been received. He spends many hours just reading to his grandson, and now Robert says that his retirement years are the best years of his life. Instead of spending money on trips and golf, Robert has found a new purpose and is currently creating a Web site that will help other families who live in the area navigate the maze of options, specialists, and care available for children with autism spectrum disorders.

NEOPHOBIA, THE FEAR of doing new things, contributes to the high death rates among men following retirement, according to Dr. Larry Dossey.

TAKEAWAYS FOR YOUR LIFE LIST

- Plan for retirement ahead of time, including how much money you'd like to earn from investments, part-time work, and other potential income sources, where you'd like to live, and the activities you'd like to pursue.
- George Vaillant, an expert on aging, suggests that you have a role model or "expert friend," who has successfully navigated this chapter of life, to help you through this transition.

A STUDY OF twenty-eight thousand Americans between the ages of eighteen and eighty-eight found that the happiest people are the oldest, with the chance of being happy increasing 5 percent with every ten years of age. Overall, about 33 percent of Americans say they are happy at age eighty-eight, while only 24 percent of those between eighteen and their early twenties say they are happy.

A Few Goals to Consider

Here are a few more interesting goals we've seen on life lists that focus on work, retirement, and money:

❑ Join a women's investment group and learn how to buy a stock.

❑ Find out my credit rating and make sure it's as high as it can be.

❑ Buy identity theft protection.

❑ Learn money management software and pay bills online.

❑ Take a "vocation vacation" and try on a new career instead of lounging on a beach.

❑ Build a retirement home that will accommodate the entire family, and make it an easy-to-get-to haven for future getaways for everyone in the family.

❑ Go on a safari.

❑ Start a blog about retirement and use it as a forum to connect with others.

16

THE SURROUNDINGS THAT SHAPE YOU

Home is the most popular, and will be the most enduring,
of all earthly establishments.
—CHANNING POLLOCK

Τ HE LAST OF the sixteen areas that we will consider here involve our surroundings, which include our homes, our neighborhoods, and our communities. Sometimes we forget how much these different parts of life impact our
health, happiness, and zest, but research underscores how big a role they actually
play. In the following section, we explore why goals in these realms are on many
life lists, and how we can enhance our life lists by always keeping an eye on our
quality of life in these areas.

Home

Few people would disagree that the place that we call "home" has a big impact
on how we feel about ourselves, our lives, and the way we greet each day.
Ideally, a home is a welcome respite from the world, and a place where we can
simply unwind, be surrounded by loved ones, and pursue hobbies that we
enjoy. The importance of home to our well-being may be on the increase; social
scientists and market researchers have found that people are spending more
time "nesting" in their homes and less time venturing outdoors to play or exercise. With the Internet and the rise in social networking, we can learn, socialize, work, and play indoors, as well, which can be useful or unhelpful,

depending on how much we moderate our use of these potentially isolating options.

People who set life list goals around changing their home typically want to move, spruce up, or unclutter the environment in which they live. They might also have conflicts with a roommate or family member, which can make the house feel unwelcome. Overcrowding also can create problems, including stress, unhappiness, and even serious social problems, such as delinquency. Regardless of the type of challenge that arises, though, our clients always want resolution to these dilemmas because satisfaction with where one lives can influence our contentment with life in other areas, such as how we feel about play or our relationships with others.

HAPPY FAMILIES USUALLY have homes described as "comfortable" and "warm," with ample space for family members to have privacy, if desired. Happy families also have houses described as "peaceful," with few, if any, raised voices.

Sample Home Goals

Many clients have money goals that overlap with home goals. For example, a large number of life lists we've seen have goals such as "Save money for my first house" paired with "Pay off credit card debt." Sometimes we find that the goals connect learning, play, or creativity goals with home goals, as did one client who decided to set a goal of creating a perennial garden on her front lawn that would beautify her home, put her into a state of flow, help her learn new things, and give her an opportunity to design a colorful, ever-changing creative mix of flowers and grasses.

> Julie loved bright colors and felt like her tastefully painted white walls, chosen by her decorator, did nothing to lift her spirits. So she set a goal of making her bedroom reflect her personality, and painted the walls a bold, vibrant green. The drapes went from understated to bright yellow, and the TV cabinet was transformed into a multicolored extravaganza of painted flowers, sayings, and other happy objects. The bed went from comfortable to elegant with the addition of thousand-thread-count sheets and down pillows sheathed in bold colors. Although Julie didn't spend a fortune on redoing her sanctuary, she says that her bedroom makeover is one of the best things she's ever done for herself, and she spends more time there now than she ever did before.

Deirdre's house was a complete mess when she started her life list, and she knew that uncluttering and rearranging things would give her a fresh start on tackling other goals on her list. She bartered with a friend for help uncluttering, and agreed to create a Web site for her friend's new business if she would come over and spend two days throwing things away, donating bags of clothes and toys to charity, and rearranging furniture for a more open feeling. After going through these steps, Deirdre was a new woman. She exulted to her friends that not only did she feel lighter and happier in her house, but she had found an heirloom that her mother had left her in the process, and that she'd been searching for. "I think my mom approves of my efforts to get organized," she said. Even Deirdre's children were happier about the big cleanup, and they focused more on the new play areas that had been created and not on the numerous toys that had just disappeared.

THESE THREE APPROACHES to home, neighborhood, and community can help you zero in on your goals:
- **Love it means that you find new ways to appreciate and accept your surroundings instead of trying to change them.**
- **Leave it means you either leave, or make plans to leave, with careful goal setting and accountability strategies.**
- **Fix it means you improve your surroundings by changing some of the things that you want to be different.**

TAKEAWAYS FOR YOUR LIFE LIST

- Your home contributes mightily to your happiness and outlook on life, and how you feel when you are there is an indicator of whether or not you need to set goals around changing it.
- Simple changes like a coat of paint, a garden project, uncluttering, and fixing the air-conditioning might be the inexpensive fixes you need to feel happier about your home.

Neighborhood

Don't buy the house; buy the neighborhood.
—RUSSIAN PROVERB

Closely tied with your satisfaction with your home is how you feel about your neighborhood. Research has shown that characteristics such as noise, attractiveness of buildings, yard upkeep, the mixture of homes and businesses, and green space all affect neighborhood satisfaction. Ed Diener and Marty Seligman have also found that investing time in neighborhood relationships has happiness payoffs in several areas at once, leading to improved quality of life.

In one study of women and girls, the long-range effect on their mental health of living in impoverished, crime-ridden neighborhoods was significant, including high rates of depression. Researchers found that moving to safer neighborhoods "works as well as Prozac" in terms of improving one's outlook on life. Another study showed that women are also less likely to exercise if they live in poor neighborhoods, leading to higher obesity rates.

Sample Neighborhood Goals

Quite often we see life list goals focused on neighborhood involvement, the idea being to feel safer and more connected to one's neighbors. Here are some case studies:

Vivian was new in the neighborhood, but with two young children and no family nearby, she felt isolated in her surroundings. She set the goal of walking around the neighborhood in the mornings while her neighbors were getting their children off to school and walking their dogs. Vivian struck up conversations with many of them, mentioning that she was new in the area and was looking for other young stay-at-home moms with whom to bond and form a playgroup. Eventually, Vivian's morning walks and neighborly greetings became so familiar that she was entrusted by some families to take in their newspapers and mail while they were away, which made her feel more at home in her neighborhood. At the same time, Vivian found the community of young mothers she was seeking, while creating a variety of friendships with people of different ages.

Jill had a similar problem. She worked all day and had little time to get to know her neighbors. Through a community e-newsletter, Jill learned that there would be a creek cleanup near her home, and that neighborhood volunteers were needed. She decided that this would be the perfect way for her to meet other adults on the weekends, contribute to the improvement of the area, and get some exercise. Now Jill participates in several neighborhood clubs when she has time, such as bake sales and garage sales, and feels much more connected with her neighbors than she had before.

TAKEAWAYS FOR YOUR LIFE LIST

- Your neighborhood and its appearance can help or hurt you, both mentally and physically.
- Connections with neighbors can strengthen your commitment to your neighborhood and make you feel that you belong.

Community

A community is like a ship; everyone ought to be prepared to take the helm.
—HENRIK IBSEN

The city, town, and region where you live are just as important to your happiness as your home and neighborhood are. It's important that you assess the political or religious participation in the general area, the number of parks within a short drive, how long your commute to work might be, and the quality of the schools. Affordable taxes, health and fire department services, and police protection should also be on your checklist for finding a community that meets your needs.

MANY INTERNET SITES now offer the opportunity for you to select the features that matter most to you when you are relocating or considering a move. After identifying your criteria for schools, outdoor activities, weather, public services, and ease of commute, you will receive a printout of cities that match your desires.

Sample Community Goals

Moving or relocating to a new neighborhood (or rediscovering the one you already live in) can inspire new goals to put on your life list under the general heading of "Community." For some people this boils down to whether or not there are local resources for learning, recreation, retirement, and culture, such as museums, theaters, or movie houses. The next case histories are good examples of how two women came to terms with these issues:

Lydia loved her active, social lifestyle when she was a single writer living in New York City, but she didn't realize how much she missed it until she married a poet and moved to a rambling house on the top of a mountain, two hours outside the city. Opportunities to get together with people were few and far between, but Lydia mostly missed the culture of the city, which couldn't be replicated where she lived. She worked out a gradual "leave it" strategy with her husband, and asked if he would consider moving to another city that was closer to museums and other cultural venues that Lydia values, or whether they could split their time between a small apartment in the city and a house in the country, so that they could have the best of both worlds. In the end, they decided to sell the mountaintop house and move to a town closer to New York City, in addition to wintering in Los Angeles, where they both have family, and can experience the nightlife and movie culture that they both love.

When a community hospital announced plans to create a huge landfill in a beautiful wooded area in Christine's neighborhood, she got mad. Christine had worked for months with a Realtor to find a house in the neighborhood that she loved, and that was with walking distance to day-care and public school options. Instead of pulling up stakes and moving again, Christine volunteered to spearhead an organization of local activists to fight the hospital. While her children were napping, she created a Web site with information about the landfill and solicited signatures to stop it. Although she was new in the neighborhood, she quickly became well-known and was elected president of the neighborhood association because of her commitment to fight for the safety of the neighborhood. Christine's "fix it" approach worked, and the hospital agreed to find another solution to disposing of its medical waste that didn't endanger the safety of the neighborhood.

TAKEAWAYS FOR YOUR LIFE LIST

■ When you select a community, you need to know what matters most to you before putting down roots. Do you intend to go to arts festivals and museums or possibly take classes at the community college? Are there enough bike trails for in-line skating and biking? What is the history of tax increases? Does the community support good public schools and safe streets? Is there easy access to health and medical facilities? How close is the community to work? Are there parks for recreation? Try to match as many of your needs to these characteristics as you can, and use the "love it," "leave it," or "fix it" strategy if you're dissatisfied.

A Few Goals to Consider

If you have set goals for yourself in the areas of home, neighborhood, and community, you might want to consider adding some of these to your list:

❏ Have a block party once a year to meet more of the neighbors.
❏ Join a walking, gardening, or playgroup in the community and get to know other families.
❏ Volunteer to work at the local polling place on Election Day to underscore my commitment to the importance of voting.
❏ Go to basketball or football games at the local high school.

4

SAVORING THE WINS

In the final section of the book, we want to help you learn how to properly celebrate all of the successes you experience with your life list goals, as well as understand the importance of doing so. We also want you to realize that success often happens despite setbacks, and that having a resilient attitude will help you through times when you feel discouraged. You may want to refer to the beginning of the book for a refresher on how to set the best kinds of goals so that any temporary roadblocks are easily gotten around, and you fully enjoy the experience of creating and living your best life ever.

▼

17

CELEBRATING THE WINS

Happiness does not consist in things themselves
but in the relish we have of them.
—FRANÇOIS DE LA ROCHEFOUCAULD

ONE OF THE most common, and surprising, aspects of working with people for decades on goal accomplishment is that we've found that people often fail to stop and celebrate what they've successfully completed. However, the ability to celebrate how far we've come, and enjoy the triumphs that we've labored for, is more than just a good excuse for a party. This ability to savor life's victories and sweet moments is also the sign of a healthy, high-functioning, and happy person, so we'd like to share this research and its importance with you, particularly as it pertains to the success of your own life list.

Failure to Savor

One of Greta's top ambitions was to eventually leave her government job, which didn't take advantage of her creativity or flair for entrepreneurship, and open a fitness studio that catered to elite athletes. In order to reach that goal, Greta's short-term ambition was to pass a rigorous yoga certification exam, which she planned to take while her life coach was on vacation. The coach, who had worked with her for months on this goal and its importance, was eager to be kept apprised of this development, and she told Greta she wanted to know what happened, regardless of the outcome.

When the coach came back to town and checked her messages, she was surprised to find nothing from Greta, which worried her. When Greta finally called her coach for their regular appointment, her coach asked, "What happened during the yoga test? That's all we've been talking about for months, and I haven't heard a word from you. Was it because you were disappointed in the results?"

To the coach's surprise, Greta nonchalantly acknowledged not only that she'd passed the yoga certification test, but that she'd done it with flying colors.

"Why didn't you say anything?" the astonished coach asked.

"I don't know," Greta said, somewhat sheepishly. "I guess I didn't think it would matter."

This true story is a good example of how hard it is for some of us to actually celebrate our wins, even if we know other people would like to hear about them. It turned out that Greta had not only failed to share the news with her coach; she had also kept it from other friends and family members, robbing herself of precious opportunities to prolong the happiness derived from her major accomplishment, as well as make it easier for her to remember and draw upon her memories of this significant achievement whenever she needed a self-confidence booster.

This poignant lesson showed Greta how little she enjoyed or celebrated her triumphs in life, and how much she needed to work on this skill. Not only had she failed to share her good news with her coach; she hadn't told any of her friends or family members, either. Greta decided to work on learning how to discuss and share her progress and good news with others, particularly because it allowed her to enjoy the happiness of her goal pursuit for longer periods of time, and also strengthened her relationships with people who were important to her. Another benefit: Greta's friends began to share more of their good news, too, which taught Greta some good lessons about the reciprocity of friendships, as well.

Sharing Your Success with Others

By now, you have probably begun to make some real progress toward achieving your own life goals, and may have already accomplished a few of them. You might have also started some new habits that are giving you more willpower in areas that matter to you, or perhaps you've taken baby steps toward getting a new job by updating your résumé or booking a trip to see some college friends. This is all terrific and exciting forward movement.

But if you've done all of these things in a vacuum, without the support of a cheerleading section to help you to stay on your feet when your motivation is low, or help you get back up when you fall, and celebrate with you when you are victorious, then you may be hurting yourself in some important ways that could undermine your success with long-term goal accomplishment. In fact, researchers have found that sharing our sorrows and losses with other people is critical to emotional health, but they've also discovered that it's helpful to the accomplishment of our goals, as well. When we share good news with people who care about us, social scientists call this process "capitalizing." How we do this, and whom we do it with, has a significant impact on us in many ways, and particularly regarding how we choose to pursue other goals. In fact, research has found that when we capitalize with others, it:

- **Prolongs happiness.** Studies have found that sharing the accomplishment of a goal with others amplifies your happiness in significant ways, causing you to feel much happier than you would have if you had kept your accomplishments to yourself.
- **Allows you to replay your successes.** When you share your good news with friends and other supportive people about what you've accomplished, you enjoy a "mental replay" that has a positive effect on your attitude and everything else you do over the course of the day.
- **Builds social resources.** As Barbara Fredrickson found with her "broaden-and-build" hypothesis, when you share your news with friends, you build interpersonal bridges that provide you with "social capital" to call upon in the future, and show others what your "assets" are. Celebrating alone means that no one else has the ability to share in your good fortune and feel close to you, but sharing your accomplishments initiates an "upward spiral of well-being" that promotes flourishing relationships and builds reliable support systems.
- **Improves results.** Researchers have found that the broader your social network, the better you feel about what you've accomplished, and the happier you are. Sharing with your coach is great, but sharing with a network of family, friends, coworkers, and virtual buddies feels even better.
- **Boosts self-esteem.** When you replay your victories with friends, you are giving yourself the opportunity to bask in the reflected light of their admiration. The feeling of pride you experience when your friends respond positively to the goal you've accomplished is tied in with the recognition that you have done something difficult, and that others admire you for your successful efforts.
- **Makes you healthier.** The expression of positive emotions has been found to enhance health in a variety of ways, particularly your immune-system functioning.

- **Sharing equals gratitude.** In effect, when you tell your friends about one of your achievements or a piece of good luck that has come your way, you are thanking others for their help, for the unexpected coincidences that make you feel "lucky," or for what your body or mind has allowed you to achieve. In fact, expressing *any* form of gratitude has a profound impact on how happy you feel.

- **Helps you remember good things more easily.** One of the findings of the positive psychology movement has been that "bad is bigger than good," which is why it is so important to counter or offset every negative event, comment, or situation with three positive ones. Since our brains tend to remember the negative things that happen to us, it's extremely helpful to find ways to interrupt the way we process experiences so that good things come to mind more easily. Lucky for us, sharing our successes and replaying them with friends have been found to make it much easier to remember the good things and to enjoy the emotional and physical benefits of being happy all over again.

Capitalizing with the Right People

Life is like a box of crayons. Most people are the eight-color boxes,
but what you're really looking for are the sixty-four-color boxes
with the sharpeners on the back.
—JOHN MAYER

Our clients often have difficulties knowing how to share their happiest moments or greatest accomplishments with the right people or in the right way, which can foil the process of capitalization and derail all of its benefits. For example, it's been found that sharing good news with people who are genuinely interested in you, and who are not jealous of your successes, is much more likely to foster happiness than telling someone who secretly (or not so secretly) envies you for your positive accomplishments. Research has even found *that the very first response* of the person you share your good news with is an important predictor of how good you'll feel about your goal, so you must be sure to pick that person carefully. Here are a few tips to help you maximize the beneficial effects of sharing and minimize the negative ones:

- **Blood is not thicker than water.** Don't assume that just because someone is related to you they'll be happy for you when you are successful. Automatically calling your mother or your sister when you land a big account may result in killjoy statements like "Won't that type of work bore you?" or "Won't your children suffer while you're on the road working on this account?" Many of our clients have had wake-up calls after we taught them about how to capitalize with the right people, and to take special notice of whether or not the statements uttered by family members are truly supportive or not. Quite often, the people who are happiest for you are unrelated to you, so be sure to nurture and protect those close friends and social relationships regularly.

- **Don't brag endlessly.** Don't always talk about yourself when you want to share your good news. The best relationships have a healthy give-and-take in which you are just as delighted to hear about your friends' good news as they are to hear about yours. Make a point of asking your friends about how they are doing with their own goals, and remember to appreciate and celebrate their wins, too.

AS MENTIONED IN Chapter 8, there are four ways to respond when something positive happens to someone you care about. The best response is "active constructive"—an enthusiastic response where you encourage the other person to give you more details. The others are:

- Passive constructive—an unenthusiastic, "That's great" response, followed by changing the subject, ignoring further updates, and lack of sharing with others.
- Passive destructive—a negative response disguised as a positive response, such as, "It's a lovely dress, but it emphasizes your big legs."
- Active destructive—the worst of all four responses, typified by an attack or put-down when someone hears your good news.
- Keep your third ear open. If you begin to hear passive-destructive or active-destructive statements while capitalizing on your good news, end the conversation gracefully. You may have unwittingly elicited a negative reaction from someone who secretly shares your hopes and dreams, but who has had little or no success in achieving them. Get away quickly, and be conscious of the fact that some people may not always know how to react positively to the successes of others, particularly if you work in a competitive environment.

Clever Sharing

No person is your friend who demands your silence,
or denies your right to grow.
—ALICE WALKER

Many of our clients have been surprised to find that they do not have a ready-made support system, outside of their coach, who is excited about their accomplishments and eager to hear about their successes. In some cases this has been the result of growing up in a supercompetitive environment where any type of good news was greeted with envy or anger. Others simply never understood the importance of friendship as a mutual support system, and had some catching up to do. Whatever the reason, we have found that our clients who want to find new ways to share their joy with others, while simultaneously bolstering their social network, become happier and more successful people in the process of doing so.

Here are some of the ways our clients have learned to capitalize better while also building stronger relationships with others:

- **Add thanksgiving to your prayer list.** One client noticed that the notebook that was passed around at weekly prayer group meetings asked only for prayer requests that pertained to illness, fear, or problems. She drew a line down the middle of the page and wrote "Thanksgiving" on the other side, writing down the wonderful things that had occurred in her life that week. The leader of the group was open to this change, and the rest of the group was also excited to focus on good things, not just the things that weren't working.

- **Form a "mastermind" group devoted to mutual growth and success.** Many of our clients meet regularly (and by invitation only) with others, either in person or on conference calls, to help one another set and accomplish life list goals. Because they are completely devoted to helping each member who participates, these groups are ideal for capitalizing, and many say that joining a mastermind group has been a turning point in their lives and has helped them to pursue, accomplish, and discuss goals that matter to them in an environment that is welcoming and supportive.

- **Join a virtual goals group.** One of the best things about the Internet is the proliferation of goal-setting sites where people log on, list their goals, and receive "kudos" and ideas from others who share the same goal, or who have already accomplished it. If you are shy or feel isolated or homebound for any reason, one of the first steps you can take is to join a virtual social group that will allow you to capitalize in an honest and encouraging way.

Savoring Your Success

In addition to all the research that has been done on capitalization, and how it helps to create and prolong positive moods, there is a related line of research in positive psychology devoted to the ability to savor good events so that you can readily call them up later and remind yourself of not only your triumphs, but also the many blessings in your life. Fred Bryant of Loyola University in Chicago has studied this quality and what it brings to your life and well-being, and has even created a test to help you score your own capacity for savoring, including questions such as "I feel fully able to appreciate good things that happen to me" and "I feel a joy of anticipation when I think about upcoming good things."

If you are like Greta, who had trouble sharing and celebrating her triumphs with her coach, friends, and family, you can imagine how hard it was for her to savor those same events, and call them up later and enjoy them privately again and again. In fact, Greta admitted that she rarely revisited her successes, and was surprised to hear that the process of remembering and savoring them would have any impact on her life list goals. Somewhere along the line she had internalized the idea that sharing her successes with others, or even replaying them in her own head, might earn her enemies or make her too complacent to move forward on new goals, so she simply put her head down, and unsmilingly went for the next goal, and the next, and the next, never really stopping to ask herself why she took no joy from the journey.

Why Does Savoring Matter?

I think it pisses God off if you walk by the color purple in
a field somewhere and don't notice it.
—ALICE WALKER, THE COLOR PURPLE

Savoring is a key quality that many happy and well-adjusted people naturally have in abundance, but not everyone enjoys this advantage. Because of its importance to well-being and goal accomplishment, though, we teach our clients about the necessity of savoring and assign exercises to help them learn how to do it more successfully.

Savoring differs from capitalization in some important ways. Although capitalization, or sharing, is an essential piece of enjoying our triumphs, the quality of savoring goes even further, and implies something deeper and richer. When we truly savor something, like a fine wine or a well-cooked meal, we consciously take in our surroundings and experience our emotions with a powerful sense of appreciation for what is happening in that moment. Savoring also includes the capacity to plan or look forward to something—like a vacation—and enjoy the very thought of the upcoming event. It also includes the ability to look backward and reminisce about what we've already done, and take joy from those memories.

Savoring in the Moment

Walking along the seashore at sunrise while you inhale the tangy salt air might be a perfect example of savoring in the moment, but there are an infinite number of ways to suspend your thoughts and reactions by just "being," and savoring an experience so fully and with so much enjoyment that you can derive almost as much pleasure from it in your memories as you can at the time that you actually experience it. Anyone who has watched an Olympic gold medalist pause on the podium, after winning an event, just to gaze around with tears in his or her eyes, has seen an example of savoring in the moment. These "mental snapshots" are deliberately invoked, easy-to-access memories in which to bask on a regular basis.

Seldom has a better example of savoring in the moment been captured on video than when eighteen-year-old Dustin Carter made the Ohio State wrestling tournament at the conclusion of his senior year. Dustin's achievement was not just remarkable because of the intensity and competitiveness of wrestling in his state, but because Dustin is a multiple amputee, parts of whose arms and legs were removed when he was five years old in order to save his life from the ravages of meningococcemia, an acute bacterial infection.

Dustin had dreamed of making the state tournament against all odds, since the eighth grade, when he entered the sport, and had pursued an eye-popping fitness regimen to get there that would have overwhelmed most able-bodied athletes. By taking advantage of the quickness and torso strength that he had honed over the years, Dustin finally did what no one had ever done before him; he not only beat almost every opponent in the 103-pound division who faced him, but he overcame every conceivable mental and emotional obstacle to qualify in third place for the Division II state tournament in 2008.

As the crowd rose in a sustained, emotional standing ovation when Dustin's match ended—and it became clear what he'd just pulled off—Dustin rotated slowly, looking from one section of the cheering audience to the next. With tears in his eyes, as well as an expression of awe on his own face, Dustin slowly looked, turned a fraction, looked again, turned a bit more, and kept drinking in the thousands of people who were giving him such a heartfelt tribute. After years of dreaming his "impossible" life list goal, and working toward something that most people would have discouraged him from attempting, Dustin wanted to fix this moment in his memory with a lasting "mental picture" so that he would always savor this special triumph.

• • •

Savoring in Anticipation

An intense anticipation itself transforms possibility into reality, our desires being often but precursors of the things that we are capable of performing.
—SAMUEL SMILES

People who can savor the upcoming joy of a vacation, a college reunion, or birth of a child are much more likely to be resilient and happy in the moment, since they believe good things are coming their way. Consequently, they act in ways that will ensure the future they envision.

Paul, one of our clients, used the process of anticipatory savoring to keep himself from losing hope and heart while hiding behind enemy lines during the Vietnam War. During the many weeks that he was deployed looking for downed American pilots, he would think about what awaited him at home, such as a warm bed and favorite meals. He says that the many hours he devoted to this kind of pleasurable daydreaming helped him survive when most of his platoon was killed. "Believing I was going home, instead of worrying that I'd have my brains blown out that same day, probably prevented me from making careless errors or behaving in a self-destructive way," he noted thirty years later.

Another client of ours who recognized that she rarely had anything to look forward to made a point of building anticipatory savoring into her life by booking day-long meditation retreats in her calendar that would occur several months later, and she posted pictures of the retreat site on her bulletin board. Another client decided to plan the family summer vacation earlier in the year, instead of in a last-minute rush, so that she and everyone else could talk about how much fun they'd have, what they were going to see, and what books they would read as they unwound. These small prescriptions for savoring made a world of difference in our clients' lives, and helped them to be more present in their day-to-day lives, too.

PEOPLE WHO ANTICIPATE that they will attend a humorous event, and anticipate the joy they will derive from it, experience profound chemical changes in their bodies, including reduced levels of cortisol and higher levels of positive feel-good chemicals.

Savoring in Hindsight

One of the tools that have successfully raised the level of well-being among senior citizens in nursing homes is "reminiscence therapy," a form of journaling that encourages people who are approaching the end of their lives to look back with appreciation on what they've accomplished, and to share those stories with others. Not only has it been found to increase happiness, but it is also thought to be a powerful tool to help "make meaning" of our lives—a natural urge as we grow older and feel that time is running out. A study at the University of Southampton in the United Kingdom reinforced that being nostalgic is a powerful mood booster. Subjects who wrote about a time that they remembered fondly were more cheerful, after the exercise, compared to people who simply wrote about their day.

Researchers such as Sonja Lyubomirsky have suggested that it might be even more positive to replay these types of happy scenes in our heads than it is to write them down. In one of her studies at the University of California at Riverside, she asked participants to either write or think about their happiest life experience, and she found that those who replayed their happiest moments in their heads later experienced greater well-being than those who just put their thoughts on paper. "There's a magic and mystery in positive events," she explained, "so analyzing them lifts the veil and makes wondrous events more ordinary."

———————— ⁂ ————————

WHY DON'T WE always replay happy times in our heads, and naturally boost our own moods? The answer is that negative events are much easier to remember than positive ones. Elizabeth Kensinger, a psychologist at Boston College, says that her research shows that negative experiences produce more activity in the orbitofrontal cortex and the amygdala, two emotion-processing regions of the brain. This activity results in greater recall of a negative event because the greater the activity in this part of the brain, the easier it is to bring it to mind with specificity.

Our clients who have wanted to improve their reminiscing muscle have found that there are many creative ways to do this, while also helping them achieve greater goal accomplishment. Peggy is a scrapbook consultant who helps others preserve family memories, but she decided to create a scrapbook devoted to the accomplishment of her goals, which she uses as a demonstration when selling her products. She has laid out thirty of her life list goals on pages that are decorated with stickers, inspirational slogans, and pictures of others who have accomplished the same goal, and leaves the middle of the page empty until she is ready to insert a picture of herself with the completed goal. In this way she is both savoring in anticipation and savoring in hindsight, a clever way to work on both aspects of getting better at this life list skill!

Ways to Stop, Savor, and Smell the Roses, Before and After

Savoring has many profound consequences, and people who are adept at savoring have been found to be happier, less anxious, more grateful, healthier, blessed with more friendships, and even more persistent in the face of obstacles. Here are just a few of the ways our clients have improved their ability to savor:

- **Have pictures of happy times everywhere.** Scrapbooking is a positive and useful hobby because it promotes every aspect of savoring. Happy families instinctively know how to promote savoring by putting pictures in strategic places, including walls, refrigerators, key chains, mugs, pictures, photo albums, screensavers, and anywhere else you can think of. The new trend of digital frames makes it possible to run a savoring slideshow in your home or office that reminds you of the moment your children were born, the scene of your last girls' night out on the town, the joy your pet brings to you, or anything else that puts a smile on your face.

- **Learn how to meditate.** Learning a form of meditation that encourages being more mindful of your emotions and actions can dramatically improve your ability to stay focused in each moment instead of being carried away by momentary surges of anger or anxiety.

- **Throw a thank-you party.** As mentioned earlier, this is a clever and successful way to thank people who have been there for you or your family when you experience times of stress, illness, extended travel, or juggling many balls.

- **Go on a silent retreat.** When you remove all distractions from your life, such as television and unnecessary conversations and sounds, you begin to notice things that may have escaped you before, like the crunch of gravel under your feet, or the sharp scent of autumn air. This kind of quick intervention into your life can have a lasting impact and can help you understand the meaning and importance of savoring each moment of life.

- **Talk less and listen more.** When you are busy talking and thinking about what you'll say next, you are not listening to what is happening around you. When you quietly listen to others, and to what is happening around you, you are less distracted and more able to focus on what is happening, which will also have the benefit of improving your friendships.

- **Institute a weekly savoring day.** In many religions, one day a week is set aside as a sacred day of attending to God and one's moral growth. This can involve not using electricity, making elaborate meals, or shopping. The point of a savoring day, however, is to also stop and take time to take stock of your life, be grateful for your blessings, and focus on what is positive.

- **Stop making upward social comparisons.** The happiest people have a way of looking around and, when they notice that they have more than others, counting their blessings. Unhappy people look "up" and make upward social comparisons, in which they devalue their moment of triumph by seeing who has more than they have, not how far they themselves have come! A study of Olympic silver and bronze medalists found a fascinating distinction: Silver medalists were more unhappy because they tended to look "up" and regret what they hadn't achieved, while bronze medalists looked "down" and saw how much better they'd done than everyone else, which leads us to believe that a "bronze medal outlook" could be a good savoring strategy.

- **Write a holiday savoring letter.** During the holidays, send a letter that records the wonderful things that happened over the course of the year to you and your family, instead of just another picture of your children on a beach or in their Sunday finest. When you receive other people's holiday letters, take a moment to reach out to them through a call or e-mail and ask them to tell you more about something that caught your eye in the card, and then really listen to their response. The effort to help others capitalize will not only make them happy, but also will reinforce your own social resources.

- **Tell stories often.** Happy families are regular storytellers, which may help explain why savoring flourishes in these families. By retelling your children's exploits in front of family and friends, and allowing your spouse to replay his college gridiron greatness or her rowing races, you help create a familiar and friendly savoring environment that benefits you and everyone else.

Where Your Life List Is Now

You may have checked some goals off your list, and now it's time to celebrate! Jack Welch, the former CEO of General Electric, says that celebration of successful accomplishments is part of how a high-functioning company operates, so we want you to celebrate your own goals now by planning a capitalization e-mail to your friends or throwing a party for yourself. Take a look at your list, pick a few that you are really proud of, and then find a way to capitalize and savor. Be creative!

Life List Exercises and Worksheets

❏ Fill out the capitalizing worksheet called "Share and Share Alike," and add to it as you accomplish goals and share them with others (see page 250). By keeping track of this worksheet and updating it regularly, you will be able to see who you are sharing your good news with, how they reacted, how that made you feel, and whether or not it helped you create your own upward spiral of well-being. This worksheet also allows you to track how often you successfully capitalize with others on their accomplishments, which is also important.

18

HITTING SPEED BUMPS

Our greatest glory is not in never falling,
but in rising every time we fall.
—CONFUCIUS

IN CHAPTER 17 we talked about the importance of savoring the "wins" and celebrating the accomplishment of your life list goals with friends, family, and those who are invested in your happiness, and who are part of a social network that is uplifting and elicits your best efforts. Sharing your wins with the right people not only will allow you to enjoy your accomplishments for a longer period of time, but also will make you happier and more successful in other areas of your life.

But what if you've gotten to this point and have nothing to celebrate, or at least you don't think you have any wins to speak of? Or what if you went after a goal and it became impossible to complete because your circumstances changed dramatically, and you are still reeling from that disappointment? Don't despair—it's not the end of the world, nor does it predict what will happen to you in the future. Sometimes it takes a while to lay the groundwork for success to take root, but that planning can pay off handsomely when it's time. For example, one of our clients spent a full year changing her circle of support before going after any of her biggest goals because she recognized how much easier it would be to make progress when everyone around her was supportive, positive, and proactive.

. . .

Fallen Ice Skaters

There are many things we need to know and learn about dealing with setbacks and disappointments, particularly with regard to the accomplishment of goals. After all, if you are brave enough to have dreams and go after them, you need to be strong enough to deal with the fact that you won't always get what you want. In fact, no one does, so understanding that fact and having appropriate coping skills is an essential piece of your life list program.

We liken this to what often happens in an ice-skating competition, when the skater misses a jump or slips on the ice and lands on his or her rear end while the music plays on. These skaters never remain defeated on the ice, staring at the crowd in dismay. Without exception, they gamely get to their feet and keep skating, picking up their program wherever they can in order to finish with their best shot.

After the performance, they carefully analyze their mind-set, support system, and self-care, and strategize about how they can strengthen their program in order to avoid future disappointments. That's exactly what we want you to do. If you've slipped and taken a fall, let's take a look at what you can do to keep going and stay positive about achieving your goals. .

Win Some, Lose Some

Quitting smoking is easy. I've done it a hundred times.

—MARK TWAIN

As you've undoubtedly experienced, disappointments are inevitable—everyone has setbacks—so be prepared for a few speed bumps along the road to achieving your life list goals. Don't let a "lapse" become a "collapse." One misstep is just one misstep. One failure is one failure. Don't globalize your disappointment and throw your goals or life list out the window. The most important thing about having a setback is how you handle it, how you use it to define yourself, and what you do to right the ship and keep going.

Here's an example of how one man handled a massive disappointment in his life without throwing out all of his goals:

Paul Thomas is a personal trainer and martial artist in the Washington, D.C., area who grew up in the projects of Perth Amboy, New Jersey. Through aggressive goal setting and finding role models, such as his first martial arts grand master and his parents, who taught him how to persevere despite seemingly insuperable obstacles, he got what he wanted and avoided the drugs, mediocrity, and apathy that he saw all around him. In 2001, Paul won the Naturals bodybuilding contest in Las Vegas, having sculpted a powerful body without the use of steroids or performance-enhancing drugs. Several years later, he spent months preparing for another national competition, disciplining himself with rigorous training, a careful diet, and exemplary self-care. The week of the competition, however, he slipped on a patch of slick grass while he was running and took a hard fall. The moment he hit the ground, he knew his goal of competing in, let alone winning, the competition was gone. Months of hard work were obliterated in a second because of this pulled muscle. But instead of whining or being depressed, Paul went home and stayed in a room for about twenty-four hours, where he focused on making peace with his disappointment. He got all of his sadness and regret out of his system by systematically reviewing everything he had done, what it had meant to him, and what other goals he could set to keep himself focused and energized. When Paul reappeared at work, his clients were surprised to see no lingering traces of sadness or self-pity. "I did everything I could do, and I can't change a thing. On to the next goal," he told everyone who asked how he was handling the disappointment. Paul's resilience and positive attitude provided even stronger role modeling for his clients.

Love Yourself

Mark R. Leary, a professor of psychology and neuroscience at Duke University, has done research on why some people roll with life's punches, while others crumple at the first sign of a calamity. The difference, he found, is that people who have self-compassion are able to love themselves despite their failures, and see setbacks as part of the normal human condition. "Life's tough enough with little things that happen," Leary commented. "Self-compassion helps to eliminate a lot of the anger, depression, and pain we experience when things go badly for us." Leary's research has found that people who are resilient about setbacks in life share the following characteristics:

- They have fewer negative emotional reactions to real, remembered, and imagined bad events.
- They are able to accept responsibility for a negative event, but don't take on negative feelings about it.
- They don't judge themselves on the negative outcome of a failed marriage, competitive event, or bad interview, for example. They tend to see themselves kindly, regardless of whether these events turn out well or not.

If you are being particularly hard on yourself because you are basing your feelings of self-worth on whether or not you have succeeded at everything you have attempted, try practicing some acceptance, and talking to yourself as you would speak to a beloved child or dear friend. This practice of "loving-kindness" meditation, in which you send love and compassion to yourself and others, can also help free you from feelings of discouragement or inaction.

The Stages of Change

In addition to evaluating yourself more kindly, it might be a good idea to consider whether or not you have selected the right time to go after certain goals, and if your readiness for change needs to be reassessed or refocused in order for you to move ahead.

James Prochaska, John Norcross, and Carlo DiClemente are practicing clinical psychologists, university professors, and researchers who for decades have been at the forefront of studying how successful self-change occurs, and they are often the first people reporters call when they want a scientific take on New Year's resolutions. Dozens of studies over several decades have upheld their view that people who change their habits and behaviors go through predictable stages of change and that all of these stages are necessary if you want to initiate and maintain a positive shift—to stop smoking or lose weight, for example. They've found that rushing too quickly from one stage to another, or even skipping a stage altogether, will probably lower your chances of goal success.

What are the stages, and how do you know where you are? Here's a quick self-assessment from Prochaska, Norcross, and DiClemente's excellent book, *Changing for Good*:

STAGES OF CHANGE SELF-ASSESSMENT

1. I solved my problem more than six months ago.
2. I have taken action on my problem within the past six months.
3. I am intending to take action in the next month.
4. I am intending to take action in the next six months.

Answering no to all four statements indicates precontemplation.

Answering yes to statement 4 and no to everything else indicates contemplation.

Answering yes to the last two statements and no to the first two indicates someone in preparation.

Answering yes to statement 2 and no to statement 1 indicates someone in action.

An honest answer of yes to statement 1 indicates someone in the maintenance stage.

After taking this self-assessment, you should be able to see if you have misjudged your readiness for accomplishing a goal, or have failed to see the actions you have taken in other important stages, so read on for a closer look at how to assess where you are with the stages of change with regard to your own goals.

Where Are You Now?

Regardless of where you are in the process of making change in your life, our program can help you. If you find that any of the following categories apply to you, please go back and reread the chapters that specifically address these topics and take another shot at the exercises we recommend:

- **Precontemplation.** The stage in which you are stuck in one place and not ready to take action is called precontemplation. Typically, other people are aware of whatever it is you might need to change, but you are either unwilling to face it yourself or completely unaware of the issue. If you are in this stage, you might have put a goal on your life list because you think you "should" do it, or because someone else set the goal for you. If, consequently, you are not feeling successful with your goals, recheck your list to make sure you haven't put any precontemplation items (also called "controlled" or "extrinsic" goals) on your list. For example, you may be failing at certain goals such as cutting back on work hours or spending more time with your family because you never thought these areas really merited your attention, and they were on your list only to please someone else.
- **Contemplation.** The contemplation stage, in which you are contemplating the "whys" and "hows" of change, sometimes takes a while. It is a very important period, nevertheless, and progress on goal accomplishment can be real, but almost undetectable. Examples of contemplation progress include being more thoughtful about how to save money and being more aware of impulse buying, or watching your peer group go after meaningful jobs while you remain stuck in a job that is making you increasingly unhappy. If you haven't achieved a goal but have made progress in contemplation, don't gloss over it. Reward yourself for progress on your precontemplation subgoals, because, bear in mind, by completing these steps you will ultimately succeed at accomplishing your goals.

■ **Preparation.** In the preparation stage, you are readying the platform for your life list goal accomplishments. Preparation can mean clearing your schedule for a scuba diving class in six months, interviewing prospective life coaches prior to selecting one, or throwing out "fat" clothes prior to joining a gym and starting a weight-loss program. Again, preparation is very significant, and without it, you cannot leap into the next stage, which is where all the glory seems to reside. Reward yourself for preparation, and perhaps push the expected date of actual goal accomplishment back a little bit to accommodate the realities of changed circumstances in your life.

■ **Action.** Action is the glamorous part of goal accomplishment, because it is where change and victory occur. When you take action, for example, you are interviewing for and getting the job you want, becoming a regular Meals on Wheels volunteer, and going on meditation retreats, and your positive efforts at change have become comfortable habits. Taking action doesn't always result in lasting success, though. Researchers have found that it usually takes people around seven attempts to accomplish New Year's resolutions, and that only 5 percent of these people will get to the next stage of change without experiencing at least one setback. Every bit of forward progress, though, is reason for celebration.

■ **Maintenance.** In the maintenance phase, you are instilling in yourself and practicing regular habits of self-control, and overcoming stressful challenges that might cause you to slip backward. Getting to the maintenance stage and staying there is difficult, however, since many self-changers have regular setbacks, each of which must be followed with action in order for you to keep moving forward. In fact, taking proactive steps within one month of a "slip" has been found to double your chances of success in the following six months, as opposed to taking no action following a slip.

■ **Termination.** The termination stage describes the moment when you have accomplished a goal and checked it off your list, when there is no apparent likelihood of backsliding. Typically, termination means that goals such as integrating regular exercise into your life, overcoming an eating disorder, or not swearing in front of your superiors are so successful that you can put a big, fat checkmark next to that goal and celebrate like there's no tomorrow. But don't forget that the previous phases can and do give you chances to pat yourself on the back and give yourself credit for what you've accomplished. .

• • •

Resilience and Reinventing Yourself

For every complex problem, there is an easy answer, and it is wrong.
—H. L. MENCKEN

After assessing whether or not you have jumped too quickly into goal accomplishment, without going through the preparatory steps to make it stick, it's important to examine whether or not you are resilient enough to get through the inevitable hassles and stresses that are part of modern life, and which we all have to cope with at one time or another.

Some people appear to have more troubles and disappointments than most of us, but still manage to push through to get what they want. These resilient individuals have been studied in order to discover the traits and qualities they embody and practice so that those of us who crumble more easily can change, grow, and pursue our goals with more purpose and direction.

Karen Reivich and Andrew Shatte are psychologists and researchers who have studied, taught, and written extensively about resilience. The pioneering work they have done at the University of Pennsylvania's Penn Resilience Program has helped underprivileged students learn how to become more resilient and optimistic in the face of multiple challenges. Their work has proven that resilience skills are available to everyone, from CEOs to middle school students, and that with some coaching and awareness, all of us can have more resilience in our lives, regardless of our childhood experiences or predisposition to handle stress well. The research shows that people who lack resilience typically share the following characteristics—some of which might be contributing to real or perceived roadblocks to your own resilience and achievement of life list goals:

- **Poor stress responses.** People who are especially resilient do not fall apart under stress. In fact, they are usually described as "stress-hardy" individuals who actually get more zestful and optimistic when things are looking bleak. These are the ones who are typically selected to lead platoons in war and run major corporations because they stay focused on the mission, regardless of the chaos around them. Learning better stress responses will help you to stay committed to goals like losing weight and staying away from cigarettes, because emotional stress is the most frequently cited reason for relapsing. Proven stress busters such as exercise, meditation, and journal writing (see pages 35–45), can help you adjust and refocus your responses to stress and move beyond it to get what you want.
- **They quit too easily.** Persistence is the hallmark of resilient people, who, when they hit an obstacle, look for another way to accomplish the same

goal. In fact, studies have found that success increases measurably when you have two or more avenues available to accomplish the same goal, so always have a Plan B if Plan A fails. People who quit their goals are often victims of the infamous what-the-hell rule, typically seen among dieters or smokers who think that a single slip is enough reason to drop their efforts for the rest of the day—or even indefinitely.

- **They leave out important pieces of goal accomplishment.** If you set a big goal but skip the important parts—that is, the help of a socially supportive network, accountability to other people, measurable sub-goals, role models to help you build self-efficacy, approach versus avoid-ance goals, and other factors that were outlined on page 59 in the descriptions of "good" goals—then you may have set yourself up for failure. Take another look at Chapter 4 (see page 49) and revisit optimal ways to structure your goals.

- **They stay committed to an unworkable goal.** If one of your goals was to compete in your sport at the Olympics, but an accident has left you injured and unable to walk, you need to reengage in life with different and viable goals. Dave Denniston knows this. In 2001, he was at the top of the swimming world when he won the NCAA Championships in the two-hundred-yard breaststroke for Auburn University. Within a few years, he had a sledding accident that left him in a wheelchair with use-less legs and shattered dreams. After briefly succumbing to depression, he set his sights on swimming again, but as part of the Paralympic Games, which gave him a fresh set of meaningful, challenging goals. Now Denniston spends much of his time educating people about how to overcome the disappointments that arise when life hands you a lemon, and how to find a new set of goals that will reenergize your spirit and your life.

- **They don't reach out for help.** Resilient people have an amazing abil-ity to find other people who can and will help them accomplish their goals. For example, London Fletcher is a Washington Redskins football player who had every conceivable reason to live a life of low ambition and bitter regrets. When he was young, his sister was raped, beaten, and left to die on the railroad tracks. After this horrendous event, his mother succumbed to street life and drugs. Fletcher says he was saved by a bas-ketball coach at a recreation center who let him stay there as much as possible to avoid the lure of the streets, and by a benefactor who adopted Fletcher's sixth-grade class as part of the "I Have a Dream" Foundation, promising the children that he would underwrite their college educa-tions if they stayed in school and worked hard. The benefactor, Leonard Schwartz, and his wife, Charlotte Kramer, said that Fletcher just soaked up everything they offered, and was one of only twelve students out of seventy-two who took full advantage of their offer. He went on to achieve his dream of finishing college and enjoying a pro football career. Fletcher now has his own foundation and strives to help kids just like he used to be.

- **They are unhappy.** Resilient people are happier and more optimistic than others, so if you need to increase your happiness level, reread Chapters 2 and 3 on how important it is to perform happiness exercises every day, such as gratitude journaling and exercise (see page 36). You can also voluntarily change your own positivity ratio (see page 109) by deliberately ensuring that every negative event of your day is countered by at least three positive ones. Seeing a mental health professional could also be a wise choice, because prolonged sadness is not only a health liability; it will make it harder to accomplish your goals—or even recognize progress when it occurs!

- **They have poor self-control.** Resilient people do not give in to momentary urges to lash out at others, drink themselves into oblivion, or otherwise exhibit poor willpower and an inability to delay gratification. Being able to put off momentary pleasure for long-term gain is possibly the most important driver of goal accomplishment, and there are many proven ways to become better at this skill, including exercising regularly, monitoring your spending, curbing automatic urges to speed or swear for specific periods of time, or logging change behavior in a journal. It might be a good idea to go back and spend some time on the exercises in Chapter 6 (see pages 85–88) if your resilience is continually undermined by self-regulation failures such as alienating friends with your temper, or blurting out your thoughts without censoring them first.

- **They don't see things realistically.** People who are resilient are able to separate reality from their emotions, and are more likely to interpret a setback as a momentary blip on the screen. Unresilient people think, however, that a setback occurred because there was something wrong with them. If you are prone to misinterpret events as more disastrous than they really are, we encourage you to seek out someone who can help you dispute your negative thoughts (as Albert Ellis practiced in rational emotive therapy) or read some of the literature on how to think more optimistically, such as Ellis's *Feeling Better, Getting Better, Staying Better*; Karen Reivich and Andrew Shatte's *The Resilience Factor*; or Marty Seligman's *Learned Optimism.*

- **They don't celebrate little victories.** Resilient people know when to pat themselves on the back, and they don't punish themselves when they fail. In fact, punishment is rarely used by successful self-changers, according to Prochaska and his colleagues, while rewards are extremely successful. Be sure that you are savoring your small wins and capitalizing on them with the right people, because these small celebrations might play a bigger role in creating resilience than you previously thought.

- **They don't look for low-hanging fruit.** Resilient people find ways to accomplish smaller goals in valued areas when a big goal eludes them. Remember that quality of life has been shown to improve from the effect of "happiness spillover" when you make progress in another area of your life that matters to you, so be sure to always have at least three to five goals in your crosshairs as opposed to being stubbornly focused on only one.

- **They don't see the humor in life.** Resilient individuals have a way of using humor to cushion their falls and to reframe sad events in order to get perspective. If you don't have a funny bone, think about poking a bit of fun at yourself from time to time, and don't look at everything as a serious, life-and-death endeavor.

Angelo's story illustrates how important it is to always have a Plan B for your goals, and to avoid the what-the-hell effect if a goal is important enough to you:

Angelo is a twenty-one-year-old man who lives near the Delaware resort of Rehoboth Beach. Angelo saw his life dreams evaporate when his knee was "blown out" in a collision during a high school football game. As a well-recruited linebacker, Angelo had entertained hopes of going to college on a football scholarship, but in one instant, his future was snatched away. Abandoned by his parents and many of his friends, who no longer saw him as a glamorous star, Angelo lost hope and fell in with the wrong crowd. He stopped working out and gave up the idea of going to college or playing football. Then he began to date a young woman who believed in him and who encouraged him to continue rehabilitation on his knee and try to go to a smaller school than the one he had once dreamt of going to. Now Angelo is preparing to marry this woman, with whom he has two young children, and is running a forty-yard sprint in 4.3 seconds again. He works out every morning, holds down two jobs, and has sent out a new highlights reel to prospective coaches at small schools, where he has a good chance of getting a scholarship as a walk-on player within the year. Angelo is no longer the defeated young man he once was, and now understands that he still has the chance to achieve his original goal of playing football in college on a scholarship, but that it will probably happen later in his life, and in a different way, than he had originally envisioned. Learning how to be flexible and benefiting from another person's passionate belief in his abilities was all it took to transform Angelo from a guy who'd given up on his dreams to someone who has the resilience to make them happen.

Final Tips on Life List Success

In this book, we have attempted to give you the benefit of all the available research on goal accomplishment so that you can create, pursue, and achieve your goals and dreams. We firmly believe in the power of the human spirit and the vast possibilities that exist within all of us to do more than we may have ever dreamed of. Too often we find that people settle for lives of mediocrity and reactivity, and instead of being ambitious, they decide that their goals are "too hard," "too unrealistic," or "too far away" to be worth an investment of time and energy. With this book, you now know that there is hope and that your goals and dreams are well within your reach.

The connection between pursuing challenging goals and being happier is impossible to deny. We have shown you that happy people are optimistic, believe in their capabilities, and wake up every day with a variety of short-term and long-term goals that engage them and provide meaning, purpose, and pleasure in their lives. Happy people live longer, have more friends, are healthier, persist in their endeavors, and succeed more often in life *because* of their upbeat outlook on life.

By connecting the research on goal setting with the new science of positive psychology, we have given you all the tools you could ever need to move ahead in life and keep going past every setback or challenge that might occur. Our research-driven approach allows you to assess the quality of your life, create and move toward optimal goals, and take control of your life in all of the areas that contribute to making you more resilient, proactive, gritty, and hopeful. We hope you use this book well and often, and inspire those around you to create their best lives, too—which could be the best legacy any of us can leave behind.

Where Your Life List Is Now

We close with the story of a man whose resilience continues to inspire more than one hundred years after his death. This particular gentleman was born to a poor family, and he failed more often than he succeeded. He lost almost every contest he entered, and his one true love died after spurning his marriage proposal. He outlived most of his children, one of whom died at the age of eleven, causing him to wail in profound grief in the boy's room for two days. He was reviled by many people, and struggled with his own private battles with depression throughout his life. Regardless of these monumental setbacks and tragedies, Abraham Lincoln achieved his goal of becoming president of the United States, and is now remembered as one of the greatest statesmen, leaders, and men of all time.

If Abe Lincoln never quit on his dreams, and found a way to keep going forward toward the achievement of goals that were important to him and the people of his time, then you can, too.

Your best life is in your hands, waiting to be shaped, nurtured, and celebrated. Now, go and make it happen.

PART

5

LIFE LIST EXERCISES AND WORKSHEETS

This section of the book is where we give you a comprehensive set of worksheets and exercises that are designed to help you deepen your understanding of the research-backed approaches to goal accomplishment and happiness in our life list approach. We also provide a list of additional resources that you may want to explore as you continue to grow, change, learn, and live the fullest and most meaningful life possible.

▼

ONE HUNDRED THINGS TO DO BEFORE I DIE

ONE OF THE most interesting and fun exercises we can do is make a comprehensive list of experiences we would like to have before we die. This list serves as a wonderful way to keep track of the many ways in which you can conceive and achieve the dreams you have for yourself. Please complete this list, refer to it often, and check off the experiences as you knock them off!

To help you complete this list, there are some prompts and questions before each set of ten goals. If you are having no trouble filling in your list, just skip them, but if you need help thinking outside the box, you might find these questions useful.

▶ THE TOP TEN

What are ten burning desires you have for yourself?

A certain trip?
Meeting a certain person?
Achieving a certain milestone?

Top Ten Burning Desires	Date Completed
1.	
2.	
3.	
4.	
5.	
6.	
7.	
8.	
9.	
10.	

ONE HUNDRED THINGS TO DO BEFORE I DIE

▶ ELEVEN THROUGH TWENTY

Keep Dreaming

What is your next set of dreams?
Would you like to go on a safari?
Rollerblade through Holland?
Be a guest at a deluxe spa for a week?
Complete a triathlon?

Eleven through Twenty	Date Completed
11.	
12.	
13.	
14.	
15.	
16.	
17.	
18.	
19.	
20.	

ONE HUNDRED THINGS TO DO BEFORE I DIE

▶ Twenty-one through Thirty

It's getting harder, so dig deeper.

What were your fondest wishes as a child?
Where there any dreams you buried after you left school
  that you'd like to revisit?

Twenty-one through Thirty	Date Completed
21.	
22.	
23.	
24.	
25.	
26.	
27.	
28.	
29.	
30.	

ONE HUNDRED THINGS TO DO BEFORE I DIE

▶ THIRTY-ONE THROUGH FORTY

If you're stuck, think of experiences that might feel like fairy tales.

Visiting Paris in the spring?
Driving down the coast of Italy?
Visiting the ruins of Pompeii?
Scuba diving in the Red Sea or on the Great Barrier Reef?

Thirty-one through Forty	Date Completed
31.	
32.	
33.	
34.	
35.	
36.	
37.	
38.	
39.	
40.	

ONE HUNDRED THINGS TO DO BEFORE I DIE

▶ FORTY-ONE THROUGH FIFTY

What are your professional and financial goals?

Do you have a dream of retiring at a certain age?
Where? With whom?
Is there a career you'd like to explore before you die?

Forty-one through Fifty	Date Completed
41.	
42.	
43.	
44.	
45.	
46.	
47.	
48.	
49.	
50.	

ONE HUNDRED THINGS TO DO BEFORE I DIE

▶ Fifty-one through Sixty

Make sure you are listing all of the significant people you'd like to hear, meet, or study with.

Do you want to have dinner at the White House?
Meditate with the Dalai Lama?
Have lunch with Oprah Winfrey?

Fifty-one through Sixty	Date Completed
51.	
52.	
53.	
54.	
55.	
56.	
57.	
58.	
59.	
60.	

ONE HUNDRED THINGS TO DO BEFORE I DIE

▶ SIXTY-ONE THROUGH SEVENTY

Be outrageous here! What do you secretly want to do that might sound silly to others?

Play the piano at Nordstrom?
Sing in a rock band?
Walk the red carpet at the Cannes Film Festival?
Go to the Oscars?
Meet the pope?

	Sixty-one through Seventy	Date Completed
61.		
62.		
63.		
64.		
65.		
66.		
67.		
68.		
69.		
70.		

ONE HUNDRED THINGS TO DO BEFORE I DIE

▶ SEVENTY-ONE THROUGH EIGHTY

What are your deepest values and spiritual beliefs, and how would these play themselves out in the next ten experiences?

Seventy-one through Eighty	Date Completed
71.	
72.	
73.	
74.	
75.	
76.	
77.	
78.	
79.	
80.	

ONE HUNDRED THINGS TO DO BEFORE I DIE

▶ EIGHTY-ONE THROUGH NINETY

If you were given six months to live, what would you make sure you accomplished in that time period?

Forgive someone whose actions hurt you?
Go after true love, despite what others might think?
Laugh and love more, and work less?

Eighty-one through Ninety	Date Completed
81.	
82.	
83.	
84.	
85.	
86.	
87.	
88.	
89.	
90.	

ONE HUNDRED THINGS TO DO BEFORE I DIE

▶ Ninety-one through One Hundred

If you die tonight, what do you most want to have experienced, said, seen, or accomplished?

Ninety-one through One Hundred	Date Completed
91. _____	_____
92. _____	_____
93. _____	_____
94. _____	_____
95. _____	_____
96. _____	_____
97. _____	_____
98. _____	_____
99. _____	_____
100. _____	_____

ALL BUT DISSERTATION GOALS

ALL BUT DISSERTATION (ABD) indicates incompletion of a doctoral degree, and has also become a shorthand term to describe someone who fails to accomplish the last step of a long, arduous goal. ABD fits a large number of doctoral candidates in the United States, according to statistical reports of the various state and government agencies monitoring higher education. These people fail to complete their PhDs despite successfully sustaining the effort through the doctoral qualifying examinations, completing language requirements, and fulfilling residency coursework.

As part of creating an authentically fulfilling list of life goals, it's important that we revisit any of our unfinished ABD goals to examine whether or not they should be added to our list. ABD goals have a way of weighing us down, particularly if they remain as longings that follow us for years when the finish line is still within sight. However, some goals are unfinished because they didn't fit our lives and we redirected our energies. If they don't gnaw at us, they are not ABD goals.

Are there any ABD goals that you'd like to reopen and pursue now? If so, please use this sheet to write down the goals, the reason you stopped the goal pursuit (bad timing, ran out of money, changed your mind, lost confidence), and what you need to do to get a PhD in this goal.

Goal	Why Stopped	Steps to Take
1.		
2.		
3.		
4.		
5.		

"BEN" THERE, DONE THAT

THIS WORKSHEET IS in honor of one of our Founding Fathers, Benjamin Franklin, who decided to strengthen his character by taking one virtue at a time—such as modesty, humility, temperance, or sloth—and marking with an X each day he successfully refrained from bad behavior in that area.

Franklin's program worked for reasons that goal specialists of the twenty-first century understand: He focused on only one major self-control change at a time, he monitored his behavior in a journal, and he proceeded to working on the next quality only after perfecting the one before it. Franklin's well-known efforts spurred the creation of the Franklin Covey organizational system, so there's no doubt that embarking on this worksheet can help you adopt a new habit, too.

In the first column, write down the behavior you'd like to perform for at least two weeks. It should involve effort and self-control. Good examples include starting a fitness program, meditating for ten minutes every morning, being on time for every appointment, and following the speed limit. In the next column, put an X for every day that you successfully performed the desired action, and do not move on to your next change until you have completed two successful weeks.

Date	Behavior	Completed

BRIGHT LIGHTS AND BLACK HOLES

6:00 AM		1 2 3 4 5
8:00 AM		1 2 3 4 5
10:00 AM		1 2 3 4 5
12:00 PM		1 2 3 4 5
2:00 PM		1 2 3 4 5
4:00 PM		1 2 3 4 5
12:00 AM		1 2 3 4 5

Date: _____

COPY THIS FORM and use it for a week to track how you feel at various times during the day. For each time listed on this sheet, write down whom you are with, talking to on the phone, or engaging in another way, such as e-mail. Then rate yourself on a scale of 1 to 5 on your well-being, with 1 being the worst you can feel and 5 being the best. At the end of one week, you will have a good idea of which situations and which people constitute the "black holes" and "bright lights" in your life.

GOAL SUCCESS PLAN

FOR EVERY GOAL, complete the following worksheet and share it with others:

Goal: _____

Is the goal:

❑ Specific   ❑ Challenging   ❑ Approach

❑ Measurable   ❑ Value Driven   ❑ Intrinsic

❑ Accountability   ❑ Involved   ❑ Flow

What steps are necessary to achieve the goal?

_____

_____

_____

What might stand in the way of accomplishment, and what will I do to overcome these barriers?

_____

_____

_____

How will I enhance my commitment and motivation? For example, whom can I be accountable to and how can I precommit myself to action (paying for a class, for example)?

_____

_____

_____

Who else, or what else, do I need to be successful?

_____

_____

_____

What are the interim milestones necessary to chart my progress?

_____

_____

_____

Who is part of my accountability team?

_____

_____

_____

IFS, ANDS, AND BUTS

RESEARCHER PETER GOLLWITZER has discovered an elegant solution to the common problem of getting stuck on the "action" part of a difficult goal. Gollwitzer discovered that people who created an "implementation intention"—a statement of what they intended to implement when they encountered a situation or person—tripled their likelihood of goal accomplishment, particularly if the goal is challenging.

An implementation intention, also known as an "if-then scenario," goes like this:

"When I encounter *X* in the environment, I will do *Y*."
Following are a few sample "if-then" statements:

"When I sit down in front of my computer,
I will pay my bills online before I do anything else."

"When the morning newspaper arrives,
I will take the dog on a ten-minute walk."

"When I see my pedometer,
I will put it on the waistband of my pants."

In the spaces below, write down your goal and the "if-then" action that will help you make it happen:

Goal	If (something you encounter)	Then (I will do this action)

JOLTS OF JOY

THOUGH SCIENTIFIC EVIDENCE has now found that things like kindness, exercise, and meditation are proven to improve your mood, happiness boosters are unique to every individual. Make your own list of things that bring you jolts of joy, and add to it as you encounter new situations and things that enhance your delight. When you need an emotional boost, this list can serve as your reminder of things that might be added quickly and effectively to put a smile back on your face.

_____

_____

_____

_____

_____

_____

_____

_____

_____

_____

_____

_____

_____

_____

_____

_____

_____

_____

_____

LIFE LISTS ARE A RISKY BUSINESS

He who is not courageous enough to take risks will accomplish nothing in life.

—MUHAMMAD ALI

THE BIGGER THE goal, the bigger the risks you'll need to take to make it happen. Because fear is often the main thing standing between you and action, please use the first five lines to write down the risks you've already taken to get what you want, and what happened as a result. (Reminding yourself of previous bold actions that got results will inspire you to design and take fresh risks.) In the next five lines, write down five new risks you could take, and what life list goals you'd like to achieve as a result.

Risks I've taken and the results I've gotten from them:

1. _____

2. _____

3. _____

4. _____

5. _____

**New risks I'd like to take
and the goals I'd like to accomplish as a result:**

1. _____

2. _____

3. _____

4. _____

5. _____

MEDITATION AND MINDFUL
BREATHING FOR BEGINNERS

THE GOAL OF meditation or mindful breathing is to calm you and make you aware of thoughts that may be unpleasant or self-defeating, which you can explore and "cognitively restructure." It also teaches you to focus most of your attention on the present moment and what is happening inside you.

To begin your meditation or mindful breathing:

1. Keep your posture as erect as possible as you stand, walk, or sit. Keep your shoulders high and your back as straight as possible. (See your physician about how erect a posture you can assume if you feel any pain or have had any back or other pain problems in the past.)

2. Concentrate on the following:

    a. Your breath as it goes in and out of your nostrils—try to not breathe through your mouth.
    b. Your belly as it expands and contracts with the breath—you can put a hand on your belly to make this more real.
    c. The other parts of your body. This is an in-the-body rather than out-of-body experience. It is designed to make you aware of all your bodily sensations.
    d. The sounds around you.
    e. The sights around you.
    f. Your favorite mantra or word pair to utter to yourself silently as you inhale and exhale. Say one word to yourself slowly, the whole time that you inhale. Say the second word to yourself slowly as you exhale.

Some mantras that we have found useful include:

Inhale	Exhale
In	Out
Here	Now
[Say nothing]	Ah
Deep	Slow
1	2 . . . to 10
No	Thought
[Say nothing]	1 . . . to 10

[Say nothing]	One
Deep	Still
In-2-3	Out-2-3 [prevents hyperventilation]
Just breathe	Just breathe
[Say nothing]	[Say nothing]
Mer-	cy
Let	Go [of judgments, worries, etc.]
Judge	Not
My	Movie

Develop a mantra for yourself that expresses your deepest life list goals for the day and your life.

Gently and endlessly acknowledge intrusive thoughts, greet them as you might an old friend who is not a favorite but whom you know nonetheless, and then gently refocus your attention to your breath, body, sound, or mantra. It is fine to spend your whole time in meditation just redirecting your attention away from thoughts about the past or future to the present moment. End when you feel comfortable, or after a specific time period.

Meditation or mindful breathing is an excellent prelude to prayer or some other type of contemplative spiritual practice. All major faith traditions have contemplative or meditative prayer traditions that you can explore, if desired. It is very helpful to find a meditation or meditative prayer group to practice these skills with on a regular basis.

MY FLOW CHART

MIHALYI CSIKSZENTMIHALYI DISCOVERED that the happiest people are those who regularly enter into what he calls "flow," a period in which we lose track of time and are engaged in meaningful and positive activities that challenge our skills. We are most likely to enter into flow at work when we are doing something we love, but the pursuit of hobbies like gardening, bicycling, or painting are also typical flow activities.

Because flow is so positive, and people report feeling energized and happy about what they pursue while in this state, any goals that cause you to enter this state are going to be easier to achieve and more rewarding in the process.

When are you most likely to be in flow? List below the activities, situations, and people with whom this often happens, and then list what goals or values they represent. For example, Stephanie gets into flow several mornings a week when she's at her spinning class, and the goal or value that it represents is "Fitness/Health." Jeremy gets into flow while reading the Bible and praying before work, which represents the goal or value of "Learning/Ethical Behavior."

I get into flow when
I do the following   **Value/Goal**

1. _____

2. _____

3. _____

4. _____

5. _____

MY LIFE LIST MAP

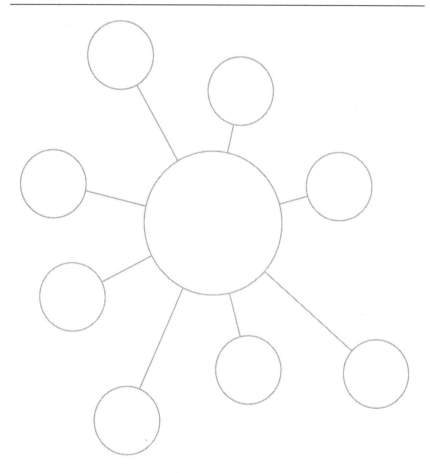

THE LIFE LIST Map will help you think about your goals in a new and visual way. In the center, write your name and the year, and then draw lines, or spokes, out from your name, identifying each major spoke as an area of life that is important to you, where you have specific goals. Draw "branches" off these spokes to identify specific goals, with steps radiating off these branches if desired. You can transform this map with colors, as some studies suggest that colors and the length of certain branches or spokes might make these goals easier to remember. Add more branches and spokes as desired.

THE PRIMES OF YOUR LIFE

WE ARE ALL subtly primed to behave and think in certain ways by our environment and the people we encounter. This exercise is designed to help you identify all the things you have in your life now that elicit positive, goal-directed behavior, and that you might even want to have more of in the future.

In the first column, write down a prime that you encounter, and then next to it write what it inspires you to do that is positive. For example, a positive prime would be seeing fresh flowers in your kitchen, and next to it you might write, "I smiled and thought about how much I enjoy tending my garden in the spring and summer months." Another positive prime might be, "Got an e-mail from my best friend with a funny joke." Next to it you'd write, "My best friend makes me feel better about myself, and seeing her name in an e-mail makes me smile and remember fun things we've done in the past."

Knowing who and what causes you to behave in the most positive, hopeful, and proactive way every day is an important tool in creating your best life, so pay close attention!

Prime	Action/Reaction

THREE BLESSINGS

IT HAS BEEN found that gratitude is one of the character traits most closely associated with happiness, and this simple exercise has been found to boost happiness levels as long as you continue to practice it regularly and with mindfulness. When you start to count your blessings and include the reasons why these blessings occur in your life, you will discover that much of what you are grateful for is due to the energy and effort you put into cultivating and stimulating positive, rewarding relationships and events in your life. The opposite is true, as well. The old biblical proverb "You reap what you sow" is as applicable today as it ever was when it comes to creating more joy in your life.

Try this exercise every night, either in written form or as a mental exercise. Ask yourself what three things happened in your day for which you feel blessed and grateful. Add why they happened specifically to you.

Do this faithfully, and you'll discover a shift in the way you go through your day and the things that you choose to notice and amplify. Strive to come up with as many as possible if three is too few.

MY BLESSING _____

Why it happened to me _____

_____

MY BLESSING _____

Why it happened to me _____

_____

MY BLESSING _____

Why it happened to me _____

_____

NOTES

CHAPTER 1

5 *If you write it down* Rachel Alexander Nichols, "Technically Speaking, Capitals' Leonsis Is a Visionary," *Washington Post*, August 5, 2001.

5 *Edwin Locke, the codeveloper* Edwin A. Locke, *The Prime Movers: Traits of the Great Wealth Creators* (New York: Amacom, 2000).

5 *Her methods were so successful* "Leadership Initiative: Mary Kay Ash," Harvard Business School, www.hbs.edu/leadership/database/leaders/mary_kay_ash.html.

6 *Cullen noted* Shankar Vedantam, "Along With Grief, 9/11 Survivors Find Resolve," *Washington Post*, September 10, 2007.

6 *Duffy elaborated* Ibid.

7 *He had been diagnosed* Nelly Tucker, "Randy Pausch, the Professor Who Gave the Lecture of a Lifetime," *Washington Post*, July 26, 2008.

7 *A survey released by the Adventure* Brigid Delaney, "The Spirit of Adventure," March 7, 2008, www.cnn.com.

8 *The British government* Ibid.

8 *People are aware that* Don Aucoin, "Crisis? More Seeing Midlife as a Quest," *Boston Globe*, reprinted in the *San Diego Union-Tribune*, September 25, 2005.

8 *It's no surprise, then* Christopher Solomon, "Michael Phelps: Inside His Plan for the Greatest Olympics Ever," *Outside*, January 2008.

8 *Kate Ziegler* Kate Ziegler, interview with Caroline Adams Miller, March 30, 2005.

8 *Eric Mangini, the youngest* Les Carpenter, "For Jets, Ex-Apprentices Now Piloting the Franchise," *Washington Post*, September 5, 2006; Tom Pedulla, "Mangini on a Mission," *USA Today*, July 7, 2006.

9 *His partner in running* Ibid.

9 *The iconic Lou Holtz* Lou Holtz, *Wins, Losses and Lessons* (New York: William Morrow, 2006).

9 *Think well to the end* Michael J. Gelb, *How to Think Like Leonardo da Vinci* (New York: Dell, 2004).

11 *He has also discovered that smokers* Nicholas A. Christakis and James H. Fowler, "The Collective Dynamics of Smoking in a Large Social Network," *New England Journal of Medicine*, 2008.

12 *Consider the case of Bob Perini* Bob Perini, interview with Caroline Adams Miller, August 24, 2005.

CHAPTER 2

17 *University of Illinois psychologist* Shigehiro Oishi, Ed Diener, and Richard E. Lucas, "The Optimum Level of Well-Being: Can People Be Too Happy?" *Perspectives on Psychological Science*, 2007.

17 *Unaddressed depression* Patricia Cohen, "Midlife Suicide Rises, Puzzling Researchers," *New York Times*, February 19, 2008.

18 *Sadly, while plumbing the depths* Martin E. P. Seligman and Mihalyi Csikszentmihalyi, "Positive Psychology: An Introduction," *American Psychologist*, 2000.

18 *In fact, Seligman was* Martin E. P. Seligman, *Learned Optimism* (New York: Knopf, 1991).

19 *Between 1887 and 2000* David G. Myers, "The Funds, Friends and Faith of Happy People," *American Psychologist*, January 2000.

19 *Since Seligman birthed* Raymond D. Fowler, Martin E. P. Seligman, and Gerald P. Koocher, "The APA 1998 Annual Report," *American Psychologist*, 1999.

19 *There is even a widely* Sonja Lyubomirsky, Kennon M. Sheldon, and David Schkade, "Pursuing Happiness: The Architecture of Sustainable Change," *Review of General Psychology*, 2005.

20 *A recent Gallup World Survey* Ed Diener and Robert Biswas-Diener, *Happiness: Unlocking the Mysteries of Psychological Wealth* (New York: Blackwell/Wiley Publishing, forthcoming).

20 *But Ruut Veenhoven* Bridget Bentz Sizer, "Happy? The Surprisingly Simple Factors That Add Up to Feeling Good," *Washington Post*, June 25, 2006.

21 *Bhutan's former king* Peter Wonacott, "Smile Census: Bhutan Counts Its Blessings," *Wall Street Journal*, March 22, 2008.

21 *Their concerns are well founded* Jules Evans, "Teaching Happiness: The Classes in Wellbeing That Are Helping Our Children," TimesOnline, February 18, 2008, www.timesonline.co.uk; UNICEF, *Child Poverty in Perspective: An Overview of Child Well-Being in Rich Countries* (Florence, Italy: UNICEF Innocenti Research Centre, 2007).

21 *There is also a new* University of Warwick, "Germany and Portugal Come Near Bottom of New Blood Pressure–Based Happiness League," *ScienceDaily*, February 28, 2007.

21 *A comprehensive study* Michael Kahn, "Middle-Age Is Truly Depressing, Study Finds," Reuters, January 29, 2008.

22 *Although most men and women* Anke C. Plagnol and Richard A. Easterlin, "Aspirations, Attainments, and Satisfaction: Life Cycle Differences between American Women and Men," *Journal of Happiness Studies*, 2008.

22 *Periodically, the National* Yang Yang, "Long and Happy Living: Trends and Patterns of Happy Life Expectancy in the U.S. 1970–2000," *Social Science Research*, 2008.

22 *We are even now learning* Edward M. Eveld, "Why Is This Family Smiling? Daily Conversation and Mutual Respect Are the Keys to Cultivating a Convivial Clan," *Kansas City Star*, May 17, 2006.

23 *There are several different ways* Ed Diener, E. Suh, R. E. Lucas, and H. L. Smith, "Subjective Well-Being: Three Decades of Progress," *Psychological Bulletin*, 1999.

24 *As Bandura described* Albert Bandura, *The Social Foundations of Thought and Action* (Englewood Cliffs, NJ: Prentice-Hall, 1986).

CHAPTER 3

29 *Sonja Lyubomirsky* Sonja Lyubomirsky, Laura King, and Ed Diener, "The Benefits of Frequent Positive Affect: Does Happiness Lead to Success?" *Psychological Bulletin*, 2005.

29 *Here is a sample of how happiness* Ibid.

29 *Social isolation hurts* David Spiegel and Catherine Classen, *Group Therapy for Cancer Patients: A Research-Based Handbook of Psychosocial Care* (New York: Basic/Perseus Books, 2000).

36 *Dr. Laura King and Dr. James Pennebaker* Laura King, "Interventions for Enhancing Subjective Well-Being," in *The Science of Subjective Well-Being*, ed. M. Eid and R. J. Larsen (New York: Guilford Press, 2008).

36 *One of the most intriguing findings* Laura A. King, "The Health Benefits of Writing about Life Goals," *Personality and Social Psychology Bulletin*, 2001.

36 *For instance, Sarah Pressman* Sarah D. Pressman and Sheldon Cohen, "Use of Social Words in Autobiographies and Longevity," *Psychosomatic Medicine*, 2007.

37 *Michael McCullough* Robert A. Emmons and Michael E. McCullough, *The Psychology of Gratitude*

(New York: Oxford University Press, 2004); Robert A. Emmons, *Thanks!* (Boston: Houghton Mifflin, 2007).

37 *Marty Seligman has*   Martin E. P. Seligman, Tracy A. Steen, Nansook Park, and Christopher Peterson, "Positive Psychology Progress: Empirical Validation of Interventions," *American Psychologist*, 2005.

38 *Oxford University psychologist*   Michael M. Argyle, *The Psychology of Happiness*, 2nd ed. (London: Routledge, 2001).

38 *He found that the prefrontal*   Henning Boecker, Till Sprenger, Mary Spilker, Gjermund Henriksen, et al., "The Runner's High: Opioidergic Mechanisms in the Human Brain," *Cerebral Cortex Advance Access*, February 2008.

39 *Researchers who studied*   Marc A. Musik, A. Regula Herzog, and James S. House, "Volunteering and Mortality among Older Adults: Findings from a National Sample" (University of Michigan, Institute for Social Research, March 1999).

39 *Laura King even said*   Laura King, "Benefits of Positive Emotion" (paper presented at the Subjective Well-Being Conference, St. Louis, MO, April 2006)."

39 *Studies of macaque monkeys*   Kathryn Shutt, Ann MacLarnon, Michael Heistermann, and Stuart Semple, "Grooming in Barbary Macaques: Better to Give than to Receive?" *Biology Letters*, June 2007.

40 *Researcher Fred Bryant*   Fred Bryant and Joseph Veroff, *Savoring: A New Model of Positive Experience* (Mahwah, NJ: Lawrence Erlbaum Associates, 2007).

40 *Scrapbookers preserve*   Barbara Kerr, "The Happy Families Project" (presentation at the 2006 International Positive Psychology Summit at the Gallup Headquarters, Washington, DC, October 2006).

42 *Forgiveness isn't always*   Everett Washington, *Forgiveness and Reconciliation: Theory and Application* (New York: Brunner-Routledge, 2006).

42 *One study found that people*   C. R. Snyder and Shane Lopez, *Positive Psychology: The Scientific and Practical Explorations of Human Strengths* (Thousand Oaks, CA: Sage, 2007).

43 *One study found that employees*   Jan Elsner, "Building Exceptional Self: From Positive Affect to Positive Effect. An Integrated Model for Putting Positive Psychology to Work" (presentation at the Gallup Well-Being Forum, Washington, DC, October 5, 2007).

43 *Once the exclusive domain*   Antoine Lutz, John D. Dunne, and Richard J. Davidson, "Meditation and the Neuroscience of Consciousness: An Introduction," in *The Cambridge Handbook of Consciousness*, ed. Philip David Zelazo, Morris Moscovitch, and Evan Thompson, pp. 499–551 (New York: Cambridge University Press, 2007).

43 *Barbara Fredrickson*   B. L. Fredrickson, M. A. Cohn, K. A. Coffey, J. Pek, and S. Finkel, "Open Hearts Build Lives: Positive Emotions, Induced through Meditation, Build Consequential Personal Resources" (University of North Carolina at Chapel Hill, 2008).

CHAPTER 4
50 *Locke, a professor*   E. A. Locke and G. P. Latham, *A Theory of Goal Setting and Task Performance* (Englewood Cliffs, NJ: Prentice Hall, 1990).

50 *If you are seeking*   Ibid.

51 *These mediocre goals*   Ibid.

51 *Subsequent work*   Jessica L. Tracy and Richard W. Robins, "Emerging Insights into the Nature and Function of Pride," *Journal of Personality and Social Psychology*, 2007.

53 *These are called "approach" goals*   Joanne M. Dickson and Andrew K. MacLeod, "Approach and Avoidance Goals and Plans: Their Relationship to Anxiety and Depression," *Cognitive Therapy and Research*, 2004.

54   *These are called "intrinsic" or "self-concordant" goals*   Daniel C. Molden and Carol S. Dweck, "Meaning and Motivation," in *Intrinsic and Extrinsic Motivation: The Search for Optimal Motivation and Performance*, ed. Carol Sansone and Judith M. Harackiewicz, 132–159 (San Diego: Academic Press, 2000).

55   *Their self-determination theory*   Ed Deci and Richard Ryan, "Faciliating Optimal Motivation and Psychological Well-Being Across Life's Domains," *Canadian Psychology*, 2008; Richard M. Ryan and Edward L. Deci, "Self-Determination Theory and the Facilitation of Intrinsic Motivation, Social Development, and Well-Being," *American Psychologist*, 2000.

57   *Gary Latham has also said*   Gary Latham, interview with Caroline Adams Miller, March 25, 2008. On behavioral contracts, see Frederick H. Kanfer and Arnold P. Goldstein, *Helping People Change: A Textbook of Methods* (New York: Pergamon Press), 1975.

57   *There's also the old-fashioned method*   "Oprah Winfrey and Discovery Communications to Form New Joint Venture: OWN: The Oprah Winfrey Network" (press release, Oprah.com, January 30, 2008).

58   *Tom Higgenson, lead singer*   Brian Mansfield, "Plain White T's Singer Lands a Date with Delilah," *USA Today*, January 20, 2008; Mike Celizic, "Muse Shares Story Behind 'Hey There Delilah,'" January 23, 2008, www.msnbc.com.

58   *For example, people who made their*   John C. Norcross, Marci S. Mrykalo, and Matthew D. Blagys, "Auld Lang Syne: Success Predictors, Change Processes, and Self-Reported Outcomes of New Year's Resolutions and Non-Resolvers," *Journal of Clinical Psychology*, 2002.

58   *An economist who analyzed*   Michael S. Rosenwald, "An Economy of Scales: Paying People to Lose Weight Helps Drop Pounds and Health-Care Costs," *Washington Post*, November 11, 2007.

59   *Csikszentmihalyi found that the happiest people*   Mihaly Csikszentmihalyi, *Finding Flow: The Psychology of Engagement with Everyday Life* (New York: Basic Books, 1997).

CHAPTER 5

63   *In the only study*   Bruce Headey, "Life Goals Matter to Happiness: A Revision of Set-Point Theory," *Social Indicators Research*, April 2008.

64   *the "Best Possible Self" journaling exercise*   Laura King, "Interventions for Enhancing Subjective Well-Being," in *The Science of Subjective Well-Being*, ed. M. Eid and R. J. Larsen (New York: Guilford Press, 2008); and Sonja Lyubomirsky, Lorie Sousa, and Rene Dickerhoof, "High Self-Control Predicts Good Adjustment, Less Pathology, Better Grades and Interpersonal Success," *Journal of Personality and Social Psychology*, 2006.

64   *King even found that simply*   Laura King, "The Health Benefits of Writing about Life Goals," *Personality and Social Psychology Bulletin*, 2001.

67   *Alison Sigethy came to the realization*   Lee Lawrence, "Backstory: Greenland or Bust—One Woman's Midlife Detour," *Christian Science Monitor*, June 14, 2006.

67   *More specifically*   M.B. Frisch, *Quality of Life Therapy: Applying a Life Satisfaction Approach to Positive Psychology and Cognitive Therapy* (Hoboken, NJ: John Wiley and Sons, 2006).

73   *The advantage of using this system*   Tony Buzan and Barry Buzan, *The Mind Map Book: How to Use Radiant Thinking to Maximize Your Brain's Untapped Potential* (London: BBC Books, 1993).

CHAPTER 6

77   *In one of the most famous*   Walter Mischel and E. B. Ebbesen, "Attention in Delay of Gratification," *Journal of Personality and Social Psychology*, 1970.

79   *Dr. Roy Baumeister*   Roy Baumeister, Todd F. Heatherton, and Dianne M. Tice, *Losing Control: How and Why People Fail at Self-Regulation* (San Diego: Academic Press, 1994).

79   *Chris Peterson and Marty Seligman*   Chris Peterson and M. E. P. Seligman, *Character Strengths and Virtues: A Handbook and Classification* (New York: Oxford University Press, 2004).

80 *The Self-Control Scale*   June Tangney, Roy Baumeister, and Angie Boone, "High Self-Control Predicts Good Adjustment, Less Pathology, Better Grades and Interpersonal Success," *Journal of Personality*, 2004.

81 *A Pennsylvania State University*   Clancy Blair and Rachel Peters Razza, "Relating Effortful Control, Executive Function, and False Belief Understanding to Emerging Math and Literacy Ability in Kindergarten," *Society for Research in Child Development*, 2007.

84 *In one study, participants were divided*   Harry Wallace and Roy Baumeister, "Effects of Success versus Failure Feedback on Further Self-Control," *Self and Identity*, 2002.

84 *A study at the University of Kentucky*   Suzanne Segerstrom and Lise Nes, "Dispositional Optimism and Coping: A Meta-Analytic Review," *Personality and Social Psychology Review*, 2006.

84 *In another study, research participants*   Matthew Gailliot and Roy Baumeister, "Self-Regulation and Sexual Restraint: Dispositionally and Temporarily Poor Self-Regulatory Abilities Contribute to Failures at Restraining Sexual Behavior," *Personality and Social Psychology Bulletin*, 2007.

84 *Finally, in a third study*   Kathleen Vohs, Roy Baumeister, and Natalie Ciarocco, "Self-Regulation and Self-Presentation: Regulatory Resource Depletion Impairs Impression Management and Effortful Self-Presentation Depletes Regulatory Resources," *Journal of Personality and Social Psychology*, 2005.

85 *Participants in another study who used willpower*   Matthew T. Gailliot, Roy F. Baumeister, C. Nathan DeWall, Jon K. Maner, E. Ashby Plant, Dianne M. Tice, Lauren E. Brewer, and Brandon J. Schmeichel, "Self-Control Relies on Glucose as a Limited Energy Source: Willpower Is More Than a Metaphor," *Journal of Personality and Social Psychology*, 2007.

85 *Participants in an Australian investigation*   Meagan Oaten and Ken Chang, "Improved Self-Control: The Benefits of a Regular Program of Academic Study," *Basic and Applied Social Psychology*, 2006.

86 *Oaten and Cheng did another study*   Meagan Oaten and Ken Chang, "Improvements in Self-Control from Financial Monitoring," *Journal of Economic Psychology*, 2007.

86 *Richard Davidson*   Antoine Lutz, John D. Dunne, and Richard J. Davidson, "Meditation and the Neuroscience of Consciousness: An Introduction," in *The Cambridge Handbook of Consciousness*, ed. Philip David Zelazo, Morris Moscovitch, and Evan Thompson (New York: Cambridge University Press, 2007).

87 *Davidson noted that improved self-regulation*   "Compassion Meditation Changes the Brain" (news release, University of Wisconsin-Madison, March 27, 2008).

87 *Improvements in self-regulation around overeating*   "Eastern Philosophy Promises Hope for Western Women with Eating Disorders," *ScienceDaily*, January 12, 2007.

87 *They also found that the eating disorder*   Antoine Lutz, Heleen A. Slagter, John D. Dunne, and Richard J. Davidson, "Attention Regulation and Monitoring in Meditation," *Trends in Cognitive Sciences*, 2008.

87 *One Canadian study estimated*   Piers Steel, "The Nature of Procrastination," *Psychological Bulletin*, 2007.

88 *Dr. Edward M. Hallowell*   Ned Hallowell, "Overloaded Circuits: Why Smart People Underperform," Harvard Business Review, 2005.

88 *Roy Baumeister has laughingly said*   Roy Baumeister, interview with Caroline Adams Miller, February 28, 2008.

88 *Self-monitoring through journals and charts*   "Study Finds Keeping a Food Diary Doubles Diet Weight Loss: Study Is One of Few Trials to Recruit Large Percentage of African American Participants" (press release, Kaiser Permanente, July 8, 2008).

CHAPTER 7

90 *Goal-setting theorist*   E. A. Locke and G. P. Latham, *A Theory of Goal Setting and Task Performance* (Englewood Cliffs, NJ: Prentice Hall, 1990).

93   *Kevin Clements, one of the best swimmers*   Kevin Clements, interview with Caroline Adams Miller, February 2, 2008.

96   *Researchers such as Abigail Stewart and Elizabeth Vandewater*   Abigail Stewart and Elizabeth Vandewater, " 'If I Had It to Do Over Again . . .': Midlife Review, Midcourse Corrections, and Women's Well-Being in Midlife," *Journal of Personal and Social Psychology*, 1999.

97   *Ellis's plainspoken style*   Albert Ellis and Robert Harper, *A New Guide to Rational Living* (Oxford: Prentice-Hall, 1975).

97   *The final outcome*   Albert Ellis, *Feeling Better, Getting Better, Staying Better* (New York: Impact Publishers, 2001).

98   *A chief financial officer from a British*   Del Jones, "Leaders Learn Focus from Crossing 'Freakout Point,' " *USA Today*, April 26, 2007.

99   *James Prochaska, the researcher who coined*   James Prochaska, C. C. DiClemente, and John Norcross, "In Search of How People Change," *American Psychologist*, 1992.

100   *A study at Ohio State University*   Lisa Libby, Richard Eibach, and Thomas Gilovich, "Here's Looking at Me: The Effect of Memory Perspective on Assessments of Personal Change," *Journal of Personality and Social Psychology*, 2005.

100   *When participants saw themselves as others would*   Ibid.

101   *We may not be aware of the energy*   Laura King, "Interventions for Enhancing Subjective Well-Being," in *The Science of Subjective Well-Being*, ed. M. Eid and R. J. Larsen (New York: Guilford Press, 2008).

101   *Laura King of the University of Missouri*   Ibid.

CHAPTER 8

103   *After surveying the patterns*   Nicholas Christakis and James Fowler, "The Spread of Obesity in a Social Network," *New England Journal of Medicine*, 2007.

104   *Dr. Nicholas Christakis, the principal investigator*   Ibid.

104   *Obesity researchers*   Gina Kolata, "Find Yourself Packing It On? Blame Friends," *New York Times*, July 26, 2007.

105   *In one study, college students*   James Coyne, "Depression and the Response to Others," *Journal of Abnormal Psychology*, 1976.

105   *A study at Uppsala University*   Lars-Olav Lundquist and Ulf Dimberg, "Facial Expressions Are Contagious," *Journal of Psychophysiology*, 1995.

105   *Professor Sigal Barsade*   Sigal Barsade, "The Ripple Effect: Emotional Contagion in Groups" (Yale SOM Working Paper OB-01, 2000).

106   *For example, studies at the Arlene R. Gordon*   Caren R. Goodman and R. Andrew Shippy, "Is It Contagious? Affect Similarity among Spouses," *Aging and Mental Health*, 2002.

106   *In fact, a study at the University of Texas Medical Branch*   John Potthoff, Charles Holahan, and Thomas Joiner, "Reassurance Seeking, Stress Generation, and Depressive Symptoms: An Integrative Model," *Journal of Personality and Social Psychology*, 1995.

106   *A study of Dutch music teachers*   Arnold Bakker, "Flow among Music Teachers and Their Students: The Crossover of Peak Experiences," *Journal of Vocational Behavior*, 2005.

107   *Dr. Daniel B. Hinshaw*   Allison Mitchinson, Hyungjin Kim, Michael Geisser, Jack Rosenberg, and Daniel Hinshaw, "Social Connectedness and Patient Recovery after Major Operation," *Journal of the American College of Surgeons*, 2008.

108   *They also suffer from poor sleep*   Louise Hawkley and John Cacioppo, "Aging and Loneliness: Downhill Quickly?" *Current Directions in Psychological Science*, 2007.

108   *After running all of the speech coders'*   Barbara Fredrickson and Marcial Losada, "Positive Affect and the Complex Dynamics of Human Flourishing," *American Psychologist*, 2005.

109 *Just one year before Losada's* Barbara Fredrickson, "What Good Are Positive Emotions?" *Review of General Psychology*, 1998.

110 *After observing thousands of hours* John Gottman, *Why Marriages Succeed or Fail: And How You Can Make Yours Last* (New York: Simon and Schuster, 1995).

111 *Subjects who wore sensitive* Barbara Fredrickson, "Cultivating Positive Emotions to Optimize Health and Well-Being," *Prevention and Treatment*, 2000.

111 *One study of animals* Rosanne Thomas, Gregory Hotsenpiller, and Daniel Peterson, "Acute Psychosocial Stress Reduces Cell Survival in Adult Hippocampal Neurogenesis without Altering Proliferation," *Journal of Neuroscience*, 2007.

113 *Researcher and psychologist Marty Seligman* "Friendship and Well-Being Study," Positive Psychology Center Online Research Program, http://www.ppresearch.sas.upenn.edu.

114 *You can make more friends* Dale Carnegie, *How to Win Friends and Influence People* (Derry, NH: Vermilion, 2007).

CHAPTER 9

121 *In the following experiment* John A. Bargh and Ezequiel Morsella, "The Unconscious Mind," *Perspectives on Psychological Science*, January 2008.

121 *Bargh presented the coffee* Benedict Carey, "Who's Minding the Mind?" *New York Times*, July 31, 2007.

122 *A multidisciplinary team* Cynthia Cryder, Jennifer Lerner, James Gross, and Ronald Dahl, "Misery Is Not Miserly: Sad and Self-Focused Individuals Spend More," *Psychological Science*, 2008.

123 *In two studies, they found that* Azim Shariff and Ara Norenzayan, "God Is Watching You: Priming God Concepts Increases Prosocial Behavior in an Anonymous Economic Game," *Psychological Science*, 2007.

123 *John Bargh was behind another priming* John Bargh, Mark Chen, and Lara Burrows, "Automaticity of Social Behavior: Direct Effects of Trait Construct and Stereotype Activation on Action," *Journal of Personality and Social Psychology*, 1996.

124 *In the first study of how priming* Amanda Shantz and Gary Latham, "An Exploratory Field Experiment of the Effect of Subconscious and Conscious Goals on Employee Performance" (paper presented at the Society for Industrial and Organizational Psychology Conference, San Francisco, CA, April 2008).

124 *A 2005 study by Indiana University* Kaiser Family Foundation, *Food for Thought: Television Food Advertising to Children in the United States,* March 2007.

124 *Elizabeth Cady, a cognitive psychology* Elizabeth Cady, Richard Harris, and Bret Knappenberger, "Using Music to Cue Autobiographical Memories of Different Lifetime Periods," *Psychology of Music,* 2008.

131 *As researchers have increasingly dug* Peter Gollwitzer, "Implementation Intentions: Strong Effects of Simple Plans," *American Psychologist*, 1999.

132 *Almost one hundred college students* Peter Gollwitzer and Veronika Brandstatter, "Implementation Intentions and Effective Goal Pursuit," *Journal of Personality and Social Psychology*, 1997.

132 *Sixty male college students* Ibid.

132 *Women who were told* Paschal Sheeran, Thomas Webb, and Peter Gollwitzer, "The Interplay between Goal Intentions and Implementation Intentions," *Personality and Social Psychology Bulletin,* 2005.

CHAPTER 10

138 *Seligman and Duckworth decided to study* Angela L. Duckworth and Martin E. P. Seligman, "Self-Discipline Outdoes IQ in Predicting Academic Performance of Adolescents," *Psychological Science*, 2005.

138   *By interviewing composers*   Ibid.

139   *He saw that the most defining*   Ibid.

139   *Another researcher added decades later*   Angela L. Duckworth, Christopher Peterson, Michael D. Matthews, and Dennis Kelly, "Grit: Perseverance and Passion for Long-Term Goals," *Journal of Personality and Social Psychology*, 2007.

139   *His observation that*   Joseph Renzulli, "Myth: The Gifted Constitutes 3–5% of the Population. Dear Mr. and Mrs. Copernicus: We regret to inform you . . . ," *Journal for the Education of the Gifted*, 1999.

139   *In the 1980s*   Warren W. Willingham, "Measuring Personal Qualities in Admissions: The Context and the Purpose," *New Directions for Testing and Measurement*, 1983.

140   *K. Anders Ericsson of Florida State University*   K. Anders Ericsson, *The Road to Excellence: The Acquisition of Expert Performance in the Arts and Sciences, Sports and Games* (Mahwah, NJ: Lawrence Erlbaum, 1996).

140   *The Grit Scale was developed*   Duckworth, Peterson, Matthews, and Kelly, "Grit: Perseverance and Passion for Long-Term Goals."

140   *Another recent study*   Priya Ratneshwar, "True Grit," *Penn Arts and Sciences*, 2007.

141   *As Duckworth noted*   Duckworth, Peterson, Matthews, and Kelly, "Grit: Perseverance and Passion for Long-Term Goals."

141   *Dean Simonton of the University of California at Davis*   Dean Keith Simonton, "Scientific Talent, Training, and Performance: Intellect, Personality, and Genetic Endowment," *Review of General Psychology*, 2008.

143   *Mary Crane is just one consultant*   "The 'Millennials' Are Coming," *60 Minutes*, November 11, 2007.

144   *The vast majority of childhood prodigies*   Robert Root-Bernstein and Michèle Root-Bernstein, *Sparks of Genius: The Thirteen Thinking Tools of Creative People* (Boston: Houghton Mifflin, 1999).

144   *Jonathan Plucker, an Indiana University psychologist*   Jonathan A. Plucker, Carolyn M. Callahan, and Ellen M. Tomchin, "Wherefore Art Thou, Multiple Intelligences? Alternative Assessments for Identifying Talent in Ethnically Diverse and Low Income Students," *Gifted Child Quarterly*, 1996.

CHAPTER 11

152   *In fact, David G. Myers of Hope College*   David G. Myers, "Religion and Human Flourishing," in *The Science of Subjective Well-Being*, ed. M. Eid and R. J. Larsen (New York: Guilford Press, 2008).

152   *A study of 315 children*   Bud Mortenson, "What Makes Kids Happy?" *UBC Reports*, February 7, 2008.

152   *From our perspective*   Ron Csillag, "Study: Spirituality a Big Part of Kids' Happiness," *USA Today*, March 25, 2008.

152   *A 2007 telephone survey*   "U.S. Religious Landscape Survey 2008," *Pew Forum on Religion and Public Life*, June 2008.

152   *The trend is towards more personal religion*   Neela Banerjee, "Poll Finds a Fluid Religious Life in U.S.," *New York Times*, February 26, 2008.

153   *A Gallup survey reported that 54 percent*   G. Gallup, *Religion in America* (Princeton, NJ: Princeton Religion and Research Center, 1990).

CHAPTER 12

156   *Unlike men, stressed-out women*   Shelley E. Taylor, *The Tending Instinct: How Nurturing Is Essential to Who We Are and How We Live* (New York: Macmillan, 2002).

156   *The Hug Drug*   Ibid.

157   *In the famed Nurses' Health Study*   Yvonne L. Michael, Graham A. Colditz, Eugenie Coakley, and Ichiro Kawachi, "Health Behaviors, Social Networks, and Healthy Aging: Cross-Sectional Evidence from the Nurses' Health Study," *Quality of Life Research*, 1999.

157 *In a Duke University Medical Center study*   Beverly H. Brummett, John C. Barefoot, Ilene C. Siegler, Nancy E. Clapp-Channing, Barbara L. Lytle, Hayden B. Bosworth, Redford B. Williams, Jr., and Daniel B. Mark, "Characteristics of Socially Isolated Patients with Coronary Artery Disease Who Are at Elevated Risk for Mortality," *Psychosomatic Medicine*, 2001.

157 *According to Barbara Israel*   Barbara A. Israel and Toni C. Antonucci, "Social Network Characteristics and Psychological Well-Being: A Replication and Extension," *Health Education Quarterly*, 1987.

158 *Four basic behaviors*   Debbie Oswald and Eddie Clark, "How Do Friendship Maintenance Behaviors and Problem-Solving Styles Function at the Individual and Dyadic Levels?" *Personal Relationships*, 2006.

159 *Research from the University of Warwick*   Nick Powdthavee, "Research Says Your Happiness Makes Your Partner Happy—but Only If You Are Married," *ScienceDaily*, 2005.

161 *A University of Colorado researcher*   Leaf Van Boven, "Experientialism, Materialism, and the Pursuit of Happiness," *Review of General Psychology*, 2005.

CHAPTER 13

163 *Dr. John Ratey of Harvard Medical School*   Shari Roan, "Exercise Is Good for the Brain," *Los Angeles Times*, March 17, 2008.

166 *It used to be*   Harriet S. Mosatche and Elizabeth K. Lawner, *Girls: What's So Bad about Being Good? How to Have Fun, Survive the Preteen Years, and Remain True to Yourself* (New York: Three Rivers Press, 2001).

168 *Happiness researchers such as Sonja Lyubomirsky*   Sonja Lyubomirsky, Kennon M. Sheldon, and David Schkade, "Pursuing Happiness: The Architecture of Sustainable Change," *Review of General Psychology*, 2005.

168 *Regardless of how much income each person*   Elizabeth Dunn, Lara Aknin, and Michael Norton, "Spending Money on Others Promotes Happiness," *Science*, 2008.

CHAPTER 14

171 *Dr. George Vaillant one of the leading researchers*   George Vaillant, *Aging Well* (New York: Basic Books, 2002).

172 *Dr. Alan Marlatt of the University of Washington*   G. Alan Marlatt and Dennis M. Donovan, *Relapse Prevention: Maintenance Strategies in the Treatment of Addictive Behaviors*, 2nd ed. (New York: Guilford, 2008).

174 *A study of 737 chief executives*   Lisa Belkin, "Life's Work: Putting Some Fun Back into 9 to 5," *New York Times*, March 6, 2008.

174 *In addition, Harvard Business Review*   Martha Craumer, "Getting Serious about Workplace Humor," *Harvard Management Communication Letter*, July 1, 2002.

175 *Robert Sternberg of Yale University*   Robert Sternberg, *Wisdom, Intelligence, and Creativity Synthesized* (New York: Cambridge University Press, 2003).

175 *Dr. Gene D. Cohen, director*   Beth Baker, "Studies Suggest There Is an Art to Getting Older: Creative Activity May Have Health Benefits," *Washington Post*, March 11, 2008.

177 *Carol Dweck, a noted researcher*   Carol Dweck, *Mindset: The New Psychology of Success* (New York: Random House, 2006).

178 *A study on creativity and healthy aging*   Gene D. Cohen, *The Mature Mind: The Positive Power of the Aging Brain* (New York: Basic Books, 2005).

CHAPTER 15

180 *Tim Kasser of Knox College*   Tim Kasser, Steve Cohn, Allen D. Kanner, and Richard M. Ryan, "Some Costs of American Corporate Capitalism: A Psychological Exploration of Value and Goal Conflicts," *Psychological Inquiry*, 2007.

181   *Richard Lazarus of the University of California*   Richard S. Lazarus, *Emotion and Adaptation* (New York: Oxford University Press, 1991).

181   *Although lottery winners tend to be happier*   Richard Tunney, "Happiness Comes Cheap—Even for Millionaires," *ScienceDaily*, December 3, 2007.

181   *People who said they were unhappy*   Ibid.

182   *In one landmark study, she discovered*   Steven Blader, Amy Wrzesniewski, and Caroline Bartel, "Identity and the Modern Organization: An Invitation," in *Identity and the Modern Organization*, ed. Caroline Bartel, Steven Blader, and Amy Wrzesniewski (Mahwah, NJ: Lawrence Erlbaum Associates, 2007).

184   *In one of the most comprehensive surveys exploring satisfaction*   "Looking for Satisfaction and Happiness in a Career? Start by Choosing a Job That Helps Others." *ScienceDaily*, March 8, 2008; Tom W. Smith, *Job Satisfaction in the United States* (Chicago: National Opinion Research Center at the University of Chicago, 2007); James A. Davis, Tom W. Smith, and James A. Marsden, *General Social Surveys Cumulative Codebook: 1972–2006* (Chicago: National Opinion Research Center at the University of Chicago, 2007).

184   *Louis Wray*   Louis Wray, founder and CEO of LiveAnew, interview with Caroline Adams Miller, April 22, 2008.

185   *Illinois psychologist Dr. Mark Frazier*   Katherine Kam, "The Art of Aging Gracefully," *WebMD*, June 12, 2007.

186   *Neophobia, the fear of doing new things*   Larry Dossey, *The Extraordinary Healing Power of Ordinary Things: Fourteen Natural Steps to Health and Happiness* (New York: Three Rivers Press, 2007).

186   *A study of twenty-eight thousand Americans*   Lindsey Tanner, "Happiest Americans Are the Oldest," Associated Press, April 18, 2008.

CHAPTER 16

189   *Happy families usually have homes described*   Edward M. Eveld, "Why Is This Family Smiling? Daily Conversation and Mutual Respect Are the Keys to Cultivating a Convivial Clan," *Kansas City Star*, May 17, 2006.

191   *Ed Diener and Marty Seligman have also found*   Ed Diener and Marty Seligman, "Beyond Money: Toward an Economy of Well-Being," *Psychological Science in the Public Interest*, 2004.

191   *Researchers found that moving to safer neighborhoods*   "Lawrence Katz Reveals the Links between Better Neighborhoods and Quality of Life," *The Yard*, 2007.

191   *Another study showed that women*   Ming Wen, Christopher Browning, and Kathleen Cagney, "Neighborhood Deprivation, Social Capital and Regular Exercise During Adulthood: A Multilevel Study in Chicago," *Urban Studies*, 2007.

CHAPTER 17

199   *In fact, researchers have found that sharing*   E. A. Locke and G. P. Latham, *A Theory of Goal Setting and Task Performance* (Englewood Cliffs, NJ: Prentice Hall, 1990); James Rodrigue, Michelle Widows, and Maher Baz, "Caregivers of Patients Awaiting Lung Transplantation: Do They Benefit When the Patient Is Receiving Psychological Services?" *Progress in Transplantation*, 2006.

199   *When you share your good news with friends*   Shelly L. Gable, Harry T. Reis, Emily A. Impett, and Evan R. Asher, "What Do You Do When Things Go Right? The Intrapersonal and Interpersonal Benefits of Sharing Positive Events," *Journal of Personality and Social Psychology*, 2004.

199   *As Barbara Fredrickson found with her*   Christian E. Waugh and Barbara L Fredrickson, "Nice to Know You: Positive Emotions, Self-Other Overlap, and Complex Understanding in the Formation of a New Relationship," *Journal of Positive Psychology*, 2006.

200   *In effect, when you tell your friends about*   Robert A. Emmons and Michael E. McCullough,

"Counting Blessings versus Burdens: An Experimental Investigation of Gratitude and Subjective Well-Being in Daily Life," *Journal of Personality and Social Psychology*, 2003.

200   *One of the findings of the positive psychology movement*   Roy F. Baumeister, Ellen Bratslavsky, Catrin Finkenauer, and Kathleen D. Vohs, "Bad Is Stronger than Good," *Review of General Psychology*, 2001.

203   *Fred Bryant of Loyola University*   Fred Bryant and Joseph Veroff, *Savoring: A New Model of Positive Experience* (New York: Taylor and Francis, 2007).

205   *People who anticipate that they will attend*   Walter Hubert, Mathilde Moller, and Renate de Jong-Meyer, "Film-Induced Amusement Changes in Saliva Cortisol Levels," *Psychoneuroendocrinology*," 1993.

206   *A study at the University of Southampton*   Peter Coleman, "Reminiscence within the Study of Aging: The Social Significance of Story," in *Reminiscence Reviewed: Evaluations, Achievements, Perspectives*, ed. J. Bornat (Buckingham: Open University Press, 1994).

206   *In one of her studies at the University of California*   Sonja Lyubomirsky, Lorie Sousa, and Rene Dickerhoof, "The Costs and Benefits of Writing, Talking, and Thinking about Life's Triumphs and Defeats," *Journal of Personality and Social Psychology*, 2006.

206   *Elizabeth Kensinger, a psychologist at Boston College*   Elizabeth A. Kensinger, "How Negative Emotion Affects Memory Accuracy: Behavioral and Neuroimaging Evidence," *Current Directions in Psychological Science*, 2007.

208   *A study of Olympic silver and bronze medalists*   Victoria H. Medvec, Scott F. Madey, and Thomas Gilovich, "When Less Is More: Counterfactual Thinking and Satisfaction among Olympic Medalists," *Journal of Personality and Social Psychology*, 1995.

CHAPTER 18

212   *Mark R. Leary, a professor of psychology and neuroscience*   Mark R. Leary, Eleanor B. Tate, and Claire E. Adams, "Self-Compassion and Reactions to Unpleasant Self-Relevant Events: The Implications of Treating Oneself Kindly," *Journal of Social and Clinical Psychology*, 2007.

213   *Dozens of studies over several decades*   James Prochaska, Carlo DiClemente, and John Norcross, "In Search of How People Change," *American Psychologist*, 1992.

213   *Here's a quick self-assessment*   James O. Prochaska, John Norcross, and Carlo DiClemente, *Changing for Good: A Revolutionary Six-Stage Program for Overcoming Bad Habits and Moving Your Life Positively Forward* (New York: HarperCollins, 1995).

216   *The pioneering work they have done*   Karen Reivich and Andrew Shatte, *The Resilience Factor: Seven Keys to Finding Your Inner Strength and Overcoming Life's Hurdles* (New York: Broadway, 2003).

RESOURCES

www.carolinemiller.com
    This comprehensive site is for people who want to learn more about Caroline Miller and her work with goal setting and positive psychology. The site is filled with research, free worksheets and newsletters, upcoming events such as speeches and coaching groups, and how to join her coaching practice. Podcast interviews with leaders in the field of goal accomplishment and positive psychology are free and available for download, too.

www.baylor.edu/michael_b_frisch
    Mike Frisch's Web site offers information about Quality of Life Therapy and Coaching, the Quality of Life Inventory, and other resources pertaining to this line of research.

Goal-Setting Web Sites

www.your100things.com
    This fun and interactive site is Caroline Miller's goal-setting and social-networking site that allows people to create and maintain lists for goal accomplishment.

www.43things.com
www.superviva.com
    These two sites offer forums for goal setting and goal accomplishment online.

Positive Psychology Web Sites

www.ppc.sas.upenn.edu
    The Positive Psychology Center at the University of Pennsylvania is a one-stop resource for anyone who wants to learn more about the history of positive psychology, find resources for teachers, or explore a wide variety of links around the world on this topic.

www.authentichappiness.com

This invaluable site is filled with free assessments, such as the VIA Signature Strengths test, the Grit Scale, the Authentic Happiness Inventory, and much more.

www.ippanetwork.org

The mission of the International Positive Psychology Association (IPPA) is to promote the science and practice of positive psychology and to facilitate communication and collaboration among researchers and practitioners around the world who are interested in positive psychology.

www.appreciativeinquiry.case.edu/

Appreciative Inquiry is an approach that seeks to identify the strengths of organizations, and then build fresh solutions through a positive framework.

www.bus.umich.edu/Positive/

The Center for Positive Organizational Scholarship is located at the University of Michigan's Ross School of Business, and is committed to advancing research in the emerging field of Positive Organizational Scholarship.

www.enpp.org/

The European Network for Positive Psychology is a collective of European researchers and practitioners with shared interests in the science and practice of positive psychology.

www.cappeu.org/index.aspx

The Centre for Applied Positive Psychology exists to advance the research and application of positive psychology—the science of optimal human functioning, or "the study of people at their best." They describe part of their mission as enabling individuals and organizations to realize and harness their strengths.

Positive Psychology Leaders' Web Sites

www.rotman.utoronto.ca/facbios/viewFac.asp?facultyID=latham

Gary Latham is the cofounder of goal-setting theory, and his Web site offers a comprehensive list of his research and published works.

www.edwinlocke.com/

Edwin Locke is the cofounder of goal-setting theory, and this site lists his books, newspaper articles, and other links to his work.

http://www.psych.uiuc.edu/~ediener/

Ed Diener was one of the first to study happiness, and is now one of the world authorities on the topic. His site is filled with his research and other lively information about positive psychology.

www.faculty.ucr.edu/~sonja/

Sonja Lyubomirsky's Web site is filled with information about her book *The How of Happiness*, her research, and other helpful insights around happiness.

www.unc.edu/peplab/barb_fredrickson_page.html

Barbara Fredrickson's Web site features her work at the Positive Emotions Lab at the University of North Carolina, as well as her research into well-being, the positivity ratio, and other components of happiness.

www.sas.upenn.edu/~duckwort/

Angela Duckworth's research into the quality of grit and how it pertains to goal accomplishment is essential knowledge for goal setters.

www.happinesshypothesis.com/beyond.html

Not only is Jonathan Haidt's book *The Happiness Hypothesis* excellent, but his Web site gives people ideas about how to use his book and other topics they might want to explore in this arena.

www.psych.rochester.edu/SDT/theory.html

Richard Ryan and Ed Deci are the creators of self-determination theory, and this site gives you an excellent background into their theory and how it fits with goal accomplishment.

Other Helpful Happiness Web Sites

worlddatabaseofhappiness.eur.nl/

This Web site contains current information on the world database of happiness.

www.happinessclub.com/index.html

This site contains information on "happiness clubs" all over the world, as well as how to form your own.

http://swbresearch.netfirms.com/

The Subjective Well-Being Research site offers people a chance to participate in online research on personality and well-being.

ACKNOWLEDGMENTS

WHEN A PROJECT is birthed so quickly, as this one was, lots of people have to rush in with support and encouragement to make it happen.

When I had to leave town to write the first part of the book, several people graciously offered their beach homes in Maryland and Delaware to help me out—Merri Goldberg, John and Trish Long, and Lori and Tony Shore. Lloyd T. Clark, Jr., who didn't even know who I was, but heard I was in need of a quiet place to write, offered me his home in Hidden Valley, Pennsylvania, and although I wound up at the beach, his generosity lit up my heart, and he deserves to be acknowledged.

Rochelle Melander, possibly the world's greatest writing coach, made me accountable for daily page output, and sent dozens of e-cards to buoy me during some lonely months.

My coach, Judy Feld, kept me moving with astute suggestions and guidance, while my agent, Ivor Whitson, earned my unending gratitude for taking early-morning and late-night calls while on vacation with his wife, Ronnie. Ivor was the most critical linchpin of the book, and I'll never forget his strength and kindness. Jennifer Williams, our editor, worked on nights and weekends to give me extra days, and somehow managed to stay focused and calm regardless of what was happening.

Paul Thomas, the finest personal trainer and martial artist I've ever met or worked with, kept my body and mind in shape for this assignment, while Louise Kupelian graciously taught me jazz piano in the afternoons to ensure that my brain stayed in harmony. My amazing Web designer and Web host, Debbie Mahony, made sure that I kept my virtual presence alive and vibrant during this long stretch, and her partner, Chad LaGrone, did the same, particularly as word seeped out about this book and my sites began to crash from heavy traffic.

The ladies of my goal-setting and accountability group dummied up mock covers to keep me smiling and kept me going with e-mails, phone calls, and in-person monthly support. They are Karen Collias, Melanie Ferguson, Carol Loitman Greenspun, Judy Holland, Nancy Mitchell, Lisa Oswald, Victoria Pickering, and Dana Rice.

Sasha L. Heinz was an angel, enthusiastically providing me with any piece of research I needed at a moment's notice, despite her own busy life as a PhD student at Columbia University. Kathryn Britton, another one of my brilliant classmates from Penn's MAPP program, stepped in at the last moment to help with sourcing and analysis, which was both generous and kind.

My clients graciously allowed me to take three months off from my coaching practice for this project and cheered me on from the sidelines, too. Their patience and support were touching.

Finally, my family—my husband, Haywood, and my three children, Haywood IV, Samantha, and Bayard—were stalwart supporters as I disappeared on nights, weekends, and for approximately one full month of their lives. Every time I was stuck and needed an anecdote, they would supply me with ideas, sports stories, and research to buttress my points. Their love for me, and their excitement about this book, sparkle on every page.

As I point out in this book, gratitude is one of the most powerful ways to enhance happiness, and my gratitude to everyone listed here is heartfelt. Thank you, all.

CAROLINE ADAMS MILLER

INDEX